The Ochre and the Blue

The Ochre and the Blue

*The Story of the Missionary Work of the
Free Church of Scotland
in South Africa in the Twentieth Century*

Bill and Elizabeth Graham

•

FREE CHURCH OF SCOTLAND
PUBLICATIONS

© BILL AND ELIZABETH GRAHAM 2009

ISBN 0-9544591-9-9

Published in 2009
by
Free Church of Scotland Publications
15 North Bank Street
Edinburgh EH1 2LS

•

PRINTED BY
J.C. PRINT LTD., BELFAST

CONTENTS

Preface

THE South African people group known as the amaXhosa live mainly in the Eastern Cape Province and surrounding areas. The Free Church of Scotland has been working alongside the Xhosa people there for over a hundred years and this has resulted in the establishment of the Free Church in South Africa.

We, Bill and Elizabeth Graham, worked with that church from 1976–1996, a momentous period in the life of South Africa, and for us a rewarding experience for which we will always be grateful.

The International Missions Board of the Free Church of Scotland commissioned the account we give in this book. It is not the whole story of the Free Church in South Africa. Missing from it are the many Xhosa-speaking Christians in the Free Church whose lives and testimonies have not been recorded. However, where such information has been available, we have used it. So the story is based on Free Church of Scotland missionaries working in South Africa during the 20th Century. But we dedicate this book to our African brothers and sisters in the Free Church in South Africa in testimony to the privilege succeeding missionaries have experienced in working alongside them.

About the book's title, *The Ochre and the Blue*: the amaXhosa have long been known as 'The Ochre People' from their custom of colouring their traditional blankets with a reddish clay. In the days when wearing such blankets was common, the blankets were discarded when the people became Christians. Nowadays the traditional garb of ochre garments has become for the Xhosa what tartan is for the Scot. Blue has become the colour for Free Church 'uniforms' worn by members of the various Free Church organisations.

Bill and Elizabeth Graham
Edinburgh, 2009

Acknowledgements

IN the course of writing this story we have drawn freely on materials contained in the missionary publications and General Assemblies of the Free Church of Scotland, minutes and other materials from the courts of the Free Church in South Africa as well as from the International Missions Board. Wherever possible we have used the published articles of the missionaries to illustrate the work they were doing at different stages in the church's life.

We are indebted to our good friend Mr Ernest Brown for his editorial help and advice and his enthusiasm for the subject. He has a great love for the Free Church in South Africa. Dr Anne Urquhart collated many references in the Free Church of Scotland publications which were extremely useful in collecting the material for this book. We are grateful to our daughter Anne Norrie for editing and preparing the material for printing, to Alex Macaskill for typesetting the manuscript, to Alister MacInnes for the cover design, and to Ernest Brown, Helen Brand, Mrs A. Murray and Evan Macdonald for some of the photos.

We thank the Lord and the International Missions Board for the privilege they have given us of serving in the missionary work in South Africa – years of deeply satisfying service.

1
How it all began

John and Helen Ross set out

IN the April of 1823 a sailing ship was battling it out on its long journey from Britain to South Africa. Among those aboard were a young newly wed Scottish couple, Rev John Ross and his wife Helen Blair. He had his roots in the parish of Creich, in Sutherland, and had been set apart in the Tron Church, Glasgow, the previous month for missionary work, under the auspices of the Glasgow Missionary Society. He was the first fully qualified and ordained minister of the Church of Scotland to go to South Africa. He was of Highland temperament, quiet, shy, slender in build, and a scholar and thinker. She was quite the opposite. She was from an Ayrshire family, strong, frank and hospitable, able to see to all the practical matters about a house and farm, and unfailingly courageous and cheerful. But as regards mission work, they were of one mind – they were always a team.

On one Lord's Day as the voyage progressed, John Ross was conducting worship on board ship. Suddenly shots rang out. A pirate ship with fourteen guns was approaching. Their ship had two guns and was totally unequal for such a fight.

John continued with his sermon and, concluding with prayer, pronounced the benediction. Then all prepared for battle. But just as they did, the pirate ship turned round and sailed away, leaving them to convene a service of thanksgiving. As John remarked, "If men were not blind, the finger of God might have been seen." It seemed that God had work for John and Helen to do for Him in the Eastern Cape region of that vast and beautiful land to which they were sailing.

John and Helen Ross were a team within a team. There were already other missionaries serving in the Eastern Cape district of South Africa. One of those missionaries, Rev John Brownlee, met them at Cape Town in the autumn of 1823. He had arrived just six years earlier, in 1817, and they were serving with the London Missionary Society. He, and later his sons, made a great contribution to the work of the Gospel and the help of the Xhosa people in the area around King William's Town. When the travellers had recovered after the long sea voyage, the Brownlees and the Rosses set out together in an ox-wagon through the Karoo heading for the Tyumie Valley, in the Eastern Cape. They spent long weary days jolting along at the rate of two and a half miles an hour for over 650 miles over rough country with no roads. They saw few white people, but they did meet lions, elephants, ostriches and buck.

Wasting no time

The travellers arrived at Tyumie Mission Station on 16 December, 1823. Two other members of the team of missionaries were there to meet them, Rev W. Thomson, and Mr John Bennie who had gone out two years earlier in 1821.

The following day John Ross lost no time in getting to work. He unpacked and set up a printing press which he had brought with him, and fifty copies of the alphabet were available two days after. Within two weeks, he had printed the Lord's Prayer in Xhosa, a small spelling book, a portion of Brown's Catechism and some hymns in Xhosa composed by Mr Bennie, who became known as the father of Xhosa literature. By 1825 they were making good progress in the translation of the Scriptures. But John Ross's favourite work was always evangelism.

Meanwhile we can imagine his wife seeing to the washing, baking bread, cooking and making a home in their simple mud and wattle house in the beautiful corner of the Tyumie valley. It was not all sunshine for them in Tyumie however. Three little children were buried nearby during the years 1825–1828. After the death of the third child, Mrs Ross said, "Sometimes I think I could wish that the veil was withdrawn that I could see my three little infants, with enlarged souls, enjoying that eternal weight of glory which Christ purchased for them." Two sons and two daughters, some born later, survived.

True Presbyterians

On 1 January 1824 the first Mission Presbytery was formed, the following being present: Rev W.R. Thomson, Mr John Bennie and Rev John Ross, clerk – and Rev John Brownlee was present but not a member of the Presbytery, since he was a Congregationalist.

Six months later John Ross and John Bennie left the Tyumie and went ten miles to the southeast, to a very densely populated area to work amongst the many Xhosa people there. They called their new home station Lovedale after Dr Love, who was Secretary and a prime mover in the Society which had sent them out, the Glasgow Missionary Society. With the help of the people there, a church was built in two days. It and their houses were just rough round thatched huts, the church hut having no windows.

Missionary methods and policy

On the long trek by bullock cart from Cape Town, John Ross had visited Genadendal, an old Moravian mission station first founded in 1737 but re-established and expanded in 1792. It lies about 100 miles to the east of Cape Town. There he saw the value of industrial training in helping a people who in some ways had not long emerged from barbarism to enter the modern world. So, only a year or two after his arrival, a request was sent to the Society in Scotland for a "missionary-hearted, fully qualified medical man, and missionary artisans, able to teach arts and crafts". A catechist and two highly qualified artisan missionaries answered his appeal, and William Chalmers, James Weir and Alexander Macdiarmid came to join the growing team in the Eastern Cape Province of South Africa.

John's grandson, Brownlee J. Ross later, in a book written in 1925, described the missionary methods and policy thought out and laid down by his grandfather and the other missionaries in the early days, which, as he says, "to the present day remain the best":

1. Evangelistic work – the foundation for all else – church services, Sunday schools, constant preaching from village to village, and personal dealing with individuals.

2. Education, including agriculture, arts and crafts, and native literature.

3. Medical work.

4. Building up a native church by sessions and Presbytery, and the training of native office-bearers and preachers.

The beginnings of Lovedale Institution

John Ross moved in 1828 to establish or re-occupy other mission stations – Balfour, Burnshill, and finally, in 1830, Pirie, where he remained for the rest of his life. But before he moved, he saw the foundation set for the institution of Lovedale which later became a famous school, known throughout Southern Africa for the standard and scope of its education. Lovedale was opened in 1841 – it was called a Seminary but it offered a general education as well as classes in specifically Christian subjects. Dr Stewart, Principal of Lovedale, speaking at a Missionary Conference in London in 1878, (the year of John Ross's death) said, "The primary aim of the Institution is to Christianise, not merely to civilise. The conversion of the individual soul to God is a result of the highest value. It is our greatest anxiety, and is esteemed to be the one most worthy of efforts and to which all other efforts are properly and justifiably subordinate." Out of Lovedale grew Fort Hare University, (where Nelson Mandela among other Southern African leaders studied) which still stands not far from the old stone Lovedale building.

Xhosa wars nearby and Church war afar off

As the Bantu people moved slowly south and west and the white settlers moved slowly north and east, a series of clashes could be foreseen. These were the result not only of the pressure by both whites and blacks for more land, but also of drought, cattle thieving and suspicions on both sides. During these wars, fought in what is now called Ciskei, the missionaries' buildings and possessions were often destroyed, as for example at Tyumie and Pirie. On one of these occasions in Tyumie in 1834–35, the settlement was left in ruins. All that is left there are the graves of the three little Ross children. Later, Lovedale was built as a fine big stone building and still stands. Four times over the years the Ross family had to flee for sanctuary into King William's Town where the Brownlees were now working. Their home and contents were burnt — but rebuilt.

As a Scotsman with a Highland background John Ross developed a remarkable insight into the way the people thought. He found himself having a great affinity with the African chiefs and people as he faithfully preached the Gospel to them. Many times he tried to avert war, and he was much loved by the people who knew him.

Meanwhile back home in Scotland in 1843 his Church was involved in a war of sorts of her own. In that year what is known as the Disruption occurred in the Church of Scotland when hundreds of ministers and congregations left that Church to form the Free Church of Scotland. The main reason for the Disruption was the unwarranted interference of the civil courts in the affairs of the Church, insisting that the Established Church was bound to ordain and induct men to the parish ministry whether the people wanted them or not. All the Scottish Presbyterian missionaries on the South African field with the exception of two entered the Free Church. The Glasgow Missionary Society which had sent out most of the missionaries closed down. So, along with the rest, John Ross became a Free Church missionary. (For the full story see *The Heritage of our Fathers* by G.N.M. Collins).

As far as the missionary work was concerned it continued as before. One tragedy that did affect the work of the mission came to be known as the *National Suicide*.

The National Suicide

One day in May 1856 a Xhosa girl of about fourteen years of age named Nongqawuse went down to the river to draw water. When she came back she reported that she had seen some men who were not at all like ordinary men. When her uncle Mhlakaza heard this, he decided to go down to the river to see for himself if she was telling the truth. Yes, he reported, he had seen them too, and he returned four days later at their command to receive instructions. Amongst these men was his long-dead brother.

At this time many of the cattle of the Xhosa tribes were dying from a lung disease which they thought was caused by the witchcraft of the English settlers who were beginning to move northward and eastward, meeting the black nations who were moving southward and westward. But the good news Mhlakaza said these strange men told him was that if all the Xhosa people would slaughter all their cattle and eat all their crops and seed, then something wonderful would happen. On 18 February 1857 a great hurricane would arise and would sweep into the sea all the white men and all the Xhosas who didn't believe him, but great and strong cattle would appear and much food would be given to those who obeyed. A blood red sun would rise and re-set in the east.

Many people were strong believers in superstition and they followed the advice of Mhlakaza and ate all their cattle and food. Many had already died of starvation before the day came at last. The crowds waited and waited. Nothing happened. No red sun rose and set in the east.

When it dawned upon them that they were utterly ruined, despair overcame them. They were driven to seek help and shelter from the very white people they had hoped they would never see again. Hundreds of thousands of cattle had been slaughtered, and at least 25 000 people are said to have perished from starvation. Mhlakaza himself died, but Nongqawuse lived. Until the day of her death, she would never speak of the matter, which came to be called the National Suicide, so it was never known whether she was really deluded, or whether it was a ploy on the part of her uncle and the chiefs to stir up the people to make a great attack on all the white people once and for all.

The government of the time had foreseen what would happen and had been storing up grain to help the starving masses. Many farmers and Christian missionaries did all they could to help. The Xhosa people were never the same again, as they came to live and work on the farms of the white people instead of living as powerful tribes under their chiefs in their own territory. But the significance of this terrible tragedy in Christian terms is that it opened the hearts of the people as perhaps nothing else could have done to the power of the Gospel. About nine years later a great revival swept an estimated 6,000 souls into the Kingdom of God.

Other missions

Of course the Free Church was not the only church serving among the amaXhosa in the Eastern Cape and Transkei (often called 'The Territories') at this time.(AmaXhosa is a blanket name for various peoples who today speak the Xhosa language. Included among them are the Mfengu (Fingoes) whose acceptance of Christianity sometimes outstripped that of other Xhosa-speaking tribes. Political and other considerations were often the reason for this.) Methodists, Anglicans, Congregationalists and the Berlin Missionary Society were doing sterling work in different areas. Schools were set up, churches built, and later hospitals were established. These lasted until very recently.

John Ross and his sons

In Pirie John had his study, a thatched hut, built a little apart from the house, beside a much-used pathway. Here he often persuaded passing men to turn aside and rest, while he spoke to them of the one true God, and learned what he could of their language, customs, and religion. Two sons of John and Helen Ross, Bryce and Richard, made a valiant contribution to mission work in the area in later years.

As John Ross grew old, his love for the Lord's work was as alive as ever. His grandson, Brownlee Ross, tells of how, with his son

Bryce now working in Pirie, the old missionary was free to devote himself to his favourite evangelistic work. Long years afterwards he met "a venerable native preacher of the Wesleyan Church" who said: "I am overjoyed to shake your hand. To this day I can see your grandfather as I saw him long, long ago. His habit as he preached from village to village was, to turn aside to the place where we watered the cattle at noon, and small boys though we were, and unworthy of the attention of a grown man, he gathered us round him and spoke always of the love of the Father in heaven. I learned the Lord's Prayer there beside the water when I was a naked little boy, when not a soul of my family knew anything of worshipping God. Even now I can see him, a kind-faced friendly man, whom we all knew as a friend. You will live if you follow in his footsteps."

His grandson goes on to recall memories of holidays spent at Pirie in the early 1870s when his chief problem on Tuesdays and Thursdays was to make an early escape and be well into the forest before 9 a.m., the reason being that at 9 a.m. the old man's pony was brought to the door, and the grandson if present had to lead it from village to village, and listen with care to address after address, as an examination was probable on the way home. If his grandson was not there at nine sharp, a start had to be made and failing the grandson a local boy or even a domestic servant led the pony.

So as the old missionary sat by his door looking over to the Amatola hills, he had much cause for thankfulness. The last of the Xhosa wars swept over him in 1877 but the station was not destroyed and his sons were active helpers in the work of the Lord. The Free Church cause in South Africa looked set to flourish. The institutions of Lovedale and Blythswood (a similar establishment in Transkei) were famous throughout the surrounding countries. John Ross passed quietly to meet his Lord in 1878, after fifty-five years of faithful service.

And the work did continue to expand. Kaffraria was a name given to the land where the Xhosa-speaking people were settled, especially in the area south of the Kei. Originally the term 'Kaffir' was an Arab term for all Africans who were non-Moslem. It came to be used in the Cape Colony in South Africa as a term for the black people and, while not initially intended as a derogatory term it did come to bear a racist connotation and is not used today. In historical contexts, however, it is used without implying any form of insult. So in 1897 there were 137 Free Churches in the two Presbyteries of Kaffraria and Transkei, with 11 ordained missionaries and 4 Xhosa pastors. There were 28 European 'artizans' and lay evangelists, and 6508 members with 2500 people in candidates' classes. In 1898 there were 101 schools, with 182 teachers and 7288 pupils. There was one hospital (at Lovedale) and two Teacher Training Colleges.

But two years later – there was no Free Church there at all. Nothing, except a fond memory which lived on in the hearts of some of the Xhosa people and would not go away.

2

Why is there no Free Church?

The year was 1907. The place was Knox Mission, about 20 miles from the town of King William's Town, in the Eastern Cape region of South Africa. An ox cart, kindly lent by the local Chief, Songo Kama, trundled slowly up to where a gathering of African Christians waited patiently. Out of it stepped two Scottish clerics, Principal James McCulloch and Professor John Macleod. Some days before, they had arrived at the port of East London and had been let down from their boat in a basket, not because they were being rescued from danger but because there was not sufficient depth of water for their ship to dock. They were met by a delegation of African Christians who were proud to have belonged to the Free Church in years past and who were puzzled by the fact (they were told) that there was now no longer a Free Church. Why?

Church Turmoil in Scotland and South Africa

As we have seen, between the years 1843 and 1900 the Free Church mission in South Africa had expanded well. Then in 1900, back in Scotland, most of the Free Church united with the United Presbyterian Church and formed a large new denomination, the United Free Church of Scotland. A small number of ministers, twenty-six in all, did not enter this Union and continued to be the Free Church. Their reason for not going in to the new denomination was that they could not agree with the vital doctrinal changes which had been made to bring about the Union. What did these changes mean? Among other things these changes allowed ministers and elders to hold views which meant they did not have to believe the Bible to be the true and inspired Word of God, and allowed them to disagree with the doctrines of the Church as found in the Westminster Confession of Faith.

What happened to the Free Church's mission in South Africa then? All of its missionaries but one in South Africa left the Free Church and went into the new United Free Church. Naturally, the African Free Church Christians were confused. Where had their Church gone? What had happened to it? They were told that there was now no longer a Free Church. So most of them went along with their missionaries and went into the United Free Church. These matters were widely reported in the South African Press at the time, so it was not difficult for the African Christians to find out that not all that they had been told was true – there was indeed still a Free Church in Scotland. Some did not see why they could not still be Free Church also. "But," they were then told, "no missionary will ever come to you from that Church." Courageously, they decided to write to Scotland to find out the situation. From the reply they received, they knew that there was a Free Church, but it was still in some confusion – no doubt absorbed in fighting legal battles in court and in the House of Lords for the right to exist. Letters continued to come from Africa to Scotland assuring the Free Church that there were many Xhosa people in South Africa who were still loyal to her and wished to remain so.

Will there be money for missions?

This must have caused mixed reactions in the small denomination, struggling to come to terms with what had happened and not sure how much responsibility should be taken on for a new start so far away in South Africa. For many months everything was still in confusion as everyone had to wait till the Report of the Royal Commission was published, which had to apportion buildings and money between the United Free Church and the Free Church. Would there be enough money to even think of overseas mission work as well as the rebuilding of the Free Church in Scotland?

Unsettled times

There were other considerations too. The years around 1900 were troubled years in the Black population in South Africa. There were strikes and political unrest. This was also reflected in the churches. Understandably many Africans resented the way some White missionaries held on to the leadership roles in the churches and were reluctant to give them up to Black colleagues. There were secessions from several of the mainline denominations and these developed into a number of African Independent Churches. These were looked on with suspicion in the early days. The pre-1900 Free Church work in South Africa had been affected in this way when Rev Peter Mzimba broke with the church to form the African Presbyterian Church. So when some Free Church people refused to enter with the majority into the United Free Church, they too were treated as politically disruptive and they found themselves ostracised by their former colleagues. Along with letters from the remaining Free Church Christians came a letter from Rev Peter Mzimba, asking for more contact with the Free Church. Similar letters were to come from Rev R. Damane from Qumbu, Transkei, and the brothers Ntsikana and Burnet Gaba from Pirie near King William's Town.

Word also came to Scotland that the future of the cherished Institution of Lovedale was in jeopardy as the South African Government was proposing that it should become an "Inter-State Secular College". The Free Church in Scotland did not want that to happen either.

Rev J. McCulloch's first visit in 1905

In order to get first-hand information on the whole situation, in October 1904 the Foreign Missions Committee of the Free Church decided to send two delegates to South Africa. As it happened, only one of the delegates Rev (later Principal) James McCulloch, was able to go, and on 29 July 1905 he set sail for South Africa. This was his first of two visits, and it must have been a lonely experience, and one heavy with responsibility. His mission was "primarily to survey the Mission Fields in the interests of the Free

Church and, in particular, to see whether there be not room for the Free Church to carry on work for the Master without interfering with agencies already in the field". It was not all plain sailing. His visit was quite widely reported in the Press and misinterpreted. He was accused by the United Free Church (both in South Africa and in Scotland) of causing mischief by going out when he did, by sowing seeds of discontent among the Africans who had belonged to the pre-1900 Free Church. This was quite unfair, as it was these Africans themselves who had asked for the Free Church to come back and to work among them again.

Mr McCulloch returned to Scotland armed with a petition signed by four thousand Africans asking the Free Church to send missionary help, as they wanted to continue under the Free Church banner and not under the United Free Church. Probably there would have been personality clashes and disagreements between the two sides, but there is no doubt that the Africans who wanted to remain with the Free Church did so because they wanted to adhere to the doctrine of the church in which they had been nurtured rather than enter into the 'new' church. There had been a gradual change in the ethos of the church prior to 1900 and it seems that even in the schools run by the church at that time there was a lack of spiritual and Bible teaching which was giving cause for concern.

So now, what was to be done? The Foreign Missions Committee of those days was in a dilemma. They were not sure if it was a good idea to go back into the area where they had been working, as it might confuse the African Christians there. At the same time, Mr McCulloch had also visited Rhodesia (now Zimbabwe) where, it was stated in the 1906 General Assembly, "Such a virgin field seems specially to call for fresh Mission enterprise, such as, in God's providence, there is a prospect of the Free Church being able to enter upon." While this was being considered, letters continued to come from concerned people in South Africa giving further details of numbers and congregations in both Transkei and in areas to the south of Transkei (often referred to as the 'Colony') of those who still wanted to be Free Church.

To get a better understanding of this developing situation two delegates were again appointed to go to South Africa with the commission to visit all congregations who wanted to adhere to the Free Church and to convey to them the cordial greetings of the Free Church of Scotland. They were to give the assurance of the Church's sympathy and admiration for all who had held steadfastly to the principles of the church. Clearly more Africans had become aware of the situation between the Free Church and the United Free Church and several congregations wanted to come back to the Free Church and be recognised as such. They wanted missionaries to be sent and the Free Church Presbytery of Kaffraria to be re-established.

The 1907 Delegation

So once again Mr (now Principal) James McCulloch packed his bags and set off for the boat to South Africa – but this time he had the welcome company of Professor John Macleod. And that is why these two Scottish clerics came to be stepping out of the ox cart belonging to Chief Songo Kama, at Knox Mission, in July 1907. They used the ox cart to make a round of visits to congregations who wanted to be Free Church. The position of the Church at home in Scotland was made clear to all. They were assured of the sincerity of the people who gathered in each place to meet them. In the light of that the delegates sent back a cablegram to Scotland: *"Visited 19 sub-stations 6000 people movement genuine, resuscitation necessitates ordination 2 Gabas, they acceptable, Both well."*

Now this required a decision and a reply from the Free Church in Edinburgh. After a lengthy, and sometimes heated debate in the Foreign Missions Committee and in a Commission of General Assembly convened on 14 August, 1907, permission was given for the resuscitation of the Presbytery of Kaffraria and a little bit of history was made.

Re-birth of the Free Church in South Africa

The date for the phoenix-like rising from the ashes of the Free Church Presbytery of Kaffraria was Wednesday 21 August 1907 and it took place at Knox Mission. At Knox everyone in the church had wanted to be Free Church, so it seemed to be a natural centre for events. The two delegates from Scotland and one elder, Mr Philemon Mpunzi formed the roll of the Presbytery and it was agreed that Mr Ntsikana Gaba and his brother Mr Burnet Gaba should be taken on trials for ordination. Both of them had been probationers of the pre-1900 Free Church. At the same meeting the delegates met with over sixty representatives from various outstations and invited their recommendations as to where the two pastors, when ordained, should be placed. Eight days later on Thursday 29 August the two brothers were ordained, Rev Ntsikana Gaba to the Pirie District and Rev Burnett Gaba to the Burnshill District, with joint charge of Gqumahashe and Tyumie. Professor Macleod preached in the open air to the assembled congregation from Psalm 132 verse 15: *"I will abundantly bless her provision; I will satisfy her poor with bread."*

And so the Presbytery of Kaffraria was reborn – tiny but alive. Because there was only one acting elder in the congregation of Burnshill the Presbytery appointed William Gaba, (Mr) Alice Msele and Joseph Mafu to be assessors to the Kirk Session of Burnshill.

So when the two delegates departed for Scotland they left behind them a Presbytery, Kirk Sessions, elders – a fragile but replanted Free Church – and a fund of goodwill.

Principal McCulloch and Professor Macleod were warmly welcomed home after a job well done. Their reports of their visit were appreciated for the way they were able to contradict many unfair statements being circulated by those ill disposed to the Free Church both 'at home' and in South Africa. Both men spoke highly of the calibre of the laymen they had met in the South African church and of the many encouraging signs for the Church to continue its work there. It was now agreed that the church should look for a suitable missionary to undertake work in South Africa in fellowship with the church there.

Early Progress

Meanwhile, in South Africa, the Free Church was getting down to business. They started by forming Districts.

In the early days of mission among the Xhosa people, when a congregation was established in a main centre, or a mission station was set up, gradually several 'out stations' or preaching places would be opened and these along with the main congregation would constitute a District. Normally there would be one minister, one Kirk Session and one Deacons' Court in the District.

It is interesting to handle the early Session and Deacons' Court books – yellow with age now, the first entries penned by one or other of those two delegates from Scotland, Principal McCulloch or Professor John Macleod. They are followed very competently by one or other of the two brother ministers, the Gabas, and they outline the early stages of the resurrection of the Free Church of Scotland in South Africa. One of the first things one District's Deacons' Court arranged to do was to levy a toll of one shilling from each congregation to give to Chief Kama to say 'thank you' to him for the loan of his cart which had transported the two deputies all over the district as they assessed the situation and set up fledgling churches. In all they had petitions from 825 members, 257 candidates and 2966 adherents all wishing to remain with the Free Church.

Early impressions

What impressions do we get from those yellowing minute books of a century ago?

The first is faithfulness to the truth. The people met faithfully, often wherever they could find a meeting place as all their buildings had been taken from them. There the Gospel was preached. They instructed candidates for membership, they held prayer meetings and other special meetings, and they watched the life of their people and tried to be faithful in disciplining their flock and encouraging them to live Christianly.

The second thing which is so striking is the covenant family faithfulness of our God. Again and again names arose in the course of the business of the church, and the amazing thing is that one hundred years later these are still the surnames which will be written in the Kirk Session minute books of today in those same villages and districts. Still we find the Tyekelas, the Tahos, the Makapelas, the Mdledles, the Ntulis faithfully serving as elders or as leaders among the women. Truly our God is faithful to his covenant children.

Thirdly, the problems they had to contend with were so deep and numerous. Many of the new members had recently come from a life of heathenism. We find the Kirk Sessions dealing with cases where a man had sacrificed a cow to appease the forefathers because he was troubled by eye disease; a man had given a goat for sacrifice to the boys who were undergoing circumcision; then we find a request for guidance – should a Christian parent let his boy go to the circumcision 'school' with all the other boys of his age? The answer to this was short; NO! But this did not mean he was not to be circumcised. That would be unthinkable. He would be condemned to a life of perpetual 'boyhood' in the eyes of his people and would not be allowed to take part in any communal matter. So the advice given was that he should be circumcised but should be kept in a house or store near the home rather than going to the bush to be lectured to by the village elders. Often a girl came before the Session because she had "run off with a man", or a man appeared because he had made a girl with child, or had married her without her parents' consent. And often, often and often the complaint was 'adultery'. So the offender's name was erased from the roll of communicants, and he or she had to come before the Session in penitence three times before being considered for re-admission to membership. Gossiping, using foul language, fighting also featured in the Sessions' "bad books". In all these matters the brethren were trying to be faithful to the truth as it is in Scripture.

But there were encouragements along the way. Once it was reported that after a girls' prayer meeting in Dyafta congregation twenty-three people professed conversion. Three times in a short space of time there were conversions recorded in Dyafta.

So – by 1908, the Presbytery was up and running, evangelists had been appointed in some congregations, schools were organised in spite of severe difficulties in getting suitable buildings, and the people had been told that a missionary would come to help them.

ON REFLECTION

With hindsight, of course, it is easy to say things should maybe have been done differently.

It was relatively easy to establish a Presbytery and to see the Free Church's missionary work in South Africa up and running again. The matter had been discussed in Scotland, both in Committee and in the Commission of General Assembly. But had enough thought been given to the **continuance** of the Church there?

For example:

• What provision was to be made for the training of ministers?

• What financial policy was to be adhered to? Was the Church in South Africa to be encouraged to be self-sufficient from the outset or was it to depend on the 'mother church' far away?

• What was the relationship of missionary staff to the African Church's own ministers and Presbytery?

We do have to remember that the year was 1907 and not 2007. Missionary policy was in many ways different then. Also, most of the people closely associated with missionary policy had departed from the Free Church. Even so, perhaps greater thought should have been given to the long term development of the work now begun as this would have determined the next steps for the 'home church' to take.

3

Enter Mr Dewar

Back in Scotland the search for a suitable missionary began. The Foreign Missions Committee put out a notice; "The Committee earnestly request any whose heart may be inclined towards the mission field to enter into communication with them without delay." Several names came before the Committee and eventually the Committee recommended the name of **Rev Alexander Dewar** for the position. This recommendation was ratified by the General Assembly in May 1908.

It has to be said that making such an appointment did not please everyone. There were those who felt the needs of the home church should receive priority over the foreign field. But, as Professor Macleod pointed out at a Synod meeting in Glasgow on 9 April 1908, "What is needed on the mission-field is men of faith, courage, prayer, resource, and common sense. To starve the mission-field is not the way to insure success at home." Again, in the General Assembly of that year it was stated that, "there is no antagonism between the clamant necessities of the congregations at home and of those abroad. Rather, they (i.e. the Foreign Missions Committee) look upon the deepening interest in Foreign Missions as fitted to strengthen and consolidate the church through all her borders".

Mr Dewar himself was not in Scotland at the time, so could not be interviewed in person. He was in Burma as a Chaplain with the Burmah Oil Company. He was born in 1864, a native of Lochgilphead, Argyll, so he would have been about 44 years old at this time. His application for missionary work in South Africa was not his first experience in this context. He had been ordained by the Free Church in 1893 and appointed a missionary at the

Livingstonia Mission in Nyasaland (now Malawi). Following the events in Scotland around 1900, Mr Dewar left the mission in Nyasaland. It was then that he went to Burma. But they say, "If you have drunk of the water of Africa, you will always come back." And so he forwarded his application for service in South Africa and awaited the outcome. Letters of recommendation about him were sought and found favourable. Rev Alexander Stewart who knew him well described Mr Dewar as "a man of downright honesty, of earnest evangelical zeal, who laid the emphasis on the right place in mission work. His supreme aim was to win souls for the Redeemer. He had a striking thoroughness of method and a capacity for taking pains. He was a man of marked firmness of character, and if disposed to err, it was on the side of severity". (Ouch!) "He was a man of marked independence of character, but he did not say he was a perfect man." Well, where would you find a perfect man?

And so a letter or cablegram intimating that his application had been successful was posted to Burma and a reply of acceptance was received.

On his return to Scotland from Burma, arrangements were made for him to speak at a series of public meetings to introduce himself to the people. It would have made good listening if we could have been present at these meetings.

In his previous time in Africa on the Nyasa/Tanganyika plateau, at the sources of the Congo, Mr Dewar had to do pioneering work, and build his own station. Being the first missionary to the people living there, he had to reduce their language to writing. After furlough he had a most successful term at the north end of Lake Nyasa. We are told that in all his work his wife was a most valued and talented helper. He was also a keen observer of the flora and fauna of the areas through which he travelled and was an excellent horseman. The Dewars had two children, a boy and a girl.

In 1904 he came home to Scotland, but it was not by the conventional route. "Desirous of seeing fresh country and new tribes, he did not return home by the usual Shire/Zambezi route, but setting his face northwards, travelled right up through the dark continent, sailing up Lake Tanganyika, then across Kiru, the passage of which had to be made in a dug-out. He was a few weeks travelling through the Congo Free State, passed through the cannibal country, and up Lake Albert Edward. He was eight days in the Congo forest, and saw the Ituri pygmies in their own home. Leaving Lake Albert, he sailed down the Nile to Khartoum, and thence to Cairo, completing a most interesting journey – being the first white man to accomplish it without an armed escort." His loyal wife and family nevertheless went home by the more conventional route, but nearly lost their lives by drowning on Lake Nyasa!

In 1908, after the Burma interlude, and after making himself known to congregations of the Free Church in Scotland, Mr Dewar was inducted to the South African field by the Free Presbytery of Edinburgh on 19 October. He and his wife Emmeline and their two children Rex and Margaret travelled to South Africa on 31 October 1908. Their first destination was to be King William's Town and from there he could consider what would be the best centre from which to carry out his work and to report to the Committee. His salary was to be £330 per annum and he was to be the Superintendent of the Mission.

So – enter Mr Dewar. Thirty-five years later, Mr Dewar was still in King William's Town, still superintending the Mission, and, though others had come and gone, he was still on his own in the field.

Getting to grips with the task

The Africans had warmly welcomed the appointment of Mr Dewar and they were awaiting his arrival with excitement and antici-pation. Mr Dewar wrote:

"My arrival seemed delayed, and their opponents had not hesitated to take advantage of same, boldly asserting that no mis-sionary would ever be sent from Scotland by the Free Church, and telling our people they might as well expect their fathers to rise from the dead as look for a Free Church missionary from home. Some said if such were to happen they would renounce Christianity and return to their red clay, while others, more bold, said they were willing to cut their throats if such a man should appear, so confident were they – or at any rate, wished to appear so – that no man would come ... (Our people's) faith and patience had been put to a severe test."

On 30 November, soon after his arrival in King William's Town, Mr Dewar had his first meeting with the Church people he had come to serve and who had waited so long for this day. The meeting was held at Pirie, and one of the elders, Mr Makubalo, provided a horse and trap for the journey of about 10 miles from King William's Town.Two other riders accompanied them and these were joined by others along the way until the cavalcade numbered about thirty. Rev Ntsikana Gaba welcomed him, Rev Burnett Gaba and friends from Burnshill were also there and informed Mr Dewar that they looked forward to him going to Burnshill the following day. A large crowd followed the party, gathered as they were from several out-stations. Choirs from different schools were also there to welcome the new missionary. They were pleased to have a Free Church Missionary in their midst. "They gave me a splendid reception, and made me feel quite at home and among old friends", wrote Mr Dewar. At the end of that momentous day he wrote: "Altogether, it was a most hearty gathering, and the people felt it was a glad day."

Sure enough the following day another gathering was held at Burnshill about 20 miles from King. Mr Dewar was an expert horseman and this journey was made on horseback. Tall and erect, there was no trundling in a slow ox wagon for him. On the way he was accompanied by a cavalcade of elders etc, the leading man of which would shout to bystanders, "This is the man they said would never come. Now here he is and see him." Rev Ntsikana Gaba joined him and as they entered Burnshill, riding two abreast, "what a shout of welcome and loud hurrahs arose from over a thousand voices!" Mr Dewar wrote to the Foreign Missions Committee, "It was a right royal welcome, and I could only wish that you (Prof Bannatyne to whom the letter was written) and the members of the Committee, together with the delegates who had a large share in bringing this event to pass, had been present to see and share in it. If the number of those present, and the expression of their feelings, can be taken as any indication of the spirit and courage which animate our Free Church natives, then it augurs well for the future of our work in South Africa. I felt God had done great things in permitting us to take part in such a service, and prayed that He would bless us still more in days to come and make us worthy of this great work."

So began Mr Dewar's long service to the Church there.

Looming problems

It was as well that the new missionary had had the encouragement of the great welcomes as there were many problems awaiting him and the African colleagues with whom he was to work.

a) *Buildings*
One of the most important considerations for the Free Church after 1900 was the provision of buildings for both worship and schools. The Free Church had lost all its buildings to the United Free Church. The Executive Commission, which had been set up to deal with this matter in Scotland, said that it had no locus in the disposing of mission buildings. The churches in South Africa were responsible for the provision of schools and now the Free Church had lost all of these also. In spite of repeated pleas to Government officials no sites were granted for the erection of new school buildings for several years. It was quite apparent that officials had been advised to refuse requests from the Free Church. This was a distressing situation because in different villages Free Church children were refused entry to schools run by the United Free Church. The whole business surrounding the provision of buildings came to have a completely disproportionate importance in the early years of the twentieth century.

b) *Mode of worship*
Another important matter that had to be looked at was the mode of worship in the Free Church in South Africa. The people were used to singing mainly hymns. There was only a limited number of Psalms rendered into metre for singing. One of the points raised in

favour of Mr Dewar's appointment had been his "notable service in translating several portions of Scripture in the native dialects (in Malawi). His attainments in this direction are plainly of special value, in view of the necessity of an adequate metrical version of the Psalms for the missionary requirements of the Free Church." However it was to be many years before the whole Xhosa Psalter was put into metre for singing, and in the meantime the people happily sang hymns with enthusiasm and harmony. Mr Dewar had so many tasks tugging at his time that the learning of the complex Xhosa language must have had to wait. Indeed, he never felt confident enough to preach in Xhosa but used an interpreter to the last.

c) *Applications to join the Free Church*
A problem of quite a different nature was the question of dealing with requests from ministers and congregations from other denominations who applied to come into the Free Church. We remember that Rev P.J. Mzimba, who had left the church before 1900 and formed his own group of churches, had made a tentative approach. He had a well-organised denomination but several from his Church wanted to come back to the Free Church. One such group was from the Tsolo area in the Transkei region. They wanted to come to the Free Church under their minister, Rev R. Damane. Such additions to the Free Church sometimes created problems but others fitted in extremely well.

d) *The employment and payment of evangelists*
Before long another problem arose about the employment and payment of evangelists. Rev Burnett Gaba said that the church had promised the salaries for 8 evangelists and these were now employed. This had been tentatively agreed to by the home Committee and it had been made clear that no appointments were to be made on a permanent basis until there was a missionary Superintendent in place. It was not the Committee's intention to fund the African workers. "The Committee have in view, that the Mission should, as early as possible be self-supporting as far as native agents are concerned, and Mr Dewar is requested to furnish

a report as to how this can be effected." This was very wise advice. However, in the meantime the Committee did send money and this established a precedent that they found extremely difficult to go back on. A church whose workers are paid by a distant 'parent' church takes so much longer to become self-supporting and independent. Not easy when the church members are poor, but the earlier they can learn to set aside a small amount for their own leaders the better.

Mr Dewar was also asked to get as much information as possible about sites for church schools and what titles would be necessary for these. He supplied an impressive list of twenty congregations (Pirie and Burnshill were the main places, and the others were offshoots, as it were) and soon was able to add more from Transkei.

Mr Dewar tells of an incident at a Presbytery meeting held at Knox. One old Chief said, "I am a member of the Free Church and have worked for it. At Tyumie, in my father's time, we had Mr McDermid as our teacher, Mr (Rev) Laing coming to dispense the Lord's Supper. When we crossed the Kei, the Free Church followed us, and a missionary, Mr W. Donald, was settled among us. He was succeeded by Mr Erskine. We built a church and I gave land to the Free Church. The land was granted by the old people. Mr Erskine has now brought in a new church, but I will die a Free Churchman and my funeral must be attended by Free Church people."

Knox was the one place where all the people adhered to the Free Church but even there the United Free Church would not allow the Free Church to use the church building (which the people had built at their own expense). How extremely sad that the troubles of the mother church 6000 miles away had to be fought out on the mission field!

Mr Dewar continued to visit the various congregations, among them Mnyameni where he experienced for the first time an *Imvuselelo*, a "revival" service. These services are evangelistic in nature. Some "Red" people (heathen) attended the services but "on the whole they were hard to reach".

In all the places visited by Mr Dewar in the course of the year the story was the same. The lack of buildings for church and school was a vexing hindrance. At Dyafta, where there were many Free Church people, the schoolmaster of the United Free Church School, Mr Henry Ntshona, belonged to the Free Church and so most of the Free Church children attended his school. Before long he was dismissed and most of the pupils left. Several attempts were made to try to find a solution to the problem of buildings but eventually the Free Church was told that the United Free Church authorities were not prepared to negotiate in any way about the Free Church's use of buildings in South Africa. In the course of 1910 the Free Church decided that they would not proceed any further with efforts to gain access to any of the buildings now claimed by the United Free Church. When this was reported to the African people they were obviously disappointed, but "in spite of their disappointment they all heartily resolved to adhere to the Free Church, and expressed their willingness to do their best in erecting necessary buildings". (Dewar to the Foreign Missions Committee) No doubt it was the best thing that could happen for cementing the church together.

On safari

In the month of May 1909, Mr Dewar, accompanied by Rev Ntsikana Gaba and Elder Philemon Mpunzi (who was an evangelist in the part of Transkei to which they were going) undertook a journey round the church stations in Griqualand, Transkei, to see for himself what was the true state of affairs as far as loyalty to the Free Church was concerned. He left his horse behind and boarded the train – a much slower mode of travel. Let him tell the story in his own words as he gives us a good flavour of what life and land were like in those early days:

> In going to the Transkei, the train arrangements are such you have to leave King William's town in the evening, wait a considerable time at the first junction a few miles off, stop at every little wayside station, then pull up about 9 o'clock at Amabele junction where you remain for the night.

Next morning, while still dark, the train starts at 6 o'clock. Soon the sky begins to brighten and we can see we are travelling through rich grazing country. The farms are large and carry many sheep. Trees are few, although in some places the indigenous thorn tree has been protected and adds a beauty to the otherwise bare grass land. In some of the river courses and ravines the original forest growth is preserved. This not only makes the scenery more varied but must be of great value in conserving the water supply, in keeping the soil moist and the pasture green.

The train follows a winding course – the line keeping the natural level, instead of as at home, going through cuttings and along embankments or over bridges and viaducts.

We stop at many little wayside places to put down a passenger, or more often a few packages. The sun is now above the horizon and we get a nice view.

The farmhouses are easily recognised with clumps of trees and the cultivated fields showing up a brighter green. In the distance can be seen the ocean – the connecting link between here and home. Passing a fruit farm and nurseries we soon reach Komagha where the train stops sufficiently long to allow of passengers having breakfast. It is a small township pleasantly situated in a valley or hollow.

The train now ascends until in a short time we are at the top and on the edge of the high ground overlooking the great rift or valley of the Kei. The sight is a grand one. The river itself is hidden from view, but the huge wall forming its left bank rises sheer up, exposing the different strata. Beyond, are the distant stretches of the Transkei uplands and behind these again are the mountains of Tembuland. On this side of the Kei, are huge irregular mountain masses, one or two looking like islands rising up from the valley below. The sides are very precipitous having a perpendicular drop of hundreds of feet. Great must have been the upheaval when the Kei valley was formed.

The train has to make its way down to the river level far beneath us. The line must have given the surveyors a lot of work. It goes round many hills and crosses the connecting necks; now and again it doubles on its track, yet all the time descending, until, when near the river, it has some zigzagging or reversing. (At one point) a temporary bridge has been built. It is entirely of wood, the trestles resting on concrete foundations. The feeling one has as the train crosses is that the structure is very insecure. We felt this more on the return journey, when, after heavy rains, the river was swollen and the waters dashed against the concrete bases; as the heavy train simply crawled across, the timbers creaked, and we felt as if each moment the bridge would give way and land train and passengers in the depth below.

We crossed the river and had the same winding out and in and up hill to get on to the general level again. Going up the Toleni valley the scenery is very fine, and the Toleni Falls – as the full river rushes over the rocky edge into a deep pool far below – is a sight well worth seeing.

After passing some large plantations we come on to the great stretches of grazing country. In a short time we are at Ndabakazi – the station for Cunningham and Blythswood. (Both ex-Free Church institutions. Cunningham was a mission station staffed for many years by Rev Richard Ross, a son of Rev John Ross of Pirie. Blythswood, a school similar to Lovedale, was opened in 1877 among the Mfengu people who largely paid for the building themselves). This is a rich part of the country and seems to be well populated. Soon

we were speeding downhill on the way to Butterworth
– the present terminus of the Transkei line ...

On the mail cart

It was expected that a trap or ponies would be waiting
our arrival but not finding them we made our way to
the market square in the hope of meeting them there.
The time was going and unless we wished to stay
overnight in Butterworth, we had to arrange for our
getting to Idutywa. The mail cart was about to start,
so, booking our seats, and stowing ourselves as best
we could among the mail bags, began another stage of
the journey.

The route for the first part was up and down hill,
but our cart, drawn by six mules and in charge of a
competent Kafir, (an acceptable term at that time)
made good progress. The dust enveloped us as it rose
from the dry road. The country was bare of trees,
hence it was a pleasing change to us to pass by a large
plantation of wattles, I think. They grow readily and
quickly, and besides being a source of profit, greatly
relieve the monotony of the landscape.

There were not many huts to be seen, but here and
there were farmhouses and trading stations. Halfway
to Idutywa we got a fresh team, and as the road was
good we went quickly on. Soon the sun went down, the
cold night air made itself felt and we experienced the
benefit of our rugs.

Carrying His Majesty's mails gave us the right of
way, and each time we came up on an ox wagon, our
driver would sound his battered bugle, which at once
caused the road to be cleared. We drew up at Idutywa
about 7 o'clock – having been three hours travelling.
Our driver was well up in his work; he had been some
years on the route, knew every turn of the road and
handled his large team well.

(A few days later, while still in Idutywa, Mr Dewar records that on its way back from Umtata the post cart was trying to cross a steep drift after much rain and the driver and five of the six mules were drowned)

On foot by moonlight

We were not yet at our journey's end, Philemon (Mpunzi) our evangelist who, with Rev N. Gaba accompanied me, saying we had five or six miles in front before reaching our destination. Fortunately, the night was good and there was clear moonlight, but it was very cold. As we walked, I was reminded of my Central African experiences where we had no train or post cart. Here however we had no fear or thought of wild beasts.

On arriving at Sangqu's (the headman of Ngc-ingwane) about 9.30 we found he had not received Mr Gaba's letter informing him of our visit. He was delighted to see us and at once got up from bed and made arrangements for our accommodation at the kraal of one of his people about three miles away. As we approached this place, the dogs announced our arrival. Usually, one can afford to think lightly of native dogs, but not so in this district, where each family lives at a distance from its neighbour and possessing many sheep and cattle they require not only good watch dogs, but animals that will attack any stranger who approaches, especially at night.

The people got up and gave us a hearty welcome and placed their best house at our disposal. It was of corrugated iron and very small. Having been on the journey since early morn and getting in cold and tired at 11 p.m. after a tramp across country we were soon ready for a good night's rest ...

First sight of Ngcingwane

Mr Dewar goes on to tell how a public meeting was arranged by Headman Sangqu and his counsellors for the following Saturday. The headman killed two oxen and the people gave 23 sheep and goats for the feast. The weather became wet and cold, but changed on the Saturday to allow the people to meet at the chief's place. Mr Dewar says:

> Sangqu sent his two traps – each drawn by a pair of ponies – to convey us to his kraal. About twenty men accompanied us on horseback. As we drove up, the crowd gave us a grand welcome. I conveyed to them the greetings of the Home Church and its continued interest in them and explained how matters stood at the present time. Sangqu and his elders responded telling how they and their fathers had been brought up in the Free Church and wished to remain in it.

They had built a church and school at their own expense, and felt aggrieved at the loss of these buildings, but were anxious to build again if a site could be obtained. They had applied for this the year before but were put off. During the next week Mr Dewar went to the local magistrate but could make no headway.

He goes on to describe services held the next day:

> Next day we had our regular services in the hut, and although the people had in some cases a good way to travel in the cold and wet, the place was crowded out, there being 121 inside and a few standing about the doorway. We examined some candidates – including two of Sangqu's sons – for admission to Membership. The people were greatly encouraged and felt that work would go on again. The following week a communion service was held, when, in spite of cold and wet weather, the place of worship was again crowded. Some children and adults were baptised, the latter being admitted to membership as were some who had been baptised in infancy. It was a solemn and refreshing time, the

people felt the work was being re-established and they went away strengthened and rejoiced.

The following morning at 4.15 a.m. they were up and about and on their ponies an hour later in the dark and intensely cold morning. A tired but very encouraged missionary arrived safely back to his wife and family in King William's Town about 10 p.m. that night.

A Journey to Jamangile's place

In September of the same year, 1909, Mr Dewar undertook a similar journey to the far away stations in Griqualand East, in particular to visit a very old chief – Jamangile – in the Tsolo district, who had said he had all along been a Free Churchman and he wished to remain one, and when his end came, that the church should bury him.

He lived at the bottom of a deep broad valley, about 1000 feet down. Again the people had built a church with their own hands and had lost the right to use it. They felt very aggrieved, especially as many more people were worshipping in the hut at Jamangile's place than were in the church, hearing the U.F. minister. They rejoiced in the services taken by Mr Dewar and he left feeling great sympathy for them.

He went on to Embokotwane, riding the twenty five miles or so over the broad plain. He says, "This place reminded me much of some of our Highland valleys. The river flowed over stones, boulders and sand and made the same music as the home streams." The Sabbath after his return to Jamangile's place he had a baptismal and communion service there. Fifty-one members communicated. The second service had to be held in the open air under the shelter of a shady tree.

The old people were sad to see him go the next day. "One old man who could speak a word or two of English said he and his companions were now old and soon they would be in their graves and that meantime they had no white missionary and if one should be sent to them by the time he came they would be underground. At the service he broke down as he was praying."

So Mr Dewar parted from the North Transkei friends wondering how he could move mountains to help them, and returned home after nearly four weeks away to ponder.

Problems and encouragements

There were busy times for the Kirk Sessions and Deacons' Courts in those early years. They had to cope with many problems that arose from the lack of buildings, lack of communion sets, Sunday School facilities and so on. Along with this there was the sad procession of discipline cases that seemed to come before every meeting of the Sessions. The Presbytery discussed this difficult matter at its meeting in October 1909. Why did some sins or offences come up time and time again? They decided to warn members about their behaviour and to caution those who prepared candidates for membership that they should take greater care when they admitted people into membership and that they should be well taught in the way of Christ and his Church. In the communities as a whole, immorality was rife, even long-standing cultural values were breaking down, many non-Christian practices were common, even among those who were professing Christians. But in the midst of all the problems there were encouragements. Souls were being saved and the church built up.

In one letter back to Scotland, Rev Ntsikana Gaba wrote on 3 July 1908, "Recently the following numbers gave themselves up to the Lord. Twelve at Whiteville, seven at Dyafta's, two at Knox and one at Rankin. Among the converts six were Reds (heathen). This is a guarantee, that those of the Home Church do mention us constantly in their prayers at the throne of grace."

Looking back on the first decade of the post-1900 Free Church in South Africa we see much to encourage but also much that makes disappointing reading.

The church had withstood the severe trauma that resulted from the Union, more people were applying to come into the church, including some ministers as well as their congregations and, in spite of the lack of buildings, schools had been opened and church services were held in many places. A new missionary superintendent was at the helm, preaching the Gospel, visiting the scattered congregations and trying to get sites for buildings and salaries for teachers. But, as we have seen there were many pastoral problems which hindered the work just as much as the lack of buildings did. Divisions among the African folk brought their own distress. However overall there was much to feel thankful for and there was optimism for the days ahead.

ON REFLECTION:

The home Church's finances were extremely limited after 1900 and care was taken to get the services of a suitable missionary to superintend the Field in South Africa – **but**:

1. Would it not have been both Biblically correct and eminently practical, if the church was going to re-establish work in South Africa, that **two** rather than one, missionaries should have been sent? The geographical spread of the field as well as the need for someone to talk things over with would suggest that this would have been better.

2. We acknowledge the sterling efforts of Mr Dewar in those early days as he gathered information, preached the Gospel in so many different places and pleaded the Church's cause before magistrates and other officials who were often quite unsympathetic and even dismissive.

4
Exits and Entries
1910–1920

Mrs Emmeline Dewar's story

During the settling in time in South Africa, Mr Dewar had been riding about and getting to know everyone and having adventures in his travels. His wife Emmeline, from all accounts a sweet and spiritually minded lady, was at home with their daughter Margaret (Queenie for short) and their son Rex. But late in 1909 and early 1910, they rented a four-roomed house in Mnyameni and took an ox wagon ride to get themselves and all their goods there to stay during the school holidays. In the March 1910 *Instructor* (The Free Church's magazine for young people), Mrs Dewar writes a vivid account of their journey there and the good time they had with the folk of that beautiful village in the hills of the Burnshill District:

> On Friday, December 24 the waggon with its twelve oxen rumbled up to our door (in the town of King William's Town). It was pouring rain, and had been for the last twelve or fifteen hours, but as everything was packed we thought we had better make a start.
>
> We locked our doors, and bundled into the waggon about 4 o'clock, and sat upon tin boxes. Oh, dear! Oh, dear! The rain still came pouring down, so the waterproof covering had to be kept tightly fastened; the heat became intense, and the jolting for a time seemed unbearable. We could not for a moment let go our hold

of the framework for fear of our heads being thrown against the side. Before long darkness came on; we had forgotten where we had put the candles; and had we known, it was perfectly impossible to get at them ... At 12.30 am we stopped, and the oxen were outs-panned – handsome, patient beasts they were, glad to be out of the yoke for a time. The boys kindled a fire on a brazier right under the waggon. We could hear the crackling, and see the fitful glare through the opening in the boards below us. We tried to sleep, but the coldness of the night, and our uncomfortable position among all the boxes effectively kept nature's sweet restorer away.

We learned afterwards that the dear oxen had been very wicked; they had made their way to a native's garden, and were making good use of their time. Before our boy could get them again he was forced to leave the screw jack behind, to ensure the fine of 6d. a head being paid for the damage.

We were distressed to see our boys wading through the mud, constantly attending to the brake at the back. The leader, a slight boy of about ten years old, looked more like a walking scarecrow than anything else. He had on a huge pair of trousers – his whole body could have slipped easily through one leg – and a man's coat that barely hung on his little narrow shoulders, the sleeves constantly hampering him when using the long whip or attending to the brake. His name was Willie Johnnie, and a sharper, more capable, cheerier small boy, it would be hard to find.

Before long we heard Mr Mpengo's voice, and glad we were to chat to him, and find that he had thought-fully ridden out to meet us and see us safely across the rivers and more difficult parts of the road. Oh! The jolting and the tossing and the cramped cold feet ... We (i.e. the writer, Mrs Dewar!) mildly suggested 'turning back' and enjoying home comforts, but as this word has never found a place in Mr Dewar's vocabulary, we had to yield to the inevitable. We were thrown from one side to the other in the most alarming way, Margaret and I being terribly sick in the midst of it all. But the worst had happily come to the worst! Mr Mpengo told us the roads further on were simply impassable, and being so slippery it was too risky to attempt – we must stay at his village. We got out with great delight and enjoyed the cosy hut and fire ... We had a warm welcome from Mrs Mpengo, her daughter-in-law, and a friend, an evicted Free Church woman – the spiritual pillar of the place. The waterproof covering had not been properly fixed, and our feet and bed-clothes had all become soaked. We were glad to get our shoes off and dry our stockings by the pretty log fire.

Mnyameni at last

The next day, though it still rained, the people gathered in the centre room, and we had service morning and afternoon. It was the first meeting the children and I had attended with the natives, and we were glad. The next morning we walked leisurely on to Emnyameni, the two children riding on the pony. We were again very warmly welcomed by Mrs Mdledle and her family of two sons, three daughters, daughter-in-law, and grandchildren. They were still busy whitewashing her whole house, and freshly manuring the floors. A cup of tea was prepared in her own comfortable, commodious, well-built hut, which we thoroughly enjoyed.

It is the custom for the sons to bring their wives home to their father's village, and they are expected to help in every way just like a daughter. If they are not happy, and think too much is demanded of them, they go back to their old home and another cow has to be paid before they return. Probably nine or ten cows have already been given before the marriage. During our visit the younger son rode off with his elder brother to see his fiancee, and get the father to name the day. They took with them a cow, the ninth and last of the purchase price ...

Mr Mdledle had passed away five months before our visit, and his loss was still keenly felt by his widow and the district generally. He had been an outstanding character; becoming blind soon after his marriage he had superintended and enthused the whole of the people around. He was the Free Church leader, and one of his last acts was to have the seats in the temporary church fixed. He would ride with others all the way into King William's Town and back, and his memory and sense of hearing were wonderfully acute. Mrs Mdledle told me he often could tell her who people were that she failed to recognise, simply by remembering the voices.

Several times I found myself wishing the home friends could be with us. Religion, labour, and love were all united and pictured in this happy valley. Mrs Mdledle, the mother in Israel, had a sweet face, mellowed by her recent bereavement. She was surrounded by her grown-up sons and daughters, and her little grandchildren were all running and hiding behind her, and often fast asleep in her arms ...

On Sundays she was one of the most devout hearers, inspiring the speakers and superintending the Sunday School between the two services. She used the 'Mother's Catechism' for them. It was a pretty sight to see all the young girls around her under the shady trees.

We shall not forget the Sabbaths. We were wakened in the mornings by the lowing of the cattle, the grunting of the pigs, and the crowing of the cocks. The view from the open door was a change to us. The 'sitting room' opened straight on to the veldt, the silent grand mountains rising in front, and the river hurrying musically down below on its way to the sea. The bright green of the grass and the rich burnt sienna colour of earth contrasted so beautifully, while the handsome forests nestling in every hollow added a deeper green to the picture. The eye was rested and feasted too.

Soon the bell was heard – a piece of an old plough served to call the people together, struck by a smaller piece of iron ... There they came over hill and dale, looking so small in the distance, yet God's people – finite creatures – in many of whom He, the Infinite, was dwelling, guiding, restraining, and yet inspiring them. They gathered, as many as could, in the hut, and the singing, to me at least, was strangely touching. The melody was there, a psalm tune, some rare classic but borne along in a sea of harmonies, each one seemingly a law to himself, the women often taking the tenor an octave higher, and some of the men filling in with a wonderfully rich bass. The last verse invariably repeated, and several notes were put in to connect one line with the others of the verse ... Several reds were there and listened most attentively.

On New Year's Day we were invited to listen to the choir. Afterwards we all played with the children on the village green, a level piece of ground close to the church – girls, boys, men and women all had their turn and were not forgotten ... Before parting we thanked God for the beauties all around us, and the health and strength to enjoy it all. It was a lovely evening, the mountains standing silent and grand, the cattle all slowly winding their way home, and the evening star, telling the milking time, shining out in the opal sky.

These people are full of sentiment and conviction, they are strongly attached to the Church of their forebears. They often said their fathers and grandfathers were staunch Free Churchmen, and they wished to remain so. They feel it terribly, not being allowed to enter their own buildings, and for so long to be cramped in a hut, or under the trees ...

Enter Mr Matayo

In that same village of Mnyameni, Mr William Matayo was a teacher in the early days of 1909. He had been dismissed by the education authorities for adhering to the Free Church. He was not even given the quarter's salary due instead of notice. In 1909 the Foreign Missions Committee gave him a grant as an evangelist, so he seems to have done both jobs very conscientiously and well and he was liked by the people. He was anxious to get some books or literature which could help him with his preaching, and Mr Dewar asked some folk in Scotland to send some out if they could. He taught the Free Church school under many difficulties up in Mnyameni in the Burnshill District, possibly helped by two young female teachers. He used a round hut as a schoolroom. Imagine fitting in a school with 111 on the roll into a round hut! But they were well taught.

When Mr Dewar rode up the hill in late 1910 to pay a visit to the school to examine the pupils he had great praise for the teacher and his pupils. Each pupil was examined, and in all the subjects the results were good. He remarks, "We had counted on this school doing well, but the children did much better than was expected. In Standard 4, Composition (English) was exceedingly well done, while in Arithmetic many gained full marks. Mental Arithmetic was not quite so good. English Dictation and Reading were very satisfactory. Xhosa Reading and Dictation – weak in most schools – had been well attended to. The same good work was done in all the Standards. Bible knowledge was fair, but more attention is being given to this subject, and the parents were urged to supply their children with Bibles or Testaments ... They were far in advance of the other schools." Some of the pupils were very poor and clad for the occasion in their father's best jacket. The problem was that since the Free Church school did not get grants,

Mr Matayo was dependent on fees from his pupils' parents, and money was so scarce at that time. Mr Dewar appealed to folk back home to help in this situation by sending shirts and dresses or cloth *('dark blue cloth with a small white pattern')* in the boxes they were sending out.

One day, early in the morning, Mr Matayo had a visitor. He tells us "Last Wednesday, a young man came very early at dawn while we were still in bed at my dwelling house. He said on Communion Day he was greatly troubled in his mind in seeing some of the women baptizing their children without their husbands as if they were widows, and he remembered his little ones, three of them, who would have been baptized by his wife long ago but he refused her (permission) to perform those rites on her children, simply because he said to her, 'Wait a little till I am also admitted to Church privileges. I thought then I would continue in the Catechumen's class, but the pleasures of the world hindered and kept me back. Give me lessons at once so that I may know the grounds I must tread'. So I did" (adds Matayo).

Chief Jamangile's death

Mention is made by Mr Dewar and Mr Matayo of 'Jamangile's place'. He was the 'kindly old chief' who lived near Tsolo in Griqualand East, Transkei, and who had all along been a Free Churchman and wished to remain one, and who said that when his end came, the church should bury him.

Now on 19 May, 1910, his end did indeed come. Mr Dewar writes:

His son (Jali) in telling me of his father's death, writes thus: "My father was happy, very happy, at the hour of death, he was always praying day and night. We are comforted with his words. He told us that his way is free, and that he was anxious to go and stay among his old Missionaries of the Free Church where his father and mother are. His soul was taken up on high in the evening of 19 May. Three times a day he was praying alone at his place. He was buried by a very great number, over 300 ... These are his last words:

'You, Jali, must obey my ministers belonging to the Free Church. Keep them, and give them (give heed) to everything they want when they have come here. Never separate with the Free Church ministers ... I myself, Jamangile, was waiting for them to come over and give communion.'"

Then his son Jali reassured Mr Dewar that he would be loyal to the Free Church and belonged to it. Even if the church his father had built and which was taken by the United Free was now lost to them, they would support the Free Church in the building of another.

This gives a taste of the strength of feeling and the loyalty which people had at that time to the church of their fathers.

Visit of Rev Dr Maclean

People were on the move even a century ago, and one encouragement for the newly revived Free Church was a visit from Dr Maclean in the summer of 1910, while on his way to visit Australia. The Rev Dr Donald Maclean was minister of Free St Columba's Church, Edinburgh, from 1905–1918 and was later a Professor and Principal of the Free Church College.

Mr Dewar took Dr Maclean on a tour of as many congregations as he could. They visited Knox, where a good gathering had assembled and Dr Maclean gave a message of greeting from the home church before preaching a "very helpful sermon to an attentive audience". That night they stayed at Debe Nek Hotel, but did not sleep very well. "Only a thin wall separated our room from the stables, hence, with horses so near, and rats making merry in the low ceiling overhead, sleep kept far away."

Then it was on to Pirie, Burnshill, Alice and Gqumahashe, and Lovedale School. On every side he was asked why had they given up the property to the United Free Church? He did his best to answer that one! Mr Dewar says, "His coming was like a breath from home, fresh from our Highland hills, and we greatly enjoyed his company and fellowship."

Dr Maclean himself said on his return, "What South Africa needs is not so much an elaborate and highly developed system of education, mainly secular, as the Gospel of Jesus Christ." "Mr Maclean's words clearly imply a mistrust of Lovedale's more modern methods, and a plea for the aims and methods of the great Evangelical preacher whose name it bears, Dr John Love," was the comment made.

What happened to the Presbytery?

The Presbytery meeting of 1910, held on December 7 at Knox, decreed that the next Presbytery for ordinary business should meet on 1 March 1911 at Pirie. However, just a week before the meeting was due to be held Mr Dewar had sent a notice to say the meeting should be in Burnshill. Tensions were still there over the applications for church sites. Rev B. Gaba insisted that they should be registered in the name of local trustees and not in the name of the Trustees of the Free Church of Scotland. So it is not surprising, given these tensions and the slowness of communications, that Mr Dewar was the only person who turned up for the meeting. In good ecclesiastical language he recorded in the Presbytery Minute Book: *"At Burnshill, the first day of March 1911, on which date the Presbytery had been summoned to meet, there being not sufficient members to form a quorum – the Moderator alone being present – the next meeting was appointed to be held at Burnshill on 7 June 1911."*

However, here is a problem. The date of the "next" meeting of Presbytery recorded in that minute book was on the 5 June 1954 (when the Presbytery was 'resuscitated' by order of the Free Church of Scotland General Assembly). It is obvious, however, that Presbytery meetings did get held for some of the intervening years, sometimes in Transkei, and the business of the Church continued. The record of these meetings is lost.

Assembly deliberations

In the Free Church of Scotland General Assembly of 1911, a large share of time and attention was given to Foreign Missions. Reference was made to the need for at least £1000 to help with the cost of new school and church buildings in South Africa.

Also what needed to be clarified to both the Church in Scotland and in South Africa was Mr Dewar's position on the South African field especially with regard to the Presbytery. He, as the representative sent out from Scotland, was to be the Superintendent of the whole work, so that he could keep the Church in Scotland abreast of the needs on the field and listen to the wishes of the South African church with reference to practical administration. It was decided that he was entitled to be present at all meetings of the Church courts and to have the right of access to all documents of those courts. All native pastors and agents had the duty of loyally recognising the position occupied by Mr Dewar as their missionary Superintendent.

But the Superintendent's role did not fit easily into a Presbyterial system and it was his relationship with the Presbytery that caused tensions in South Africa and some unease at home.

The Pain of a Splinter – exit Rev Burnett Gaba

It was very difficult to get sites for churches, especially if they were also to be used for Free Church schools. Mr Dewar spent much time trying to secure such sites. The local African ministers did their best as well, but Government authorities would only recognise a White man's signature.

Tensions were evidently arising between the African ministers and Mr Dewar as to who would hold the title deeds of such churches – were they to be in the name of the Free Church of Scotland or local trustees? A letter was sent in May 1910 from Rev Burnett Gaba to Scotland asking the Foreign Missions Committee that "in future, the property be vested in this body, (the Presbytery of Kaffraria) and that title-deeds be issued in their name, as local trustees, or in the name of the congregation to whom they belong".

In April 1911 the Foreign Missions Committee received another letter from Rev Burnett Gaba:

Dear Sirs, … We have had difficulties to face in the work arising from certain reports spread abroad by a certain elder that an attempt to form an independent church was being made by the Deacon's Court if they did not get titles in their name. The hindering of the getting of sites and buildings by Mr Dewar's conviction that these reports were true, added still more to these difficulties.

And we cannot express in words how glad we were in the midst of these trying circumstances, as we read the letter from the Foreign Missions Committee encouraging us to build new churches as early as possible; ... We were likewise greatly pleased in learning that the Rev D. Maclean (who had visited recently) said something in expression of our loyalty to the Home Church, and of his kind recollections about his visit to Burnshill. Our longings to have new places of worship, enhanced by the desire of the Church at Home that we should build at an early opportunity stirred us to send in our applications for the Church Building Sites, to the Assistant Resident Magistrates. One of them however advised us to get Mr Dewar to countersign the petitions ... It was to our great disappointment that Mr Dewar should deny our having anything to do with this important work of getting sites, claiming this duty as his exclusive right, which he could do by himself, not in fellowship with the Deacons' Courts and the Presbytery.

Feeling then that the satisfaction of the Church at Home, as well as our own, that we should have buildings soon, was thus put off, we decided at our meeting of Deacons' Court held 11th April, that we should make temporary arrangements by getting our brethren to offer their building sites where they can, on which we could erect temporary buildings that could serve as accommodations on communion seasons, as well as on Sabbath days. Our people have been exposed to wind and rain now for six years, while those of them who are in poor health feel quite unable to resist the effects of such exposure.

Then followed the names of 11 other elders or deacons.

Obviously there were strong disagreements between Mr Dewar and Rev Burnett Gaba and some of his elders. Looking back after 100 years we do not know all the reasons for this or whether there were underlying tensions of which we know nothing. But how we wish the matter could have been resolved by negotiation or the intervention of an intermediary but it was not to be. Rev Burnett Gaba left the Free Church and went on to found his 'own' church, the Ntsikana Memorial Church. Ntsikana was one of the early Xhosa converts to Christianity. He was a Xhosa bard and one of his hymns, the 'great hymn', (reminding us of the Columban hymns with their emphasis on nature) is an abiding favourite in Xhosa Christianity to this day.

So, sadly, it was exit Rev Burnett Gaba.

Not all the office-bearers in the Burnshill District followed Rev Gaba in leaving the Free Church. Mr Gaba was accused of trying to get buildings registered in his own name or the names of some of his supporters with a view to setting up his own church. But one can't help feeling a degree of sympathy for the people wanting buildings to be registered in the name of local trustees. After all, they had built buildings in the 'old' Free Church only to be turned out of them when the United Free Church was founded. They did not want that to happen again. Yet 100 years later the International Missions Board is **still** trying to get Free Church of South Africa buildings re-registered in the name of the African church!

Enter Rev William Murray

At the same meeting, on 1 September 1911, of the Foreign Missions Committee at which Mr Gaba's letter of resignation was received, an application for service in South Africa was received from Mr William Murray who had been serving for 22 years as an artisan missionary at the Livingstonia Mission in (what is now) Malawi. As well as being an experienced builder Mr Murray had also been engaged in evangelistic, educational and, sometimes, medical work and was an elder in the native church in connection with Livingstonia.

The Foreign Missions Committee warmly recommended Mr Murray's application and they agreed that he should be ordained as a minister of the Gospel and go to serve in South Africa as soon as possible. Mr Murray, a native of Rogart, Sutherland, was well liked and respected by those he had worked with in Livingstonia.

Mr Dewar said: "I have a high regard for Mr Murray, and besides being delighted to see him in the service of our church, would count it a pleasure to have him along with me out here."

Mr Murray's ordination and induction took place in Glasgow on 28 February 1912 and he sailed for South Africa with his wife and family on 2 April – the same month as the ill-fated Titanic set sail for America. The Murrays came to live in Keiskammahoek, a village in the middle of most of the Burnshill District.

He was 'in harness' right away. Mr Dewar introduced him to the Deacons' Court of the Burnshill District on 27 April 1912. Realising the pressing needs of the large congregation at Mnyameni, he prepared a plan for a church building there, along with projected costs, for the meeting of the Deacons' Court on 7 June 1912. The main problem was to get official permission to have a site on which to build. The people had already started to make bricks for the building.

A Xhosa Wedding

Mr Murray sent back this interesting account of his first Xhosa wedding soon after his arrival. This was at Amatole, a church perched on top of a hill in the Burnshill District. A daughter of Elder Mahoba of Amatole was married to a man from Wolf River nearby.

> After some delay, all seemed to have come in. In the front seat was the bridegroom, whom I recognised, and by him sat a young girl, in neat white dress, with some gum flowers in her hair, but who looked rather young for a bride. But no other one appeared to take her place ... I looked out, but no one was to be seen, so

I said, "Let us pray". The door was closed, and when opened after prayer, to my amazement there was the bride, about forty yards away, coming from the huts, at a snail's pace, magnificently dressed in white veil, orange blossoms and all, and a page carrying her train, and a woman in attendance, whose principal work was to lift her dress under her toes as it was a little too long. I was taken aback, but in quiet firm tones told them all to stand up to receive the bride; at the same time I went outside the door to meet her (and cool myself) as if it were part of the service. When she was seated, I gave out Ps 133 to be sung, and when the people present began to sing, she began to cry and sob, and before the Psalm was sung, three other girls broke into sobbing, and others showed signs of following suit. I saw that if allowed, the whole female side of the house (sixty to seventy) would be in hysterics, so looking sternly at the girls, told them to be quiet. They could hardly restrain their sobs, although some of the men present also tried to dry their tears. I let the bride weep, as, poor body, she no doubt felt parting with her freedom. When a measure of quiet was restored the ceremony went on, but I had to ask the bride the usual questions several times before she could reply.

The next difficulty cropped up when it came to place the ring on the finger. She had on a very tight-fitting glove, and the ring was too small to go over it, so it had to be removed. They tried in vain; what with perspiration and heat it was immovable. Finally I went to their help and got it off by turning it over the hand and the ring was firmly placed on the finger, the register signed, blessing asked, and they went out happy, and I took their photos!

Enter Rev R. Damane

The Foreign Missions Committee received an encouragement again in the form of an application to come into the Free Church from Rev R. Damane. Mr Damane was a respected Xhosa pastor who had previously served the pre-1900 Free Church, had left and joined Rev Mzimba's church but now wanted to come back to the Free Church. Indeed, he was already organising people who, like himself, wanted to come back to the church of their fathers. The Commission of General Assembly in Scotland accepted Rev Damane as a minister in August 1912. He was to have a seat in the Presbytery of Kaffraria, under the superintendence of Rev Dewar and was to serve in Tsolo, his home place, in Transkei. People in several areas of Transkei had indicated their desire to come back to the Free Church, especially around the Mt Frere area. It was reported from there that "the Hottentots in the village also want to come into the Free Church – their fathers' church"! Mr Damane also mentioned some conversions among 'red' people, sometimes one, other times two to five or six at a time.

Steady work

Meantime, steady work was going on in the congregations. In 1912 there were 22 places where Free Church people were meeting, children and adults had been baptised and 93 people were added to the communicant membership of the church. Two full-time evangelists were working alongside the two African ministers – Revs Ntsikana Gaba and R. Damane. There was also reference to a work of grace at Mnyameni and Ngqumeya, where 16 people had professed conversion. 'Red' people (called 'red' because traditionally they wore ochre red blankets) were being converted, meetings had been held in Transkei and an old friend of Mr Dewar's from Livingstonia days had been greatly used in 'revival' services in Transkei.

One of the two evangelists was called Mr Philemon Mpunzi. He was appointed as evangelist at Ngcingwane and the surrounding area and he carried out an effective ministry there.

In one of Mr Dewar's letters, dated September 1912, he told of a service at Ngcingwane, Transkei. Present at the service was Rev J.

Jolobe. Mr Jolobe, a recognised Xhosa poet, was later to be asked to render many of the Psalms into metre for singing, adding to the work previously undertaken by Rev John Knox Bokwe and Mr William Gaba (father of the two ministers). It had been hoped that the Metrical Psalms would have been adopted by other denominations, but this did not happen. All the other churches sing Xhosa hymns, occasionally along with some of the Psalms.

Boxes and bells

The first of many boxes of goods had arrived from Scotland for African children and others. The replies of thanks came with a request for more in larger sizes! The ladies of the church in Scotland were getting going and only the Lord knows the great help they have been to the people in the church in South Africa over the years. After the arrival of one box in 1916 Mr Dewar's letter of thanks mentioned a box of shortbread which was keenly looked for and enjoyed by the Scots in King William's Town. It also included a gift from the Free North of three pairs of socks for Mr Murray and himself! But mostly the boxes contained children's dresses and boys' clothes and pencils and scissors and other articles which were used as prizes in the schools and were very welcome. Among those goods received from Scotland were communion sets and a bell donated by Mr Peter Denny, Dumbarton. The bell had originally been on one of the Clyde steamers, the "S.S. Lochfyne". Mr Dewar (a native of Lochgilphead) wrote to Mr Denny thanking him for the bell and wrote, "I can almost imagine I smell the sea breezes of that well-known loch!"

The Opening of Ngcingwane Church

This bell was installed in the newly built church at Ngcingwane, Transkei. Both Mr Dewar and Mr Murray had spent a great deal of time and labour, hands-on, helping the builder and the local people to erect a good strong church, when a site had been made available at last. There was great rejoicing on the opening day on 25 October 1917. That day was wet, wet, wet. The opening went on, but as fewer folk could attend, it had to be followed some time later by another 'opening' in May 1918 so that enough money could be gathered in to offset the building costs. However, on the first opening day a large ox, fifteen sheep, maize, and pumpkins were donated, as well as donations of money (£200). In the taking up of the collections a donor would announce he or she was giving a goat, pig or fowl, or a bag or half bag of maize. So that was where the bell from the Clyde steamer was installed, and it is still calling the faithful to God's house in sunny Africa to this day in the congregation of Ngcingwane in Transkei.

Mnyameni opens its church at last

The congregation of Mnyameni in the Burnshill District had also at last succeeded in building a beautiful big church, after years of being denied a site, and having to meet in all weathers in the open air. (Did they use the plans drawn up six years before by their very new missionary, Mr Murray?) Before the opening day there was a lot of whitewashing, preparing of food and getting everything spick and span. On that day, 19 July 1918, some 683 gifts were received, ranging from one penny to sheep or maize. The building opened free of debt, and a good feast was enjoyed by all as 19 sheep were given for the meal. On the way home from Mnyameni, Mrs Murray's horse bolted after getting a fright from a galloping horse which came upon them from behind. After a frantic ride downhill Mrs Murray's pony shied and she was thrown, her ankle catching in the stirrup, resulting in a severe dislocation of her left ankle. She recovered well from the injury and the experience, and Mr Murray records how much kindness they received from the doctor, a retired matron, and many of the folk in Keiskammahoek. The Murrays had six children, so it can not have been easy for Mrs Murray to be much among the women and girls, but she was obviously doing a good and rewarding work there.

The Down Side and the Up

Woven in and out of the accounts of this decade were many hardships and difficulties for missionaries and pastors and people. There were several severe droughts during this time. A drought is such a painful time for everyone, in a situation where most people lived on the land and off its produce. Cattle, almost a currency, become skeletal and die by the side of the road. Women and girls have to walk great distances to find water, returning with heavy pails on their heads. There is no extra money for school fees, uniforms, books, or for church collections. Problematical for the church too was that men had to leave the land and go off to Johannesburg or other cities to find work. Mr Dewar had employed two men as evangelists (at £10 per year) in order to enable them to stay at home and also to devote more time to pastoral work. When the heavens are still cloudless, prayers for rain are said, and until the Lord answers, one must just endure. Then if and when the welcome thunder clouds gather and the rain sheets down, the earth turns to mud and then to grass and the beauty of the spring flowers.

But the drought brought even more problems. As people had become undernourished, they fell prey to diseases – typhus, measles and whooping cough. On Mr Murray's return from building works at Ngcingwane in Transkei he found a typhus epidemic raging in his Burnshill District. The death toll was 'appalling'. Schools were closed and gatherings for services were not allowed for fear of spreading the infection in the crowded and badly ventilated huts where the people had to gather since they were not allowed sites for building.

Drought outside and in

Sometimes it felt as if the drought had entered the souls of the people too. Mr Dewar spoke of "the indifference of the great mass of the red people, the lukewarmness of some of our members, and the want of a sense of responsibility on the part of some of our office-bearers". Christian life was not easy. Church people were surrounded by very many unbelievers and a culture that had, at its roots, many practices that were in opposition to a Christian way of life. Sometimes professing believers gave in to the pressures around them and would consult witch-doctors, offer sacrifices to the ancestors, attend beerdrinks, conduct heathen rites after the birth of a child and so on. Without being in the shoes of a new believer in those circumstances one can have no idea of the pressures of extended family and clan to conform to the traditional family customs. The Kirk Sessions tried to deal with all these problems, asking those who had succumbed to un-Christian practices to appear before the Session, often being brought back two or three times and being exhorted to repent and mend their ways. The sin of adultery was rife, elopement was common (often as a way of avoiding the bride-price), and polygamy was still a problem. What do you do with a man who has two or three wives and becomes a Christian? Do you say he cannot become a member unless he puts away his extra wives and their children? Then they suffer. Do you admit them all to membership if they wish to be members? Do you give baptism to the children? Other churches would if we did not. There were many problems.

But it was not all doom and gloom. The ladies of the South African church were getting going too – they were meeting every week in spite of all the problems they had in finding places to gather. Some girls also joined their meetings. Mrs Murray's arrival in Keiskammahoek had been a great encouragement to the women in the Burnshill District. In the May 1918 Assembly in Scotland members heard that from Pirie District came news of 39 conversions; seven at Knox, six at Tyusha, six at Mdisa and smaller numbers at each of the other places. In December of that year, Mr Dewar mentions some 51 had professed conversion. In spite of all the teaching over many years, old customs still had a strong hold on the people, so encouragements like these were very welcome.

Mr Matayo's safari

Around this time, Mr William Matayo, teacher and evangelist in Mnyameni in the Burnshill District decided to visit the Transkei. He sent a letter which was printed in the Instructor of July 1918 describing some of the adventures which he had on this trip:

He says:

> I took two days at Joqwana with Somhlahlo. We kept prayer meeting only. The delay was caused mainly by rains ... Somhlahlo accompanied me with his horses,

although he is not strong enough after his fall from his pony. Pains in the head are still troubling him. It appears that the joints of the skull were shaken a bit ... He also lost two mares and a colt. They were inside the Bunga Camp; lightning struck them dead ...

We crossed the Nscu river with much difficulty. Water is very heavy and reaches our legs and boots although on horseback. It causes much anxiety while you are in the middle of the stream trying to keep the head of horse up not to come in contact with the water and the swing of the stream ... We were glad to escape when we reached the other side.

On Sabbath, yesterday, I took the morning prayer. In the forenoon we had a large gathering of old and young. The attention was keen and interesting. After service was over, I took the Catechumen class and found them backward in knowledge. I took the Sabbath school scholars and catechised them. I found them to be well instructed in Catechism, also the first ten chapters of 1 Samuel. And the memory work in fifth chapter of St Matthew's was very good ... In the afternoon again the service took place, when we had about the same number of people as in the forenoon. Now I drove my address particularly to the unbelievers. In the evening after supper we had a special service in the hut of a blind man. Some of the members of his family are still in red blankets. Here we gave liberty to office-bearers and others to work and we had one convert. We had very good accommodation from the teacher's wife who provided for us, and we felt at home.

They went on from Jamangile's place and met with a terrible storm. Mr Matayo takes up the story:

The flashes of lightning were now beginning to cause anxiety in our minds. We made our way to a hut, where we alighted and opened the door of the house, and no one was present to admit us. We tied our horses on the kraal post and we stayed inside. The rain began to pour in torrents, and thunder clappings were extreme.

As soon as thunder passed we put our saddles on. We proceeded forward lest the rivers might prevent us in crossing them. But the very first stream we crossed the water was very high ... At last we reached the Nscu, the giant river whose stories of damages to human beings made us shudder and fear. It showed itself by the waves that we could not dare to go in. A Pondomese was already present who was a good swimmer. He asked us if we wanted help. We said, "Yes, how much do you charge?" "Sixpence for a man and sixpence for a horse." He took horses first, and took us by means of a box above the drift. We paid him two shillings. Here we watched many young men from Johannesburg being carried over the stream by means of this box. We passed Bedlana at dusk and reached the ford when it was dark, the water deep and heavy ... We were wet on reaching Somhlahlo's.

And poor Mr Matayo concludes: "I slept not with toothache."

All through these troubled years of trying to get sites and buildings and schools in the teeth of opposition, quiet and steady and courageous work was going on and souls were being saved and congregations built up.

The Great War and the Great Flu epidemic

The 1914–1918 First World War did not impinge very much upon the life and work of the Mission, although some men from the area were taken to form working squads for British forces in Europe. Sadly many were lost at sea when their ship went down near the coast of Holland.

On 29th September 1916 Mr Dewar writes to say that sites were being granted, which was cause for rejoicing, but prices were so high on account of the war that they would have to delay building until prices settled downward again.

But in January 1919 the terrible flu epidemic hit the world and our areas in South Africa did not escape. Mrs Dewar wrote:

The scourge storm has swept over us here and the days have been filled with sadness and apprehension ... Among the poor natives the mortality has been excessive, the elders and deacons being many days, from morning to night, either helping to dig graves or burying the people ... Before Mr Dewar returned from the Transkei he was in the thick of it, visiting, cheering, advising and encouraging them to take quinine instead of expensive patent medicines. He came back when victims were suffering in great numbers in King William's Town ... I visited my district every afternoon, besides, like every one else, sending puddings to the depot, hospital and my special patients ... Mr Murray had five (of his family) down at once, but all are about again. Six hundred natives, I think, at the Hoek (Keiskammahoek) alone fell victims to the epidemic. At Dyafta the Deacon's wife and her three children passed away.

Those who were well were digging graves and others helped to make coffins. It was reported that in Cape Town sheets of newspaper alone had to suffice for burials. Churches and schools closed for a time. Some said 1125 people perished in Mr Murray's area of Keiskammahoek alone. In Idutywa, Transkei, 2000 deaths were recorded. The Pirie congregation lost 28 members, all but one being women. Mr Matayo, teacher in the Mnyameni school, tells of his grief at what was happening and the havoc the plague was causing among the people. "The country is very gloomy, everything looks sad, people are in terror."

And yet there was gold in the darkness. In Mr Dewar's report of June 1919, he also tells of the positive spiritual awakening which followed the flu in different places.

Mr Murray also said at this time:

You will be glad to hear that at Mnyameni and also at
Ngqumeya, what is to all appearance a work of grace
is going on among the people. Ever since the influenza
epidemic in October and November last, a number of
people at Mnyameni seemed to be in earnest in regard
to spiritual matters, and recently over fifty of them
professed conversion. The majority are young people,
but there are among them people of advanced years.
We hold meetings for some time now at Ndonga, a
place a few miles from Mnyameni, and a great many
people gather each Tuesday afternoon. The people of
the place are 'reds', or heathen, but they also come to
the meetings and listen very intently. I was told of one
Red, from far away up on the slopes of the Hogsback
Mountains, who was in anxiety about her soul, and
who dreamed that she was to go to the first service
that was held in her vicinity. On the Monday she heard
about the meeting to be held at Ndonga the following
morning and she came, and as I was speaking on the
words, "Behold the Lamb of God that taketh away the
sin of the world" the Spirit was present to wound and
heal. For a time it was difficult to proceed, she was in
such agony. Others were also in tears. I trust it was a
service blessed to several. The Headman of the village
clears away whenever he sees us approach, lest he
may hear the Gospel. He is learning to become a witch
doctor, and is afraid he may be 'apprehended', as Paul
puts it ... One result of the movement is the sale of the
Scriptures. I could do with a little bookstore ...

But it seems Mr Murray had soon to record problems with false
preachers, and a falling away of spiritual earnestness after the
hoped for harvest of souls following the flu epidemic. There was
the continuing problem over sites making things difficult.

Yet during that year, (1919) 39 adults had been baptised and
98 children, and 102 had been admitted to membership. There
were about 450 children in church schools. The membership

of the church was altogether 854 plus 287 candidates and 253 adherents.

Mrs Dewar's tragic death

On 2 July 1919 Mrs Dewar died in sad circumstances. She and Mr Dewar and their son Rex were crossing the road in East London in the evening of that day when a car came suddenly upon them in the dark. She was killed instantly.

In reporting her death, Mr Dewar spoke of his and the children's loss of "my best and dearest earthly friend, the wise, trusted, and helpful counsellor of half a jubilee". He said, "Since her conversion, thirty-five or so years ago, she had given herself wholly to God. He had endowed her with many gifts and graces. These she had used to the full in His sweet service. Naturally timid and highly strung, afraid of a horse, cow, or dog, or even a spider, yet she willingly faced the dangers of Central Africa – very different twenty-six years ago to what it is today – whether as regards malaria, wild men and wild beasts, dangers by river, road, lake and ocean, enduring much discomfort and even hardship – all for sake of her dear Lord whose she was and whom she sought to serve."

Mr Murray also wrote of how much she would be missed by the Africans, who felt the blow keenly, and of all her evangelistic effort in King William's Town. She was engaged in temperance work and in all schemes for social purity of the young.

She was buried in King William's Town, and a great many people attended her funeral.

An exit phase

Sadly, during this period there were tensions in the church and between the Mission Superintendent, Mr Dewar, and some of the African pastors and evangelists. Rev Damane resigned from the Free Church in 1916 and Evangelist Mpunzi was suspended from his duties at the end of 1915. In 1917 Rev Ntsikana Gaba was disciplined by the Presbytery and he ceased to be a minister of the Free Church.

Even the worthy teacher/evangelist from Mnyameni, Mr William Matayo, made an exit. It seemed that he had lost the confidence of the people of Mnyameni, and he left the Free Church. However, he was immediately snapped up by the local missionary of the United Free Church in Burnshill. These sad events weakened the 'work-force' of the church. They also caused embarrassment to the Foreign Missions Committee, especially in those cases where personality clashes came to the fore. One of the difficulties in the situation regarding the African ministers and evangelists was the way they sometimes wrote directly to the Foreign Missions Committee in Edinburgh, bypassing the Missionary Superintendent on the field. This placed both the Superintendent and the Missions Committee in a very difficult position. The Committee had to uphold the position of their Superintendent and insisted that all correspondence had to come to the Committee through him.

In 1920 the General Assembly of the Free Church of Scotland agreed to the following: "The General Assembly ordain that the Presbytery of Kaffraria shall be attached to the Southern Synod of the Church." This meant that when there was dissension in the Presbytery of Kaffraria, an appeal could always be made to the Synod to help resolve the issue, rather than sending letters directly to the Missions Committee.

Mr Dewar went back to Scotland on overdue home leave in mid-1920 along with his children, and stayed until 1922, and Rev William Murray assumed sole responsibility for the oversight of the work. He must have felt quite forlorn after the exits of most of his African colleagues and the departure for Scotland of his only European colleague. During this period he expressed the conviction that the church needed to train African men for the work (initially as Evangelists) for "better work, and deeper and more lasting could be done if we had the right class of man as Evangelist to live for a time with the people and help them in their homes. The European Missionary is in too much of a hurry for this". How right, but perhaps ahead of his time, he was in these sentiments.

The end of this decade, 1910–1920, was marked by a lot of civil unrest on the part of the African people. There had been a near famine in certain areas and prices were very high. Mr Murray wrote that ... "A great deal of unrest prevails, and strikes, fomented apparently by paid agitators, are of frequent occurrence."

But there was, however, underlying encouragement in the work with more reports of conversions and overall 76 new members were added to the church in 1920.

ON REFLECTION

A sad reality throughout the years in the South African Church has been the steady flow of ministers and congregations who have applied for membership in the Church, have stayed for a while and then departed again.

Why has this happened?

Sometimes mistakes were made in admitting people in the first place because not enough was known about them.

Finance was at the root of the problem at times. Ministers had hoped for a good remuneration if they came into the Free Church and were disappointed. As a church we have not really provided adequately for our ministers or evangelists.

One gets the feeling that the incomers did not feel welcome in the Church because they were in some way 'different'?

Sadly sometimes doctrinal problems caused the parting of the ways and maybe, at times, personality clashes.

Disciplinary matters also arose leading to ministers or evangelists being suspended or dismissed.

But while we note the problems let us also rejoice in the continuing work of Christ's kingdom.

5

Despite the disappointments 1921–30

The years of this decade of the twenties were a struggle for the mission in South Africa. There were comings and goings of missionaries, which must have had an unsettling effect on the work.

Weary waiting for help

Mr Murray, feeling the responsibility of it all, describes the distances in a letter: "When you look at a map of South Africa, you will see the vastness of the field in which the Free Church works, and the number of stations which are dependent on one man – from Gqumahashe near Lovedale to Jamangile's away up towards Umzimkulu or Kokstad. In the Pirie district there are eight preaching stations, in the Burnshill six; in the Transkei at least eight and one near Lovedale." The distance between the two farthest apart was about two hundred miles. We can understand Mr Murray's feeling of helplessness.

He travelled about taking communions, describing sometimes a severe drought, sometimes complaining of lack of attendances due to the boisterous weather. In Ngcingwane, (Transkei), he says, "The people are weary waiting for help – either a European pastor, or a native evangelist." He says forlornly, "I am sorry there is little hope of anyone coming to help in the work here. There should be one (missionary) across the Kei as well as one or two in the Colony."

On reading this appeal back in Scotland, Mr Dewar was consulted as to his views on a missionary being stationed in Transkei.

He said that although the natives wanted this, he did not commit himself regarding the desirability of meeting their wish! A very strange opinion.

The Report which Mr Murray sent back to Scotland for the Assembly of 1921 was described as "in characteristic style, with light and shade, a faithful transcript of the situation in the field – what a well-known missionary, Miss Amy Wilson Carmichael would call: '*Things as they are*'".

Mr Murray was explaining that some difficulty had been experienced on account of a Government scheme which excluded Free Church Schools from State support. Nevertheless, good work was being done in the schools. He sent back a letter to the Instructor of July 1921 in which he asks if the Scottish children would like to see a 'native' school in South Africa. In his description he takes us right into the spirit of his work and incidentally gives us an insight into the spirit of the man himself. He says:

A School in South Africa

Let me transport you to a town of corrugated iron roofs and white-washed brick walls, with the broad streets laid out with various kinds of trees, in which the oak and pine predominate.

As we have a long way to go, we start before 6 a.m. with horse and gig, and soon leave the town behind, and see the smoke for morning coffee ascending from house after house, and are soon out in the open country, with some mimosa trees and other bushes skirting the road. We soon come to fields in which we see maize and Kafir corn, and a few plots of beans and peas. Then we see some cattle going to graze, with two or three diminutive herds looking after them.

The country is at first level, and we go over the ground fast, but as we proceed we come to an incline, and we walk up the hill, for our horse has to bring us back this evening. We see many villages to right and left of us, clusters of grass thatched round huts like bee skeps and we see the women going to their gardens, hoe on shoulder, many clothed in red blankets, others tidily dressed in nice cotton frocks. Some are already in their gardens – as the African is an early riser – and as they warm to their work, the blanket is laid aside, so that their arms and body may be free for the swing of the hoe.

The School. But we press on. The hill is surmounted and we go merrily along, and by 8 o'clock we see the place we desire. It looks near, but it takes us to 9.15 to get there. As we near the School we see the teacher and some pupils furtively looking for us, and as we draw up by the door, we hear the hum of lessons. We unharness, and knee halter our horse (lest he take French leave) and let him out to graze. We enter, and there we find little tots, with a sheet pinned to the wall, spelling two and three letter syllables, and up to Standard 3. Some have books, some have books and slates, and some have neither. There are thirty-four all told.

Mr Murray then begins to examine. As an amateur at this he felt it 'formidable'. But 'to begin is half the battle', so to some he gave out test cards in arithmetic, he set some to writing on their slates, and he began to see the little ones through their lessons on the wall. As they did fairly well, they were sent out to play, while he addressed himself to the Standards which got reading, writing, arithmetic, Scripture and Catechism.

The Prizegiving. With great relief, the examining was over by 2 p.m. and then came the prizegiving.

On the table lie dresses, overalls, pieces of print, pencils, reels of cotton etc sent out by kind friends in Scotland. As they are called they come and select each one his or her prize, and it is amusing to watch the struggle as to what to take – dress or print or shirt. By 3 p.m. they have all received their prizes, and even the small tots get something, a slate-pencil or a needle or two ...

You notice that there are few boys; they are away looking after sheep, goats and cattle. We now start for home, and as it is afternoon we proceed slowly, and look around. You see some farms, nicely kept and prosperous looking, and one or two stores. You see many of those who were in the fields wending their way homeward ...

But our talk made us forget the pace of our horse, and here we are at home. I hope you enjoyed yourselves ...

Mr Murray's Travels

Mr Murray could not stay home too long while he was responsible for the superintendence of the whole mission field during Mr Dewar's absence. He sent to the *Monthly Record* an account of a three week tour of the Transkei work, visiting the congregations and holding services, Communions, baptisms etc. He mentions an evangelist, but doesn't give his name. He mentions the long ride to Qelana which took eight hours to negotiate, "but the highland scenery of Qelana dispels all sense of weariness, and the air is fine and cool". (Is there a hint of memories of the hills of home in Rogart?) He was obviously warmly received wherever he went.

He reported too on meetings he held in the Pirie District nearer to home in King William's Town (where he was based during Mr Dewar's absence). There had been a full house (church) with two new members. There was good and bad news from Knox; 33 members and adherents had left the Free Church and joined a congregation with an African ordained minister; however 33 young people had professed conversion and were in the Catechumen's class. At Dyafta ten people had professed conversion and one at Mxaxo. He remarks: "This is especially pleasing in the general cloudiness around, when faith is tried and hope deferred." On 8 September (1921) he went to Keiskammahoek for Communion at Burnshill but a heavy fall of snow prevented him meeting with the people until the 10th. There were nine new members at Mnyameni, five being first of all baptized. There was a continuing problem over the church site at Gqumahashe, but wisely Mr Murray left off dealing with this problem until Mr Dewar's return! One could only do so much.

In the February 1922 *Monthly Record* Mr Murray tells of another tour in Transkei. He was taken ill with 'flu which was rife at the time and eventually had to return home without completing all he had hoped to do.

Mr Dewar's diligent home leave

Meanwhile back in Scotland, Mr Dewar was busy on behalf of the work he had left behind in South Africa. He conducted meetings in many of the congregations during his furlough, and he addressed the General Assembly of 1921, making the most of this opportunity. He thanked the Home Church for its support. He commended the stand the Africans had taken who had stayed loyal to the Free Church and commiserated with them in the difficulties they had faced as a result; some even being in prison because of their actions. The Government in South Africa had relented in recent times and had granted some sites for churches and schools, but teachers who had stayed with the Free Church and taught in their schools were receiving only half the regular teachers' salary. He mentioned problems with drink, immorality, polygamy.

But there were great opportunities and many positives and the Free Church should see that South Africa had a special claim on it. Mr Dewar recommended that Mission should go before civilization, because if it happened the other way round, the vices not the virtues of civilization would take hold on the people. But if Christianity came first, the people would be able to withstand the temptation to do the evils which civilization would bring.

Mr Dewar's farewell before setting sail once more for South Africa was held on 19 January 1922 in Hope Street Free Church, Glasgow. The Chairman, Rev J. Macleod, OBE, said, "as a Church they owed much to Mr Dewar". He was presented with a travelling rug.

Back in South Africa, in Cape Town, he met with Government and Education officials who told him that 'Native Councils' were to be set up and on these African members would sit. Now perhaps the Free Church would have an equal chance with other churches in the matter of school work?

Death of Mr Murray

With Mr Dewar back in South Africa, the Murray family came on leave to Scotland. Mrs Murray and their six children travelled first, sailing from South Africa in April 1922. Mr Murray meanwhile travelled to Malawi to revisit his first mission station and the friends he had made there. He made this journey against the advice of Mr Dewar who felt that Murray's health was not up to the journey. After Malawi he went back to South Africa, paying a flying visit to Keiskammahoek and King William's Town before returning to Scotland at the end of January 1923 'in an enfeebled state of health'. We have to wonder if he had a premonition he might never again see the places and the people whom he had loved and discipled and he wanted to take farewell of them?

For in Dornoch, Sutherland, near where he had first seen the light of day, "on the morning of Sabbath, 4 February 1923", Mr William Murray passed away, "sustained and comforted by the hopes of the Gospel". He had succumbed to the symptoms of blackwater fever, aged 57. He had spent 35 years of his life on the mission field, from 1888 to 1911 in Malawi, and from 1912 until his death in 1923 in South Africa, and they were years of good and faithful service.

Mrs Murray lived on in Dornoch until her death in December 1941. During these years she was said to have remained a missionary to the end, and had ministered comfort to many bereaved and sorrowing people, and radiated Christian peace wherever she went. A great testimony of a worthy lady.

Mr Dewar holds the fort on his own again

Mr Murray's death was a real blow to the people and the Free Church in South Africa, and must have been devastating to Mr

Dewar, now on his own again. He was now without a minister in Transkei, the Pirie District and the Burnshill District. There were two Evangelists in Transkei, Mr Mbana at Gqunu and Mr Tyekela at Qelana. Mr Mbana was later described as a man "whose health was poor, a good man, a very earnest, simple Christian, and his influence is good wherever he goes". Mr Dewar went steadily on visiting schools, taking communion services in his wide parish, and admitting members and baptising infants. He tells of encouraging responses of 'Red-blanket' women in the Pirie District, at Dyafta and Tyusha. Free education and free books had been introduced to state schools already in receipt of grants, but not to Free Church schools. One loyal teacher, Mr Ntshona, who had founded the school in Dyafta after being dismissed from his school by the United Free Church for his adherence to the Free Church, retired from Dyafta after serving there for 26 years. He would be very much missed by the people and by Mr Dewar.

Mr Dewar married Miss Charlotte Jane Waterson in the Presbyterian Church, King William's Town on 19 December 1923.

On his journeys in Transkei and in several parts of Ciskei Mr Dewar travelled on horseback. He was a very accomplished horseman. However in 1924 it was suggested that he should take advantage of motor transport and get a car. An injury when he fell off his horse at the end of that year probably helped to make up his mind on this point, but he found his relationship with motors much more unstable than with the horse!

The country was suffering a severe drought at this time during 1924 and 1925, resulting in a great loss of animals as well as crops, so perhaps it was also difficult to get fodder for a horse?

The Foreign Missions Committee received a letter from Mr Meshak Sanqu from Ngcingwane. He was very pleased that the school which met in the new church building in Ncingwane had at last been given a Government grant. His letter quoted from John Ruskin and Abraham Lincoln, and made a strong plea for the Church to supply Mr Dewar with a car to help him in his visits to the outlying stations.

The arrival of Mr and Mrs Adam Macpherson

Some time after Mr Murray's death, a divinity student, Mr Adam Macpherson was accepted by the Committee and it was decided that when he completed his course at the Free Church College he should proceed to the work in South Africa and be placed in Transkei. So Mr and Mrs Macpherson sailed for South Africa in September 1925.

What a relief this must have been to Mr Dewar, and to the African congregations who longed for more missionaries at this time! Speaking to the General Assembly in May 1925 Mr Macpherson said he craved the earnest prayers of the people at the Throne of Grace that God would abundantly bless the work he was about to begin. Just before he left, he said he and his wife were "Buoyed up with a great feeling of inspiration and hope for the future in South Africa. A cold fear might clutch them, in view of the many difficulties, but they were not going out in their own strength, but were taking with them the Divine Power which had sustained ... others."

Mr Dewar had found a house for the Macphersons in Tsolo, Transkei. On arrival in South Africa, Mr Macpherson bought a car for his missionary work. The price was £187. The Macphersons stayed for a short time with Mr Dewar in King William's Town and Mrs Macpherson was said to have been "very fit and just full of fire to get up among our people in the Tsolo District. Her missionary zeal grows with every day in this country".

Adam Macpherson wrote an interesting letter which was printed in the March 1926 *Monthly Record* giving his experiences on a first visit to Mqokelweni (Jamangile's place). First impressions are always fresh. He and his interpreter had set out on horseback on a very hot summer's day.

> At about six o'clock on Saturday evening we reached the highest point in the mountain over which we had to cross, and looking down into the valley some considerable distance beneath us, the village of Emqokelweni lay. It was necessary to walk down the steep slopes and lead our horses. Ere we had gone

far we were seen from below, and soon the word was passed that the new 'uMfundisi' was coming ... There was no small stir in the valley. An elder was the first to reach us, and his welcome was extremely cordial. Every hut we came to emptied itself of its occupants, who came out to pay their respects ...

A Touching Incident

One incident will live as long as memory lasts. At the door of a hut not far from the one I was to occupy a very old woman stood, with her head and hands raised towards the heavens whilst words poured from her lips. I was informed she was praying, thanking God for His goodness in sending a missionary to the people. I approached her, her hands came to her sides, and her eyes seemed to search for me but without avail, ... for they were now sightless. I held out my hand to her, and seizing it she kissed it back and front with great tenderness ... How marvellous are God's ways. This poor blind, unlettered old woman was rich, clear-sighted and wise in the things of the Kingdom.

A Busy Schedule and a Cordial Welcome

Mr Macpherson found that a service had been arranged that evening in one of the huts, and he had an attentive audience for that. The first service in the morning was at 6.30 a.m. – 'pleasant in the cool', the next was a session meeting at 9 a.m. followed by an examination of candidates for Church membership at 10 a.m. Then:

At 11 o'clock there was the usual morning service, at the close of which a number of children were baptised, and the right hand of fellowship given to those received into Church membership. The hut used for our place of worship is far too small to accommodate comfortably all the congregation, and in addition to those who were seated on forms, others were packed, tightly seated on

the floor, so that there was just enough room for my
table ... One rejoiced to feel ... that the seed was falling
into good ground, and in due time will, we know, bring
forth a good harvest to God's eternal glory.

There was an interval between this service and the Communion
service at 2.30 p.m. and it was filled with heartfelt speeches of
thanks to the Lord and the Church in Scotland for sending them a
teacher. The Communion service lasted from 2.30 to 4 p.m.

A service at 8 o'clock in another hut ended a very busy
day, and I was quite tired out when I lay down at night
to rest.

A severe thunderstorm raged nearly all night, and
on Monday morning it was still raining, and although
somewhat unwise to travel on the slippery mountain
tracks, we set out for home, and after numerous
experiences which in this country are considered com-
monplace, but at home would be deemed thrilling, we
arrived back here (at Tsolo).

A little note from the interpreter on this occasion, Deacon Somhlahlo, accompanied this account. It expressed great joy that at
last this minister had come. "We received our minister with kind
hands. Thanks to the Free Church of Scotland. May God bless her
for sending us our guide. Thanks to Him who is on high for his
mercies."

In January of the following year Adam Macpherson sent
another note to the *Monthly Record* recording the death of this
Deacon's wife. He says, "Her end was glorious, and if ever proof
was needed that Christian Missions are effective, it was to be found
at the bedside of this woman."

Mr Macpherson had settled well into his District in Transkei
and had become the chaplain to the prison at Tsolo as well as at
the Agricultural School there – an important school as it catered
for the sons of chiefs and headmen. He had ten preaching stations
to look after in an area in which there were three United Free
Church missionaries working. There were about 220 Free Church
members and 150 adherents when he arrived in the area. He

wished there was a church building in Tsolo itself, where he and his wife had their home.

Mrs Macpherson held a women's meeting in a large rondavel in their garden, once per month. "Her influence among the women is considerable and is a valuable aid to me in the work," reported her husband. In concluding a letter home, he said, "I would conclude by expressing it as my humble opinion that a field of great promise is before the church in Africa."

Interestingly, he and Mr Dewar were of the opinion that the traditional red blanket of the people had benefits as against the poor quality of the European style clothes the people buy when they want to be associated with church or school. The blanket was warm and could be dried easily when it rained, but often men had only one suit which took ages to dry.

Two African pastors come to join the Church

Help and encouragement also came when Mr Dewar received an application to join the Free Church from a Rev Skosana, an experienced teacher and preacher who had been ordained in 1925 as a pastor of the Christian Evangelical Church, 'whose doctrine and practice are practically those of the Dutch Reformed Church'. Mr Skosana's four congregations who came with him were in the Pearston District, some miles from Port Elizabeth, and about 120 miles South West of King William's Town and the other Ciskei congregations.

And in 1926 Mr Dewar recommended the acceptance into the Free Church of Rev Mazwi, who was a minister in the 'Native Presbyterian Church', otherwise known as 'Mzimba's Church'. Rev Mazwi was a trained teacher and after theological training had become a minister. He came of a truly ministerial family as his father was a minister and he was one of five brothers in the ministry. Mr Mazwi had about 220 members and candidates in his congregations plus adherents. He lived at Qelana, in Transkei, and so Mr Macpherson took overall responsibility for these new congregations with their minister as well as his own.

These African pastors were a welcome addition to the two missionaries who were otherwise the only ordained personnel on the field. There seemed to be no move to train Free Church men for the ministry.

Mr Dewar as Moderator of the Free Church of Scotland – 1927

Mr Dewar was asked to be the Moderator of the General Assembly of May 1927. The Church in South Africa was pleased that he received this honour. This meant that his home leave was to be brought forward, so he and his wife set out for Scotland together.

In his Moderator's address to the Assembly, Mr Dewar dealt with the missionary situation, its ideals and prospects. The African people were no longer unanimous in their praise of missionaries. The missionary was looked upon as a benevolent, but hardly beneficent, leader. He went on to say, "The twentieth century, with its manifold difficulties and problems, demanded, not only a keen insight into the affairs of native life, but, in addition the possession of true Christian statesmanship on the part of the missionary." He questioned the ultimate value of the educational institutions run by missions, considering "their limited results and the heavy drain they had been on the home authorities. The question was frequently being asked: "Might not the money presently being spent on missionary educational institutions be more profitably expended to benefit the cause if devoted to evangelistic purposes?"

He mentioned the changing attitudes among the native races and their rising aspirations. The question of independence in church affairs was one to be aimed at but not before careful appraisal as to how things in the church will be managed. Despite setbacks and disappointments, "the outlook for the Christian mission was assured".

The Arrival of Mr and Mrs John A. Macdonald

The cheering news came in 1926 that an application had been received from Mr John A. Macdonald for service in South Africa.

At the time Mr Macdonald was still a student in the Free Church College, completing his course there in 1927. He and his young wife, Elizabeth Mackay, were present at the General Assembly in May of which Mr Dewar was Moderator, and Mr Macdonald's appointment was confirmed as a missionary to South Africa, to work as Mr Dewar's assistant in the Pirie and Burnshill Districts. Mr Macdonald "made an appeal for prayer which rang true and gripped us." Mr Dewar spoke to the new missionaries. He warned them to be patient and sympathetic with their new converts, and urged the brethren in the Assembly to pray for them and not to forget them. How much they were to need those prayers in the months that followed!

The General Assembly of the Free Church of Scotland ordained that the Presbytery of Kaffraria should be re-constituted when Mr Macdonald, Mr Dewar and Mr Macpherson were all on the field.

Mr John A. Macdonald was ordained and inducted to the mission field in the Presbytery Hall, Edinburgh, on 27 September 1927 and the young couple sailed for South Africa three days later. On their arrival in King William's Town they were welcomed by the Macphersons, who would have travelled down from their home in Tsolo, Transkei. Mr Dewar was still in Scotland at this time. One of the first things Mr Macdonald did was to buy a horse and in a letter home at the end of 1927 he wrote that he had to become 'an equestrian pastor'! Both he and his wife had received an enthusiastic welcome from the people. Their home was to be in Keiskammahoek (where Mr and Mrs Murray and family had been previously) and they hoped to get a house there by January 1928. Mr Macpherson introduced Mr Macdonald to the Districts in Ciskei and then took him to his own territory in Transkei where they both took part in a service in the prison and at the Agricultural College in Tsolo as well as at a service for Europeans.

Fresh first impressions

Again, the first letters home from the mission field have a freshness and directness which may wear off with time and familiarity.

John Macdonald wrote:

Our first impression of the whole South African area was, from a Missionary point of view, disappointing. We expected to work among African natives who were more or less total strangers to the Gospel. Instead we found ourselves in a Country where there were several different Christian organisations competing with one another for membership.

He said they found the African people among whom they had come to work

... extremely friendly and most appreciative of what the Free Church of Scotland was doing in sending missionaries to them ... The principal congregation in our area was at Mnyameni in a lovely part of the country. The congregation was very well attended – the men sitting on one side and the women on the other. At communion and baptismal services the attendance was very good, and the worshippers always dressed in their best clothes. The names given to the children to be baptised were very many and varied. To give an illustration of this a parent at one such service for the baptism of his son, when asked what his son's name was, replied: "His name is Julius Caesar Christopher Columbus." On asking why he called his child that name he replied: "I want him to be a big man"!

(The present writer had the joy of receiving that 'big man' into full membership some sixty or so years later.)

Later Mr Macdonald said,

As far as I am aware, in my time there was no persecution of Christian missionaries in South Africa. An old, godly, well-informed and intelligent elder told me the reason. He said his ancestors maintained the Great Spirit was to send them men of a different colour of skin and the natives were to welcome them and believe what those strangers from another land were to tell them. This elder maintained that was the reason why Christian missionaries were not persecuted.

The Pirie Free Church congregation was re-established in 1927 when Rev John A. Macdonald and Rev Adam A. Macpherson responded to an invitation of David Mgcuwa, William Kete and their brother elders to open a preaching station there. Mgcuwa offered land on which a church was subsequently built. Among those who joined the newly formed congregation was Mr Q. Vasi, the Headman, a gracious man of high standing and excellent education, in whose veins flowed the royal blood of the ancient Xhosa paramount chiefs.

Back in Scotland

Meanwhile Mr and Mrs Dewar were very busy on deputation in Scotland. Mr Dewar had visited 122 congregations during the year he was on home leave as well as addressing several other meetings. Mrs Dewar was with him, and of her it was said that "Mrs Dewar had won golden opinions in north and south". The Dewars were farewelled in Glasgow on 26 June 1928 and they sailed for South Africa on 31 August travelling via Marseilles, the Suez Canal and East Africa. At their farewell meeting both spoke. Mrs Dewar said that civilisation was rushing into Africa faster than the Gospel, and there was danger in the last condition being worse than the first. She made an appeal to young people to consider the needs of the land of great possibilities for evil – or for good.

The death of Mrs Elizabeth Macdonald

Just before the Dewars set out for South Africa the sad news came through that Mrs Elizabeth Macdonald had died in hospital in King William's Town, on 20 August, 1928, aged 22. Her death followed an operation for peritonitis, her appendix having burst as she was being taken on an ox wagon from Keiskammahoek to hospital in King.

On the same day that the Dewars sailed for South Africa from the United Kingdom, Rev John Macdonald sailed for Scotland from South Africa, bringing his wife's body for burial in Scotland. They had been married for only a year. The Dewars and Macdonalds never met on the South African mission field. She was buried in Tain, Ross-shire, on 21 September 1928. Warm tributes were paid to her memory. Her own husband said of her, "She was a sterling missionary."

It did indeed seem a strange Providence that, not only was Mrs Macdonald so suddenly taken but that Mr Macdonald himself was to be invalided home as well. He had been advised, both in South Africa and the UK to abandon returning to South Africa on medical grounds. But, as the *Monthly Record* noted at the time, "Faith endures, knowing that 'Oftentimes celestial benedictions assume this dark disguise'."

For a time it seemed possible that Rev John Macdonald might have been able to return to South Africa to resume his work there but this did not happen.

It is a tribute to the grasp that Mr Macdonald had gained of the situation in South Africa that on many occasions in later years his advice was sought and valued when decisions had to be made regarding work on the field.

Things as they were in Transkei

Mr Adam Macpherson and his wife continued to soldier on in their post up in Tsolo in Transkei. His report for 1928 commented on the loss to the field of Rev John Macdonald. They had got on well together and had been able to cooperate in some aspects of the missionary work, especially in the re-establishing of the Pirie congregation and they both had a sympathetic understanding of the longer term goals.

Mr Macpherson's reports had been mentioning the unrest among Blacks caused by the 'Wellingtonian Movement' in Transkei. It was causing grave problems both for the churches and for the government. The movement gave rise to a severe anti-white feeling – the Pondomisi even killed their white fowls, pigs, cattle and horses! (This movement was started by a Black man who had claimed to have come from America but was in fact from Natal.)

Mr Macpherson reported that Mr Mazwi was doing well. His main station was at Tabase where he had good people. "Up to now," said Macpherson, "the work is promising throughout the four large districts of Umtata, Libode, Ngqeleni and Port St Johns."

Mr Macpherson wrote to the Foreign Missions Committee to say that there were native congregations who wanted to come under his pastoral care. He also passed on an urgent request from the United Free Church in South Africa that Free Church missionaries help with supervising UF Districts which were adjacent to Free Church districts where there was no UF missionary. On Mr Dewar's advice this was deemed inadvisable. A further request came from the UF Church, and in a cable from Keiskammahoek Mr Macpherson wrote: *"Bantu Church urge early conference here consider co-operation will Committee authorise us by cable negotiate."* The plan was for the Free Church missionary, if appointed, to act as Superintendent of the district with the care of schools etc. leaving the African congregation with its own minister and under its own Presbytery of the Bantu Church (the UF Church). However, Mr Dewar's advice was followed and the request was turned down. The situation in the Bantu Presbyterian Church was obviously causing the UF Missions Committee a lot of worry. It was also causing a problem on the field itself. In some Bantu Church congregations the people wanted European missionaries rather than African ministers over them. It certainly would have caused confusion if Free Church missionaries were drafted into situations where such tensions were present.

The Macphersons' bombshell

Then in October of 1928, only one month after the departure of Rev John Macdonald, a medical report was received by the Foreign Missions Committee from Rev Adam Macpherson with the dire news that he was suffering from neurasthenia and it was recommended that he return to Scotland, "otherwise a general breakdown is almost certain". Mr Macpherson said he proposed waiting until March 1929 and the Foreign Missions Committee recommended that he should take an immediate holiday in South

Africa "at a good watering hole"! However, Mr Macpherson did not actually take the holiday. Instead he tendered his resignation on health grounds and proposed returning to the UK. Mr Dewar, now back in harness in South Africa, reported that he had been given no indication of Mr Macpherson's medical condition or of his intention to resign and return to Scotland. It seemed such a pity that Mr Macpherson wanted to take this course. He was obviously getting on well in the Transkei, he had a good grasp of the needs of the work there and was well accepted in the communities where he lived and worked. Mr Dewar's opinion of the situation was that Mr Macpherson's decision was not made entirely on medical grounds and this does appear to have been the case. Perhaps a breakdown in relationships rather than in health.

Mr Macpherson arrived back in Scotland in May 1929 in time to address the General Assembly. In his address to the Assembly Mr Macpherson spoke of the influences working against the missionary effort. The native mind, he said, was being poisoned against White, and that includes missionary, influence. The Bantu Presbyterian Church (previously known as the UF Church) had in some places not been ready for native leadership. Some people had passed back into Free Church congregations. As to medical needs, Mr Macpherson spoke of the devastating scarcity of medical aid, and he appealed to the church to think of what could be done for the relief of the poor people among whom he had been working.

In speaking to a meeting of the WFMA at Assembly time, Mr Macpherson thanked the Association for all the help received on the Field. He spoke about the enthusiasm and kindness of the African women and the changes in their society, leading them to a more active role in the church as well as society. He passed on a message from the African church ladies to the WFMA, "Tell our White sisters that our love is with them, and we send it all to them through you. Will they not send out a little deputation to visit us?" He spoke warmly of the encouragement the women's work had been to both Mrs Macpherson and himself.

It does seem tragic that the Macphersons left the work there in Tsolo. Letters of commendation of Mr Macpherson came to the church from two Chiefs and twenty-three elders, from English-speaking parents of children for whom he had set up a school and from the Committee of residents in Tsolo. All of them spoke of the warmth, help and, in spite of failing health, his willingness to do all he could to help them.

Mr Macpherson never returned to the work in South Africa. When he recovered his health he became a chaplain in the army.

Mr Dewar on his own again

The sympathy of the Assembly was expressed for Mr Dewar who had lost his 'two lieutenants'. He was on his own again as far as white missionaries were concerned.

In 1926-27 there had been a severe drought which had affected Ciskei areas and this had caused much unrest among the African people. Infant mortality rates had been higher than ever. In some villages in Ciskei there were as many as two deaths per day as a result of the difficult drought conditions. Now he wrote in 1929 that there had been heavy rains in South Africa and there was much fever and many deaths. The districts of Rev Skosana had suffered much from a severe outbreak of 'flu and the town of Idutywa had suffered an epidemic of dysentery. Dewar had visited all the districts in Transkei, including Pondoland. This was the Port St Johns area, and this was the first visit from a European missionary since the people there had joined the Free Church in 1926, under Rev Mazwi.

Mr Dewar mentions the Women's Christian Association meetings going on well. He says, "What the Keswick and Crieff Conventions are to those attending them, such have these quarterly gatherings proved to our native women." At this stage they had no blue and white uniforms. They wore black shawls and skirts and white blouses.

In the July 1929 *Instructor,* there is a letter from Mrs Dewar. She tells about four journeys to outlying stations of the Mission, where she held the Women's Quarterly Meetings and examined a number of Sabbath Schools. She says:

"It was gratifying to see some few boys present at these examinations. We are indebted to the elder of Macfarlane for the happy idea of having a class for herd-boys at 6 a.m." Then Mrs Dewar appealed for money to buy Bibles to give as prizes each year to the children in every Sabbath School, 27 to 30 in all. The Sunday Schools were a promising feature of the work. There were 627 children enrolled: girls stayed on longer than the boys. Stephen Zondani of Gqumahashe was an excellent Sunday School teacher and gave demonstration lessons for other teachers.

Free Church day schools were operating at Knox, Dyafta, Mdisa, Mnyameni, Ngcingwane, Tsolo, and Sinengwane (Pondoland). Rev Skosana, in spite of problems, had opened two new stations while Mr Mazwi had lost 45 people to the Wellingtonians.

Medical mission work in the Free Church in South Africa – to be or not to be?

That was the question which vexed the church at home and in South Africa towards the end of this decade. In about 1926 Mr Dewar's stated opinion at that time was that there was no opening for a medical missionary in South Africa. At about the same time, Mr Macpherson wrote to say there was growing evidence of a desire in the UF Church for the extension of medical missions. It was agreed that a decision about Free Church medical work would be delayed until Mr Dewar came home on leave.

When Mr Dewar came back to Scotland and appeared before the Foreign Missions Committee in 1927 he agreed that there were openings for medical work, especially in 'the Territories' (i.e. Transkei). One area was about twelve miles from Umtata, another in Pondoland. Discussions were therefore opened up with the United Free Church about medical work after they said that they would be happy to co-operate with the Free Church in medical work "if planted in an agreed location and carried on, not for intensifying denominational division, but, as an evangelical agency co-operating with adjoining evangelical Missions". At the time the Free Church had two medical missionaries who had indicated their willingness to go to South Africa, Dr Katherine Rounsfell

Brown and Rev Dr Henry MacKay. The General Assembly in 1927 approved the move to set up medical work in South Africa.

There had been hopes that a joint medical work with the UF Mission would have been possible but as it turned out, this did not develop, due on the one hand to Dr Brown's ill health and other complications regarding Dr MacKay.

However, at a later date the Foreign Missions Committee accepted a new offer of service from Rev Dr Henry MacKay (who was a brother of the late Mrs Elizabeth Macdonald) to go to South Africa in place of either Mr Macdonald or Mr Macpherson and to open up Medical Mission work, as Mr Dewar had said that the time was ripe now for medical work to begin.

The General Assembly of that year, 1929, was addressed by Rev John A. Macdonald, Rev Adam Macpherson and Dr Henry MacKay who was to go to South Africa the following year.

The MacKays arrive and depart

Dr Henry MacKay and family sailed for South Africa on 10 October 1930, following his induction to the South African Mission Field on 30 September in Edinburgh. Mr Dewar had suggested that Pondoland, Transkei, would be a suitable place for Dr MacKay to settle. The Church of Scotland (now responsible for what had been the UF missionary work) had written to the Free Church expressing their willingness to co-operate in finding a suitable location for the Free Church missionary doctor to work. The MacKays arrived at East London on 2 November 1930 and by the 15th of that month Dr MacKay had cabled home to the Committee, *"No scope new medical mission here field overcrowded returning. MacKay."* In spite of the Committee's directive for him to remain pending further enquiries Dr MacKay and family returned to Scotland in December.

And that was the end of the medical missionary dream. At least until nearly 20 years later when Dr Andrews opened small clinics in some of the churches in the Pirie District.

So ended a decade that had promised so much but had yielded so little. There were broken hearts and obvious frustrations but despite the disappointments there remained a hope that better things were yet to come in the gracious providence of God.

And Mr Dewar remained alone once more.

ON REFLECTION

Three matters stand out for comment.

- The management and inspections of the Church's schools took up an inordinate amount of the missionaries' time in the years before the State assumed responsibility for the education of the African children. Even Mr Dewar in later years questioned if it had been the best use of his time running the various Free Church Schools.

- Sadly Mr Macdonald and Mr MacPherson went back to Scotland on the grounds of ill-health. It was an enormous loss to the South African church that they did not return when their health improved.

- Dr J. Campbell Andrews showed some twenty years later that a programme of medical work through village clinics was entirely possible and was a great benefit to the people. One has to assume that it was not really on 'medical' grounds that such work was not entered upon in this decade.

⑥
His Lonesome Battle
1931-40

This chapter is surely going to be short. This was a quiet decade, in some ways a decade of non-events.

Mr Dewar was alone again as far as other missionaries were concerned. All the hopes of medical work had come to nothing. All hopes of another missionary joining him came to nothing. The Foreign Missions Committee used all the Scriptural injunctions and all the logic of persuasion it could use but no one volunteered to fill the gap and come out to help the cause in South Africa. The General Assembly of 1931 paid tribute to Mr Dewar's **'fervour and loyalty in his lonesome battle'**.

Centenary celebrations at Pirie Mission
– memories of the Ross Family

One very special event took place at Pirie Mission in 1930. It was the centenary celebration of the founding of the mission there when, as Mr Dewar described it, Rev John Ross "pitched his tent close to the river and over against the high mountain, its steep sides clothed with dense forest". Of the day of the celebrations Mr Dewar wrote, "That morning members from our own and other churches made their way to Pirie Church, and at the services were reminded of the great things that God had wrought for them and the native peoples of South Africa. Great and many changes have taken place since then. Now there are native ordained ministers, hundreds of elders, twenty-five thousand members, as many scholars in the day schools and half as many catechumens." (The numbers refer to the Bantu Presbyterian Church plus the Free

Church). "With the passing of the years the work has not become easier. The heathenism that exists today is more difficult to combat than the more primitive that existed a century ago. European civilisation – not always for good – has had its effect." Mr Dewar was probably referring to a Government decision to make liquor more available to the Coloured (people of mixed race) and some parts of the Black population, and the vices which accompany this were to increase and do great harm.

Battling a deficit

While Mr Dewar was battling on in the cause in South Africa, the Foreign Missions Committee was having a financial struggle of its own back in Scotland. The Committee was carrying a deficit and various schemes were suggested to meet this crisis, including the proposal that every minister should take a 10% cut in stipend. The Moderator of the 1931 General Assembly, Rev Dr A.M. Renwick, sent a Pastoral Letter calling on all congregations of the Free Church to "observe a day of humiliation and prayer …" One of the "discomfiting thoughts and fears" noted in this letter was "a burden of debt cripples our obedience to the Missionary Command". The letter also noted, "Reluctance to consecrate themselves to this work is observable among young men and maidens who do not cry, 'Here am I, send me'."

Sadly, in 1932 the General Assembly 'suppressed' the charge at Tsolo so that it was no longer considered a mission station. While this was more for financial purposes to do with pension charges at home it did have a negative effect on the whole thinking about the mission work in that area when it was said "that there was no prospect of a missionary for Tsolo in the foreseeable future". In the end the deficit of the Committee was wiped out by a very generous gift from the Rt Hon. Lord Macleay.

The silence of Mr Dewar

So the lone missionary persevered in his work, visiting widespread congregations and examining schools, baptising adults and children and admitting new members … and then **silence**! About the middle of the decade Mr Dewar went off the radar for some months or years and he wrote no articles for the church magazines and refused to answer letters from the Foreign Missions Committee. Only when he was threatened with removal from the Field and no more salary cheques did he respond!

This was a pity because at this time there was a matter of great concern to the South African field being debated in the meetings of the Foreign Missions Committee.

Should the South African Church be independent now?

In 1934 the Foreign Missions Committee sent out a questionnaire authorised by the General Assembly, to gather information in order to "report upon the definite policy that should be adopted towards the establishment, organisation and constitution of indigenous Christian communities overseas as Presbyterian Churches and the relation of Missionaries on the field to such Churches".

They thought about the whole ideal of Indigenous Churches and, taken as given the fact that they would be self-governing, self-supporting and self-propagating, and that there would be differences in subordinate matters, the aim was "to see Presbyterian Churches, based upon and reverencing the Scriptures as the Word of God, and well instructed in and faithful to the Reformed Faith which is as universal in scope and efficiency as is the Bible of which it is the exposition". The Committee definitely hoped to see an independent Church like this in South Africa. But ...

Just as they realised that Mr Dewar 'needs much patience' in dealing with the various matters on his plate, so, as the Committee stated bluntly, 'the chosen phrase also applied to the Committee in their dealings with the missionary, who had persistently not answered any of their communications' over a lengthy period. So that didn't help. In fact, it delayed their decision regarding the future of the work in South Africa. In the end, by the General Assembly of 1936, the Committee decided, with regard to all fields that they envisaged "a period of loving and devoted help through the presence, for at least a generation, of Missionaries and Missionary helpers from Scotland".

There was more discussion when Mr Dewar eventually came home on leave in 1938, but nothing further was done about it. So that was the end of that idea for decades to come.

The work goes on

Although Mr Dewar was the only white missionary and there were only two black ministers, the work in the congregations and districts was going on amazingly well considering the scarcity of ministerial oversight. During this decade the statistics remained remarkably stable, both in church membership and in the schools. Evangelists were taking services in the 'red' or 'heathen' homesteads and some were becoming Christians, mainly women who were illiterate, so it was quite a challenge to teach them the Christian way of life. 'Hearers Classes' were held and the Bible was read to the people and the catechism explained.

In spite of the severe economic difficulties of this time on the field, there was progress in some areas in Transkei. Gqunu was doing well and had a new building. The congregation at Mqokolweni was large and the people were in the process of building there. At Qelana the work was encouraging. The Evangelist, Mr Tyekela, was getting old and feeling the weight of his years. He was a fine Christian. The Coloured school at Tsolo (started by Mr Macpherson) was also doing well. At Ngcingwane, church and school were encouraging but the Wellingtonian movement did make inroads there as in several other places in Transkei. Sometimes they set up rival schools. The churches felt some impact from this opposing movement. Rev Mazwi's work was affected at times. Chief Ndevu of the Pondomisi, who had been an influence for good in the church, had died and this added to Mr Mazwi's problems, which included his own ill health.

The South African Women's Christian Association continued to meet weekly, quarterly and annually in villages, districts and the whole field would come together once a year. Mrs Dewar was active in this work. She liked to help in the schools and with the WCA. An excellent decision was made that at each quarterly meeting of the Association they would hear a report on the Sunday

School work in the District, in the hopes of increasing interest in this work among the young. The ladies in Scotland and Australia had continued to send out boxes which were always welcome. But in 1933 the WFMA in Scotland decided it would be a better use of their funds to establish a Special Fund which would be drawn on to help with emergencies in our mission areas.

Rev Skosana leaves the church

Mr Skosana had conducted services which had been well received in the Burnshill District as well as his own.

However, when Rev Skosana was appointed to take oversight of the Tsolo District in Transkei, he resigned and joined 'a native church'. This was a great pity as far as our work was concerned but very understandable as far as Mr Skosana was concerned. He had come into the Free Church with 'his' people in the Port Elizabeth and surrounding areas and he naturally did not want to leave them and go hundreds of miles away to the Transkei, which would be almost like another country to him. So that was the departure of yet another African minister. He was a good man and a loss to the church.

Home Leave

Mr and Mrs Dewar were in Scotland on home leave, which was five years overdue, from April 1938 until July 1939. They were welcomed at the General Assembly in 1938, and the Committee interviewed Mr Dewar in Glasgow on 24 May 1938. He made a strong plea for another missionary to be sent out, otherwise he was afraid the work would disintegrate. When asked how he had been able to carry on the work of the mission some years without any subsidy from the Committee, he replied that a debt had been piling up for some time and he apologised for not having sent a record of the finances to the Committee. By reason of age, he explained, he could not expect to continue much longer in active service. The possibility of the Free Church Mission being taken over by another church in South Africa was discussed, but the other churches had their hands full, and Mr Dewar did not think there was another

Church in South Africa in full sympathy with the Free Church that could take over the whole of the Mission.

In addressing a missionary meeting in November 1938, Mr Dewar spoke of the two main divisions within the African race in the area in which we minister. He said one was the descendants of warlike and once dominant tribes, and the other the descendants of subject tribes. The latter welcomed European sovereignty and the former did not co-operate but withdrew into their old tribal life and customs. The work could be very difficult among these people, especially the young men.

At the 1939 General Assembly which Mr Dewar addressed, ("conscious he was addressing the Assembly for the last time"), he was thanked for his 30 years of supervising the work of the Mission in South Africa.

Rev Godfrey to the rescue

In Mr Dewar's absence Rev Godfrey of the Church of Scotland (and formerly UF Church) had been keeping an eye on things. A Wesleyan minister had also undertaken general oversight of the other Districts.

On his return, Mr Dewar paid tribute to what Mr Godfrey had done during that time, conducting Baptismal and Communion services in the Ciskei and Ngcingwane (Transkei) Districts, and in Port Elizabeth. He also acted as manager of the schools and had presided at the opening of the big, new buildings at Knox and Mnyameni. At a special service in the new Knox building the people gathered to thank Rev Godfrey for all the help he had given to them when Mr Dewar was away.

After his leave in Scotland, Mr Dewar felt "much revived in strength and elasticity of spirit" and he found that everything had been going on very well in his absence. In the Free Church Assembly of the following year, Rev W.J. Cameron reflected on the fact that during Mr Dewar's furlough, apart from the occasional help from Mr Godfrey, the various congregations got on well with their work and Mr Dewar found that nowhere had people drifted away from the church altogether, or that they had scattered to other missions operating in the area. Spiritual and material progress had been made, new buildings put up and new members added.

On the other hand Mr Dewar himself sent a long and very detailed Report to the Committee in which he stated that for the first time in thirty years the field had been without a missionary while he had been on furlough. "This was a handicap to progress and a keen disappointment to our people." Probably there was truth in both points of view.

Back in harness

Shortly after returning from Scotland Mr Dewar set out to visit all the Districts. Most of the Transkei areas had not been visited since well before his furlough. He lamented the fact that there were still so many 'reds' and so many Christians who would lapse and revert to heathen ways. Mr Dewar reflected, "Notwithstanding the many years – well over one hundred – Christian Missions have been working in South Africa, it is said that today there are more heathen than Christian natives, with the former increasing more rapidly than the latter. There remains much to be done, and this need calls for redoubled effort."

ON REFLECTION

In 1908 the Church discussed seriously the prospect of having an indigenous and self supporting church in South Africa; the matter was looked at seriously again in 1934; it was not until 1976 that the vision began to become a reality. Why did it take so long?

Prospects for further help for Mr Dewar and for medical work had appeared hopeful and then were dashed. Should the Foreign Missions Committee, rather than wondering about an indigenous church, have considered withdrawing from this work altogether, especially when it seemed no one from the home church was willing to offer for the work? Thankfully the Committee decided to continue.

7
Help at Last
1941–1950

This decade saw the end of an era, maybe of a legend, and the start of a new. It was born in grief and the dashing of high hopes.

Mr Dewar was still carrying on all alone as far as missionaries were concerned, and again he just seems to have clammed up as far as sending home any reports or answering any letters, even the most important. The General Assembly of 1941 came and went with barely a mention of South Africa. Gratitude was expressed for Mr Dewar's role there but as he had neither communicated with the Foreign Missions Committee nor sent in an annual Report there was little for the Assembly to discuss.

The strains of the Second World War were being felt on all sides and much thought had to be given to any extension of the mission work of the church at that time.

However, the decision was taken to advertise for a missionary to go to South Africa. An open letter from the Convenor of the Foreign Missions Committee which appeared in the *Monthly Record* in September 1941 ended with the words: "*Do you not think that some brave soul will give a thought to Africa and remember the lone missionary in King William's Town? Who will go for us?*"

Rev and Mrs Gregor Macleod

There were indeed two brave souls – Gregor and Elizabeth Macleod. Gregor was in training for the ministry at the Free Church College in 1941 when he responded to the appeal, and his appointment was recommended. At the same meeting the idea was still put forward that consideration be given to handing over the work in South Africa to some other body. Mr Dewar was informed of all this but as no word came back from him the Missions Committee had to determine the sphere of service allocated to Mr Gregor Macleod, seeking advice from Rev John A. Macdonald.

Mr Macdonald's recommendations were as follows:

(1) If Mr Macleod, or another missionary, were to go out to Africa, he should be given Transkei in which to work, with a centre at Tsolo, as long as Mr Dewar was still serving in King William's Town.

(2) Out of a population of 500,000 in Ciskei, only one seventh were professedly Christian. The rest professed to be heathen. Mission work was needed.

(3) Mr Dewar preached and taught through interpreters. Mr Macdonald thought a white missionary should train African workers in theology to enable them to preach to their own people, and to teach them in their own language. Then one European missionary, based in King William's Town would be enough to act as supervisor.

(4) Mr Macdonald did not know of any other body whose doctrine would be acceptable to the Free Church. He expressed his opinion emphatically that abandonment of the Mission by the Free Church would be a betrayal of loyal South African people, and he questioned whether they would accept a transference.

This was fully discussed, and in the end Mr Gregor Macleod's departure for South Africa was to be delayed so that he could take a session in Moray House Teacher's Training Centre. A place there was obtained in October 1942, but Mr Macleod abandoned the training after only ten days, saying that due to a nervous disability the classes were too much for him after his course at the Free Church College. Mr Macleod had been ordained in Tain Free Church (his home congregation) and inducted for work in the

South African Mission Field in September of that year, 1942. Mr Macleod's new bride (Elizabeth Macdonald) was also present that evening and was assured, along with her husband, of "the good wishes of the congregation which went out wholeheartedly and equally to both of them".

Meantime a passage became available on a ship bound for South Africa and so they were farewelled in St Columba's Free Church, Edinburgh, (Mrs Macleod's home congregation) on 18 November. At this meeting Gregor Macleod spoke of the journey they were about to undertake, saying *"they were not dismayed by the dangers of the journey, nor by the prospect of the sacrifice which their chosen career would entail"*. They sailed on 21 November 1942.

Tragic loss

In the sad and strange providence of God, their ship was torpedoed and it went down in shark-infested waters off the east coast of Africa. There were no survivors. The Convenor, Rev Prof David McKenzie had to convey the sad news to Mrs Macleod's father in Edinburgh, and the Vice-Convenor, Rev J.A. Macdonald, had to do the same to Rev Macleod's mother in Tain. This was a grievous loss – to their parents and friends in Scotland, to the Church as a whole, but to Mr Dewar and the South African Free Church, waiting so hopefully for their expected help to come at last, it must have been devastating.

This was acknowledged in a Minute of the Committee, and tribute was paid to the noble, generous and Christian character of the two young missionaries. It went on: *"The work which Mr and Mrs Macleod were not destined to take up now awaits other labourers, and it is hoped that the call of our undermanned African Mission will not fall in vain upon the ears of the young manhood of the Free Church of Scotland."*

Well, maybe it did fall in vain, as far as the Scottish church was concerned, for it was to be many years before another missionary went to South Africa from Scotland, but later in this decade in Ireland, Australia and by a Dutchman in Scotland the call was heard and heeded.

Rev & Mrs Alexander Dewar

Meanwhile Mr Dewar soldiered on alone. He did send in an Annual Report of 1942 and in this he mentioned the effects of the war. Rising prices, men being called up and a prolonged drought all added up to complicate the work. Rev Mazwi in Transkei was still unwell and was not able to travel the full extent of his territory. The situation in the Korsten (Port Elizabeth) congregation had worsened and many had left.

The situation on the Women's Associations front was more cheerful. Mr Dewar wrote:

> Each station had its weekly service for prayer and Bible lesson. The members also visit the sick, and hold what might be called 'kitchen' meetings and seek to interest their 'Red' sisters. Then there are the district quarterly gatherings, times of helpfulness when members tell of how the work goes on at the different places. The Annual or General Meeting – 'Synod' as the women call it – was held in October. This year it was held at Ngcingwane. Delegates came from all the stations, non-delegates also attend, men being among the number. Those from Ciskei arrive at Idutywa by train at 1.0 am, where they wait in the open waiting room till the morning, by which time the contingent from Umtata direction has arrived. Ox 'waggons' from Ngcingwane take them and their baggage – consisting of their blankets and Sabbath clothes – to the Mission Church, when they will have a busy time for the next few days.

Among the activities was a Young Girls' Rally.

> It is most encouraging to see so many young folk becoming members of the Junior Associations and taking an active part and keen interest in the work.

Mr Dewar reported that there were still applications coming from people (and ministers) from other churches wishing to be associated with the Free Church. There were signs of encouragement in the church in South Africa; the Young Men's Association was doing a "quiet and effective work"; one of the members from Mnyameni had successfully undertaken the Evangelists' Course at the Lovedale Bible School; the schools continued, having a total enrolment of 696. There were 1087 members of the church, 155 catechumens and 377 adherents. There were two evangelists working in the congregations. Rev Mazwi was able to minister to those congregations near his home.

Golden Jubilee and Glory Year – 1943

1943 marked the Jubilee year as a missionary in Africa of Rev Alexander Dewar. Fifty years before, he had arrived in Africa as a missionary. The following commendation was recorded by the General Assembly in Scotland of that year:

> The Assembly are thankful to the Most High for so loyal and energetic an ambassador for Christ, and recall with pleasure his indefatigable labours pursued with a bright faith notwithstanding his solitariness ... Their desire is that in the evening of his days he may in large measure experience the comfort and joy of the Lord and be assured that the church at home will ever keep kindly remembrance of that brave father in the faith still manfully carrying a load too great for lesser spirits.

A friend who had visited him previously wrote then of Mr Dewar's obvious rapport with the Africans and with his interpreter Mr Zokobe Taho of Knox. The writer, Mr R.C. Algie of Ireland wrote: "I like Mr Dewar. He is a born optimist – nothing can subdue his ardour. His trustworthy information on all sorts of subjects makes his company entrancing and withal he is so humble."

A Sudden Homecall

On 10 August Mr Dewar was conducting business in King William's Town when he collapsed and died. In the year of his Golden Jubilee, the call came to him to join the throng around the throne singing praise to the Glorious Lord who had sustained him through so many years of service here. And so this was the end of an era – the Dewar era – and the death of a legend.

A letter sent to the Misses Niven, Edinburgh, from Miss Madge Erskine, South Africa, (a descendant of the original Ross family) tells of the Memorial Service for Mr Dewar held at Knox Mission:

> On Sunday I was at Knox (Mr Dewar's out-station) with Mrs Dewar, Mrs Godfrey, my aunt (Miss Carrie Ross) and two other ladies interested, at Mr Dewar's Memorial Service. As I looked at that congregation and thought that they are without a missionary I felt very sad. The people seemed to me not bright as they were, they appeared sad and depressed. Is the Free Church not going to send a missionary? You know Mr Dewar had most of the people out here. What are these people to do? He has all the young people. I take the girls for Mrs Dewar as she cannot manage them as well.

Mr Dewar's Challenge

On hearing of the tragic loss of the two missionaries, Rev Gregor and Mrs Elizabeth Macleod, on their way out to join him in the work, Mr Dewar had sent a challenge to the young men of the church. He had issued a "call to volunteer in the highest and most venturesome of all services as well as to obey our Lord's last command ... Perhaps the loss of our young missionary will move the hearts of our like-minded men to undertake what he had set out to do".

And this is exactly what happened, but sadly, the help came too late for Mr Dewar.

REV AND MRS JOSEPH MCCRACKEN AND ANNE

Dr J. Campbell Andrews, while still a student, visited the Irish Evangelical Presbyterian Church back in 1934. He said:

> Two things about the Irish Evangelical Church must impress a stranger. One is the spiritual fervour of the members with whom one comes in contact. They are zealous for the glory of God in the salvation of souls.

The other is the great volume of earnest and definite prayer rising from the church to the throne above. It must be prevailing prayer because it is offered in faith, in Christ's name, to the end His glory and the good of men's souls. Such zeal and prayer must have results, and for this reason one feels that, under God, the Irish Evangelical Church is to be a means of great blessing to many.

God uses the tragedy

At their meeting on 16 November, 1943, the Foreign Missions Committee had before them an application for missionary service in South Africa from Rev Joseph McCracken of the Irish Evangelical Presbyterian Church. Mr McCracken had been licensed and ordained in April 1935. He was prepared to leave his present charge and church in Belfast, Northern Ireland in order to serve the Lord in the foreign mission field. He was married to Helen and they had one daughter, Anne. And it was the tragedy of the deaths of Rev and Mrs Gregor Macleod which motivated Mr McCracken and his wife to apply to go to South Africa to take their place. Mr McCracken's application was considered and after the Committee interviewed him it was agreed to accept his application for service in South Africa and steps were to be taken for him to be accepted as a minister of the Free Church of Scotland.

Mrs Dewar had been making arrangements for the work to be carried on since the death of her husband. Naturally, she was unable to do this for long, owing to her own ill health and her son Iain's disabilities caused by a bout of rheumatic fever while still a boy. It was agreed to ask Mrs Dewar to seek Rev Godfrey's help once again with the Mission until Mr McCracken arrived on the field. And so that large-hearted man, Mr Godfrey of the Church of Scotland, agreed to continue to look after the interests of the Free Church until **someone** would arrive to shepherd the flock.

Exactly one year after Mr Dewar's death, on 10 August 1944, Mr McCracken was inducted by the Free Presbytery of Edinburgh to the South African Mission Field. Everything was difficult and complicated because of the Second World War. There was a ban on civilians travelling overseas. Nevertheless, early in November 1944 the McCrackens did set sail for South Africa. We admire their courage under wartime conditions and with a little girl, especially as they must have had the Gregor Macleods' tragic experience never far from their minds.

A Dangerous Journey

Mrs Helen McCracken, looking back fifty long years later, described their experience thus:

> The seaside can be a very pleasant place and going onto the sea in a little boat can be a great thrill, but the sea can be a cruel thing.
>
> During the last war a young couple, Rev and Mrs Gregor Macleod, married three months, left their native Scotland at God's call to serve here in our South African Mission, but they didn't arrive as their ship was torpedoed by enemy action in shark infested waters – there were no survivors ...
>
> We followed about a year later, on what could be described as a mystery tour. No one was to know about our movements, our luggage was labelled 'Destination 5'. On arrival at Liverpool we learned that we would be travelling on 'The Themistocles', an old ship but said to be sea-worthy.
>
> After embarking, the passengers were assembled, warned about the dangers and instructed on how to behave, and every second day thereafter we had emergency drill so that we would know what to do if the worst happened. Instead of the usual ten days or so we were one month at sea zig-zagging to avoid submarines lurking in the waters.
>
> One afternoon a steward rushed in, closed and bolted the port-hole saying, "This is the real thing, get out." We quickly lifted what we had been told to have ready; warm clothing, hats, chocolate etc. and made

our way to our emergency station amid passengers running helter-skelter. The Captain, a sick man, (not seasick!) all the journey, was on the bridge and the boats were being lowered. After about ten minutes the 'all clear' sounded and we were told over the loud-speaker that we could disperse as the object cited had proved to be wreckage from another ship. Good enough news for the present, but a reminder that we might be the next, and only God, in His mercy, could take us safely to our destination, which He did. (*Evangelical Presbyterian Jan-Feb 1994*)

Safe Arrival and first impressions

The McCrackens arrived in King William's Town in December 1944 and they were welcomed by, among others, Rev R. Godfrey, who had indeed faithfully overseen the Mission work since Mr Dewar's death, and must now have been so glad to see them.

The McCrackens came to set up home in the African village of Mngqesha, where Miss Carrie Ross and Miss Madge Erskine, a granddaughter and great-granddaughter of the old John Ross still lived.

On 12 December 1944, Joe McCracken wrote home to tell of their first experiences in South Africa. He described the joy of the people that they had come, and especially that they were living right among the people.

Our present headquarters are sixteen miles out of King William's Town ... Our main purpose in living here is that we might more speedily acquire the difficult language and learn the curious customs of the people ... Our official welcome was held in the Knox Church on Saturday 16th December, when the people came from far and near, many travelling long distances and remaining over the weekend in order to be present at the service on the Lord's Day. The Rev R. Godfrey presided at the service. After a short but inspiring message on 'The City of God', elders, representing different Free Churches in the Pirie District spoke with great feeling. One, referring to the deaths of Rev Gregor Macleod and his wife, followed by the death of Rev A. Dewar, said in a most touching way, "God did not forget us! Scotland did not forget us!" ... The hearty, tuneful singing was an outstanding feature of the service.

The warm appreciation of the church was again expressed to Mr Godfrey for all he had done on its behalf.

It was not long before Rev Joe surveyed his new field and early came to the conclusion that, "the sound testimony of the Free Church Mission should be maintained and extended. The work holds great problems but also great possibilities". Mr McCracken continued, "Quite recently the Government introduced a School Feeding Scheme, the scholars receiving one free meal per day. This will vastly improve the health of the children, many of whom suffer from malnutrition and are so made liable to the many diseases that ravage this land ...

I would like to disabuse the minds of those who think this country is evangelised. Here on our field there are thousands of natives called 'Reds' who are out-and-out heathen and are practically untouched by the Gospel ... I have found the praise of my predecessor, the late Rev Alex Dewar, F.R.G.S., in all the churches. I only hope I may serve my Lord as well and as faithfully as he did."

Because of the vast area covered by the Mission, Mr McCracken said there was an urgent need for another missionary.

Future hopes of relief

One cause of hope was centred on J. Campbell Andrews, a member of the Free Presbyterian Church of Australia (later to be called the Presbyterian Church of Eastern Australia). He had felt the call to mission work at the age of 20, and had spent 8 years in Edinburgh completing his medical and theological training in order to prepare himself for this call. But the war intervened, and first came his duty to his country. He spent time in the war years serving as a doctor with the Australian Army in Northern Queensland and Borneo.

Also an application for service in South Africa was received from Mr Huite Sliep. He was of Dutch background and a member of the Dutch Reformed Church, who had come to study at the Bible Training Institute in Glasgow. He was now a student in the Free Church College in Edinburgh. In the meantime he was accepted as a missionary candidate, though after completing his training it was only in 1948 that he arrived in South Africa with his Scottish wife Helen, to take up his missionary duties.

However in the meantime, for the McCrackens in 1945, there was always hope.

Travelling with a sense of humour!

Mr McCracken's descriptions in letters home of his early travels in 1945 soon after his arrival show that he had not lost his Irish sense of humour – and indeed he never did lose it to the end of his days.

He tells us of a visit to the hillside village of Mnyameni in the Burnshill District on a very wet day when travel by car proved muddy and hazardous and crossing rivers dangerous. Some of the folk from the church brought horses to the scene and he switched to travel by horseback. When crossing the river on horseback the water almost touched the stirrups. However, they made it to the church where no one had expected him to come because of the weather. In a letter home he says,

> When the women saw us coming they began to shout and sing and soon the mountain was ringing with their notes of joy. We were greatly touched at the heartfelt joy of these people. Mr Taho told me that they said they never expected to see a white missionary again. In the cosy house of the school teacher we enjoyed some hot tea. The service began. The elders assembled, a case of restoration was dealt with. The woman confessed her sin and professed repentance, and so was given the right hand of fellowship. Next came two candidates

for Church membership. I asked them as to their faith in Christ and received satisfactory answers. Putting the question to one, "What made you think on these things?" the reply was "The Holy Spirit."

In spite of the rain, over 70 people gathered for the service which began at 12.15 p.m. and lasted until 2.15 p.m. During the time three adults and eight children were baptised in the name of the Lord. Then came a short break of 15 minutes, after which the bell was rung and 70 people assembled for the Lord's Supper. This service finished at 4 p.m. After dinner we left at 5 p.m.

It was still raining, so that the horses literally slipped down the mountainside, forded the river, and stumbled up the other side. I must have been a sight for sore eyes coming down the mountain on horseback the reins in one hand and an umbrella in the other, and the horse slipping and sliding all over the place. The situation was so ludicrous that I couldn't help laughing ... We arrived back at Mngqesha about 7 p.m. Pray that God will bless these dear souls in the heart of the mountains at Emnyameni. Next month I purpose visiting the Transkei. Roads are even worse there!! So I am told!!! Kindest regards, Yours in Christ for Africa, Joseph McCracken.

And in Transkei ...

A short time later in April 1945, Mr McCracken did go to Transkei and travelled all over the region, to see how things were with the churches. They had been without a missionary for more than two years, and in some cases there were difficulties to be sorted out, but on the whole the churches were in good heart and the welcome was most sincere.

He obviously enjoyed the adventure of having to ride by horse to Gqunu, about four miles into the mountains. "The narrow path to Gqunu runs parallel to the Tina River, and at times we had to dismount, on the advice of the natives, as they were afraid of losing their missionary in the deep waters of the Tina River!." But more importantly he adds, "During the services at this place I experienced a great sense of the Lord's presence, which could only be the outcome of somebody's prayers (date 12ᵗʰ April).

Two souls professed faith in the Lord Jesus Christ. Only one of them can read. Pray for these dear souls."

Next morning they left for Mqokelweni, a journey of 60 miles.

When we arrived at the church the people went wild with joy. They said that they never expected to see another white missionary from Scotland. This large church was crowded, and the chief of the people, a young, educated man, came to bid me welcome on behalf of his people. After numerous speeches I baptised 7 children and preached the Gospel to over 200 people. At the afternoon service there was a somewhat smaller audience at which, after preaching another sermon, I dispensed the Lord's Supper. About 120 came forward to the Table. Tears were shed at both these services but what they meant I cannot say. I hope it was the mighty Spirit of God at work. The chief, who had been in the South African Army for a period, drove me up a fearsome cutting ... We arrived back at 6 p.m., just as darkness was falling.

After sleeping in a village overnight, they left early for Ngcingwane.

The reception we received at this place beggars description. On Wednesday morning about 24 horsemen arrived ... and led the way double file while I drew up the rear in the car. When we got to the church, which is beautifully situated and solidly built of brick and concrete, about 100 scholars from the day school were drawn up in single file and facing inwards, then about 50 yards apart the members and friends of the congregation were lined up in single file facing the children and all were singing. The horsemen galloped round the children at the command of their captain and came in between children and members; of course the car had to follow and stop in the centre. We waited until the singing had finished and then I shook hands with over 300 persons including the children ... Many speeches of welcome were made, but I did not miss the opportunity of preaching the Gospel.

At the service next day I baptised a 'red' woman and her baby. This woman had been converted recently in the church.

Although we left at 7.10 a.m. the next morning for Mngqesha, quite a number of the office-bearers came to see me off. And so ended my first journey to the Transkei.

The Problem of the 'Reds'

From the beginning of his time on the mission field Rev Joe had been wrestling with the problem of the great number of heathen 'red' people – those who wore red ochre blankets and resisted the changes and the God of the 'school people'. He was disturbed to think that 53% of the people on our Mission Field were 'red' people. And we had been there more than 100 years.

One day towards the end of 1945 he went to Rankin, crossing six rivers en route, and over some of the worst tracks on our mission field. He goes on,

> It is one of our smaller churches, but yesterday we had about 50 present at the service. Arriving at the church, we noticed some boys lying on the grass nearby, so we made a bee-line for them. We invited them to come to the service, but they only laughed; however, six of them did come. Boys in South Africa are the great problem. Girls are expected to go and seem to enjoy going to church, but not so the boys ...
>
> The service had just commenced when it was rudely interrupted by a band of 'red' boys, who marched past the church singing and beating their knobkerries (clubs). The elder went out to remonstrate with them,

but they maintained a defiant attitude. After the service I looked out of the window to see if the boys were in sight, and, sure enough, I could see what proved to be about 200 young people, including girls, at some distance from the church. Having learned that they had been drinking beer, singing and dancing the whole night through, I made my way with the schoolteacher to the gathering of the young people. They were from different locations and it was evident that between two distinct parties negotiations were proceeding for a fight. Sides are chosen and they proceed to club each other, using a small shield made of grass attached to their left arm to ward off, if possible, the blows of an opponent. Nearly all these fights end in the death of some boy, many of the others being disfigured for life.

On approaching them I noticed that their attitude was definitely hostile, so, when some distance from them, I asked them to sit on the grass as I wanted to speak to them. The majority obeyed, but some were still very defiant. Just at this moment the girls, naked to the waist, ran from the hut behind us blowing whistles and shouting defiance at us. For a moment the situation was tense, for it seemed as if we might be attacked, but I began to speak to the young men, most of whom were naked, about their fighting powers and then reminded them that the Lord Jesus needed soldiers for His army to fight the good fight of faith. I tried to tell these raw heathen in simple language the great love of God in Christ. They listened very well in spite of the fact that the girls were dancing, singing and shouting about 150 yards from us. When I told them I would expect to see them in church the next time I visited Rankin, one young man wanted to know if it meant giving up all the 'fun' they were having. I replied it meant that, but that Christ would give them something better. The answer did not meet with the approval of many of them. We found it difficult to speak, the air being charged with evil ... The elder informed us that the girls, all in their 'teens, fight with sticks, as well as the boys ...

In the whole business we seemed so weak. The Church seemed so weak, and this after nearly 100 years of Gospel influence. I'm afraid it is true that we are losing ground here.

Day to day Responsibilities

As well as the care of the churches over the whole area of the South African mission field, worrying about the evangelisation of the 'reds', and being increasingly aware of the political scene where the position of the Blacks was becoming more and more oppressed and they themselves becoming more militant, Mr McCracken had the responsibility involved in being manager of six schools. This involved much work, but it gave him great influence with the teachers, the scholars, and indirectly, with the parents.

Mrs McCracken was also well occupied with work among the women and girls, a work that was making steady progress, especially in the Pirie and Burnshill Districts. Mr McCracken wrote about the Women's Quarterly Meetings:

> After a Conference Service addressed by my wife there follows the business meeting, after which the service takes the form of an evangelistic meeting, usually lasting the whole night through! The reason for this is not far to seek. The women come from all the Churches, some walking 30, 40 or even 50 miles to be present, and there being no accommodation, what better way could they spend the night than by singing, praying and preaching?

Reports of steady work

While he was the only ordained minister on the Field in 1946 he did report on the Evangelists who assisted him in the work. Simon Langa, who had been suspended for a time was restored to his

THE FIRST MISSIONARIES

Rev Zokobe Taho

Rev Alexander Dewar

Rev Wm. Murray

Rev A.A. Macpherson

Rev John A. Macdonald

Rev Gregor Macleod

"Red" people thatching a traditional house

Four boys going through initiation

Boys going to a stick-fight

Three "red" women

Rev Joe and Helen McCracken

Dr Campbell and Mrs Ruby Andrews

Mrs Lex Colville

Rev Huite and Mrs Helen Sliep

Ngcingwane
Church bell

Ngcingwane Church

Mdisa Church

Pirie Church

Mnyameni Church

Albert and Pat Sliep

Angus and Helen Macdonald

Bill and Elizabeth Graham

David and Marion Fraser

SOUTH AFRICAN MINISTERS AND MEN

Rev Bryce Taho

Rev Wilfred Vumindaba

Rev Thyson Nkwelo

Rev Nelson Mpayipeli

Rev Patrick Diniso

Rev Avery Ngaki

Rev F.F. Mva

Rev Khulile Davids (left) and
Rev Buntu Mtishe (right)

Rev Lindikhaya Piyo

Rev Clifton Xabadiya

Rev Richmond Gotywa

Rev William Ledwaba

Evangelist Makapela

Evangelist Nenemba

Evangelist Soka

WOMEN'S WORK

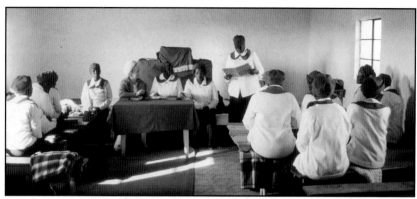

A typical Thursday — WCA meeting in progress

Women about to be admitted to membership of the WCA (blue hats and collars on the table will be put on)

Women on a mission — probably to visit a sick member of the WCA

duties in the Transkei, Mr K. Kobo was appointed as an Evangelist in Pirie and there was the good prospect of a trained Evangelist being appointed to the Burnshill District to replace the former Evangelist who had left for another church. On top of all his other responsibilities Mr McCracken was undertaking to give Mr Kobo a course of instruction in Scripture, Apologetics and Pastoral Theology. This, though onerous, was a refreshing development on the part of the missionary's work.

The visit of two deputies from Scotland

Rev Duncan Leitch and **Rev Prof R.A. Finlayson** were appointed as Deputies to visit the South African mission field by the General Assembly of the Free Church in Scotland of 1946 and eventually sailed for South Africa in February 1947. They boarded the liner 'Carnarvon Castle', (the same ship which had transported the MacKay family in 1930) and were astonished to find it completely transformed into a troop ship! They slept with many others having no privacy, in hammocks down below decks. Food was served in the novel and American way of 'self-service'. Soon like-minded Christians gathered for an hour each day for Bible study, prayer and fellowship. Many years later Prof Finlayson was amazed to hear that one of the passengers counted his words at one of these meetings as the time when he first met his Saviour, and he had later become a missionary.

Gaining impressions

Everywhere the Deputies went they experienced a warm welcome. Hundreds of people gathered, children's choirs sang, people expressed their appreciation of the Church in Scotland ... At the official welcome in Knox Church, Miss Caroline Ross gifted a farm in the Pirie District to the Free Church.

They enjoyed the hearty services and the stamina of the people who could sit for hours on backless benches, and then continue the service throughout the night! Almost always there were heathen people present – "at the back of the church or on the fringe of the gathering out of doors they sit in their red blankets listening to the message of the Saviour's love". In Rankin, where Evangelist Kobo had been taking evangelistic meetings, they met several of the 'reds' who had recently professed faith in Christ. Among these were some young lads – could they have been some of those to whom Rev Joe McCracken spoke on his first visit to Rankin two years before?

They appreciated the faithfulness of the untrained office-bearers who preached week after week in various churches. Mr (later Rev) Zokobe Taho of Knox went with the Deputies day after day, interpreting for them and giving them most useful information about the beginnings of the work. They wished to take him back with them to meet the people in Scotland but were very disappointed when the shipping line would not grant him a passage.

Some outstanding occasions

Some services were quite unforgettable – for example the first Sabbath, which was spent at a communion service at Knox, where they baptised nineteen children. *"The Communion Service reminded us of happy Sabbaths at home when, with His people we gathered round His table to remember His death, and we thought too of the table spread above, around which His people of every nation and tribe will yet gather for a communion that will have no end."*

Again they attended an African wedding, assembled with about two hundred others to await the coming of the bride and bridegroom in their ox-drawn, covered carts. The occasion was too much for Rev Joe who seized the chance to preach to the waiting company, of the love of the Heavenly Bridegroom who had paid such a valuable 'lobola' (brideprice) for his Bride – when he gave Himself on the Cross that He might purchase his Bride, the Church.

While in Alice Prof Finlayson and Mr Leitch attended the Graduation Ceremony at the University of Fort Hare. After the church service at Gqumahashe, conducted in the open-air, they met Dr Bokwe, a medical doctor and graduate of Edinburgh University. His "Christian character and missionary sympathies render him a tower of strength to every Christian enterprise in the community, and whose knowledge and experience of the medical situation were at a later date placed so freely at our disposal." (i.e.

when they were trying to ascertain whether or not there was a need for the Free Church to start a medical work.) "With him on this occasion was his aged mother, a Christian woman of forceful character and rare devotion, who spoke to us of having visited the Free Church Assembly when in 1929 she had been in Edinburgh ... The impression left with us from this visitation of the Burnshill District is that it offers a splendid sphere of service for an energetic missionary, who, with the assistance of one or more native evangelists, could do much-needed work among the very large sections of the community still unreached by the Gospel."

In Transkei the Deputies first visited Ngcingwane where, again, they were very warmly welcomed by members of the Free Church as well as representatives of both the Methodist and Episcopal churches. Later they visited widely, including Tabora, the home of Rev Mazwi, and Tsolo, where Rev Adam MacPherson had been working.

They appreciated the good work done by Mrs McCracken among the women and girls of the Mission taking note of the fact that the women dressed in the recognised Free Church colours – *"dark skirt, white blouse with blue collarette, and head-dress to match"*. In each denomination the women have their own colours. Our Free Church colours were chosen by Mrs Dewar. They dutifully attended a Women's Quarterly Meeting, saw eight women being admitted to membership of the Association and solemnly commended to God in prayer.

Prof Finlayson and Mr Leitch especially enjoyed meetings with the children. They loved the way the school children sang the Psalms and the beautiful African National Anthem, *"God bless Africa ..."* They were asked to baptise many children during their weeks in South Africa and they noted that, while many of the children had been given names that were common to boys and girls in Scotland, there were some rather different ones, such as Agrunnel, Ethelina, Waitington and even Governor! The Free Church Girl's Association was well organised under the direction of Mrs McCracken. Little Anne McCracken, aged 5, was already speaking Xhosa fluently.

The Deputies greatly appreciated the hospitality and help-fulness of both Mr and Mrs McCracken and the good work they were doing there.

Farewell

At last in Knox church on 31st May, ten long weeks after gathering in the same church for a warm welcome, it was time to say 'farewell'.

One venerable elder present then could recall the first deputies who had visited them in 1906 – Principal McCulloch and Prof Macleod – and added: "*We recall the hard times when we doubted the existence of the Free Church. God made it possible for us to believe it when these deputies arrived and promised to send us missionaries. Now, we are sure the Free Church is alive and tell them at home that the Free Church in Africa is alive.*"

Mr Zokobe Taho expressed thanks to the Scottish church for their sacrifice and interest in the Free Church people of South Africa. Then he concluded: "*Sirs, please ask your praying people to continue in prayer for us, that the Holy Spirit may be poured out upon us, blessing the professing people of God, and above all, bringing the many heathen around our doors to the knowledge of the truth as it is in Jesus Christ our Lord.*"

The occasion gave a good opportunity to pay tribute to Mr Zokobe Taho, and a presentation was made to him to recognise his valuable services, not only to the Deputies (for he had accompanied them in all their travels), but for his long service at the Church's school at Knox and his valuable help to the Mission in so many ways.

Next day all met again for the observance of the Lord's Supper.

Reporting Back

So Prof Finlayson and Mr Leitch made the return journey and arrived home safely and thankfully. On the boat they would have had plenty of time to reflect on all they had experienced and to think of what recommendations they would make to the Foreign Missions Committee and to the Assembly on their return. What would stand out? What was being done well and should be con-tinued? What would be better to be done differently?

Here are some of their considered observations and recommendations, made in an Appendix to the Assembly Report for 1948:

1. That the present division of the Field into three districts (i.e. Transkei, Pirie and Burnshill) be continued, and that a missionary be put in charge of each, and be wholly responsible for the work there.

2. That the Presbytery of Kaffraria be revived as soon as this was possible.

3. That the strong congregations in each district be developed and expanded, and from these, as centres, the heathen in the surrounding areas should be evangelised. It might be necessary eventually to discontinue work in places where the Free Church was weak and where other missionary agencies were established.

4. That the missionary should arrange to spend two to three weeks each year in each of the more isolated congregations in his district. During his stay he would (a) instruct office-bearers and candidates (b) organise and establish the various departments of the congregation's activities, particularly among the young (c) consolidate the work of the evangelists and (d) visit the homes of the people, especially where there are cases of sickness and infirmity.

5. It should be the policy of the Mission to have men of Christian character and suitable gifts trained for work as evangelists. At present these men should be trained by the missionary ...

The deputies made two other interesting observations at a different time:

In forward-looking wisdom Prof Finlayson said that

Although the final goal of all missionary enterprise was world evangelisation, their immediate aim was the establishing of the Christian Church in every mission field as an indigenous, self-propagating, self-supporting Church. The missionary was not there to stay indefinitely or relieve the Christian community of the burden that rightly belonged to them as Christians; he was there to establish, organise, instruct and foster a Christian Church which should shoulder its own burdens and recognise its responsibility to the regions beyond ...

Prof Finlayson also spoke (at the annual WFMA meeting in May 1948), of the way in which Christianity had elevated the status of women in South Africa.

They were a dominating influence in the home, and consequently in the nation. They had quarterly meetings for women, conducted with composure and dignity. The women in charge were business-like, and possessed of native eloquence, which came out in their prayers, praise, reading of the lessons and presentation of reports. Perhaps they at home had something to learn from the women of South Africa, whom the Gospel had so greatly transformed ...

With regard to medical work in the South African field which had caused so much heartache in previous years, it was recommended and agreed to "that no attempt should be made by the Free Church to build a hospital in South Africa but that Dr Andrews (by early 1948 he had arrived on the Field) could work in the Pirie District, helped by a nurse/interpreter until such time as all medical services were taken over by the state".

ARRIVAL OF DR CAMPBELL AND MRS RUBY ANDREWS AND ELSPETH

On 14 January 1948 Dr Andrews and his wife Ruby and little daughter Elspeth arrived in South Africa from Australia. Once again Knox Church hosted a warm welcome meeting, and Dr Andrews became responsible for the Pirie District.

Settling in

Dr Andrews lost no time in covering the area allocated to him and made plans for his future work there, assessing its needs and opportunities. The family stayed in King William's Town, in the house which had been occupied by the Dewars. Mrs Dewar and Iain had by now moved permanently to Cape Town, and the McCrackens had moved back to Mngqesha. (When they found a suitable house in Keiskamma Hoek they moved there nearer to the Burnshill District, which was their sphere of work).

Dr Andrews was to study the Xhosa language in his first few months, and become familiar with the new Government scheme for medical services in Cape Province.

Whenever possible, he conducted services in two centres each Lord's Day, and at the close of the services he often addressed the young people, who formed the greater part of the congregations.

In his report on his work in the Pirie District, Dr Andrews listed the things that impressed him most since his introduction to the work:

- The rigid colour bar and its implications for the Black people

- the luxury of the Europeans relative to the Africans

- the chronic droughts

- the prevalence of malnutrition and tuberculosis among the Africans and the inadequate medical services to deal with this.

- On the other hand, there was the fervour, devotion and unfailing courtesy of the Africans in the churches.

Elder Vasi

Dr Andrews mentions the loss to the congregation at Pirie of the Headman of the area and Chief of the AmaHlebe tribe, Elder Qalanto Vasi who had been a great help in the work of the Gospel there. He was "dignified, courteous, faithful to his Lord, loyal to his Church, uncomplaining in distressing illness". His funeral was attended by over 700 people and the Native Commissioner, three African pastors and two missionaries took part.

Kowana

A new congregation had been started at Kowana, a new settlement some 35 miles from King William's Town, to which people from Tyusha and Ndevana had been moved by the Government. Some of these families had already been moved some time in the past from the Burnshill area. Now they came under the Pirie District.

Medical matters

Dr Andrews wrote too of his medical work, helping out at Mt Coke Mission Hospital, not far from King William's Town, during the illness and leave of the medical superintendent of the hospital, preparing for the setting up of clinics in his own area and also seeing any patients who came to him for treatment and advice. He looked forward to the setting up of the first clinic with financial help from the Australian Church.

Dr Andrews started his district clinics in 1949. These were set up in Mngqesha, Dyafta, Knox and Pirie. Other centres pleaded for clinics too but he had to decline due to lack of available time. A loyal team of interpreters helped him at each of these places – Mr Robert Taho at Knox, Mrs Fihle at Mngqesha, Mrs Vasi at Pirie and Mrs Ntshona and Mr Albert Nqaba at Dyafta and Tyusha respectively. Prolonged periods of drought had "aggravated the malnutrition so prevalent in the native population here", he wrote in October 1949. An outbreak of measles had resulted in the deaths of many children. But the great scourge of the district was pulmonary tuberculosis, and there was no hospital for those suffering from this disease. Eye infections often leading to blindness and diseases due to lack of hygiene or polluted water supplies were also rampant. Grants had been given from the Red Cross and congregations in Australia and this had gone a long way to enable him to provide vitamin supplements, milk and other helps necessary to nourish many of those suffering chronic malnutrition or T.B. Speaking to one father about his very ill son aged 15 years, Dr Andrews had to tell him there was no hope for the boy. He would not get well but would soon die. The father replied, "Do not give up hope, Missionary, we can pray to God." The doctor wrote: "Rebuked by his faith I said I spoke merely as a doctor who sees the course of a disease and who knows that all medical treatment available to us is in vain in his case. If I speak as a missionary I say, there is hope in God, for in Him all things are possible." The father had been a 'red' man, converted the previous year and was admitted into the membership of the church. What a test to his faith he had to face in the illness of his son! Dr Andrews mentions in a later report that this boy was still living in answer to the prayers of his parents and others.

Family life in a Xhosa home

The new *'From the Frontiers'* missionary magazine of the Church printed a perceptive article from Dr Andrews in May 1950 in which he tells of aspects of life in Xhosa homes in Ciskei. Being a farmer boy himself he was especially interested in the agricultural aspect of things, and confessed to being amazed at any crop of maize being produced at all given the struggle it had to survive the vagaries of sowing and cultivation, and later, the scorching heat and drought of summer. He said maize was the staple food of the people, eaten green after boiling the cobs or stamped in a kind of mortar with a clubbed stick and then boiled for several hours until it was soft enough to eat. Or again, it might be ground to form mealie meal and cooked as porridge. Pumpkins, marrows, cooking melons, and beans were also grown, and kaffir corn was used to brew kaffir beer. Meat, unless an animal had died, was rarely eaten – mostly on special occasions such as weddings, funerals, or coming of age, or church conferences. Sour milk, or amasi, was a favourite food when available.

The houses, he explained, were mostly one-roomed rondavels built of mud and thatch, and were usually very congested. Each is occupied by a family which may include the children of relatives who are away working. There was little or no privacy. Grass mats on a dung-smeared floor formed the beds of the majority. Several might sleep under a common covering. He went on:

I was surprised at Mdisa one day when removing a case of open tuberculosis complicated by tuberculosis of the knee to Mt. Coke Hospital. I asked how many people lived in the hut. "Ten" was the answer. At night time a fire is lit to prepare the evening meal and warm the hut. It often produces a smoke which is blinding to the newcomer but of little consequence to the inhabitant. Later, for fear of intruders and of evil spirits, the door is closed as well as the window or small port which serves for one, so that any fresh air is also excluded.

Women's work

With the men often away at work or far away in the mines, and the young boys out herding the cattle or unemployed older teenager boys lounging about the locations in groups, the burden of all the work fell on the women.

Apart from ordinary household duties of cleaning, washing, cooking and sewing, and the peculiar function of bearing and nursing children, they perform most other work. They fetch water. This may have to be carried in a large pail on their heads, twice a day, a distance of up to a mile or more, usually uphill. They gather firewood, ... walking up to ten miles to the nearest forest or mimosa thicket. The bundles of wood are carried on their heads at a fast walk or even a run ... They also prepare the mud bricks and thatch bundles used in building, and plaster the walls of their homes outside and inside, often using several colours of mud and various designs for indoor decorations. Theirs also is the work of sowing, cultivating, and harvesting the crops ...

This account gives us an insight into the struggle it must have been to a member of the Women's Christian Association to appear at a Thursday afternoon meeting, possibly very late, in her spotless white and blue uniform, leaving behind many little children in the care of an older girl who will be preparing the evening mealie porridge while she attends the meeting. It also gives a hint of how hard it must have been to start to treat all the medical cases presented to Dr Andrews, with no possibility of changing the surroundings of the patient. But the work went on regardless.

REV HUITE AND MRS HELEN SLIEP ARRIVE

On 15 April 1948, only a few months after the arrival of the Andrews family, the Carnarvon Castle brought in more reinforcements for the missionary cause in the Free Church in South Africa. Disembarking at Cape Town this time were Rev Huite Sliep and his Scottish wife, Helen. They stayed the first weekend with the McCrackens and then a few days with the Andrews'.

Three new missionary couples within five years! If only the beleaguered Mr Dewar had lived to see the day!

Early impressions

The Slieps themselves in a letter to the children of *The Instructor* take up the story of their earliest experiences.

> Our first Sabbath in Ciskei we will not forget in a hurry. Mr McCracken took us out to a mission station in the Burnshill District ... But a river we were supposed to cross barred us from going farther because it was in spate and so we had to go on foot over the hill. That was our first experience of real hill climbing. But our efforts to reach the church were richly rewarded, for a great many people had already gathered around the church. We had two very fine services that day.
>
> During the afternoon service, at which the Lord's Supper was dispensed and an elder was ordained, the rain came on heavily which made us look forward with apprehension to our return journey. But, happily, it stopped again until we had ourselves comfortably seated in our cars. Then it began to rain, and it rained all the way in a fashion we never witnessed before in our lives. How Mr McCracken kept the car on the road was to us little less than a miracle. And it rained

without a stop until Tuesday morning. Great was the damage done to the already terrible roads, and on our way up to the Transkei we saw many huts blown down by the storm and rain. Meantime, please continue to pray for us, for, as you will learn from our next letter, the Transkei district is the most difficult area for the kind of work we are engaged in. We shall be glad, boys and girls, to receive some letters from you.

And so the new missionaries had a preview of what awaited them in their new work among the friendly Xhosa Christians of the Free Church in South Africa.

A Large District

The Slieps were assigned to the large district of Transkei, and so their proper Welcome was held there in Esidwadweni, near Tsolo, where Adam MacPherson had ministered in days past. Rev Joe McCracken chaired this meeting, and he had brought with him two teachers, Mr Robert Taho and Mr Theophilus Nocanda. They conveyed the greetings of the Pirie District to the new missionaries. The senior elder of the Esidwadweni congregation, a blind man, said: "I am thankful that God's servant has come while I still live though I cannot see him. We are glad to meet this man of God who with love, sacrificed to come to us people. Like Abraham he went forth, not knowing whither he went." The local chief was also present and welcomed Mr Sliep in the name of the Fingo race.

Both Mr and Mrs Sliep, in reply, said they now realised the desire of their hearts and looked forward to the work before them.

Communion was celebrated on the Sabbath, nearly two hundred being present. Rev Joe preached in the morning, using as his text the words of Martha to Mary at Bethany: "The uMfundisi is here and is asking for you." The word for 'Teacher' in the Xhosa Bible is 'uMfundisi', the title used for a minister or missionary, so it was a suitable text for the occasion. Rev Huite conducted the Communion service for his new flock himself in the afternoon.

And so a new ministry among the loyal Transkei people was launched.

Trials in Transkei

As time went on, the Slieps found there were many struggles. At one time, drought was hindering the work and it was the cause of many deaths. Also a lack of funds stopped Rev Huite from visiting his churches more regularly. To overcome this he had published a magazine in Xhosa to keep in touch with the people. This had been welcomed by some but not by all. He had given himself to study of the language and to learn how to 'think black'. Mrs Helen Sliep also was giving faithful service in the women's work.

The Slieps had settled in Umtata, the capital of the Transkei, in a house purchased by the Foreign Missions Committee in Scotland, and they were finding this good for the work as they had been able to give hospitality to several of their people who had to come to Umtata for one reason or another. Previously, in lodgings, they could not receive visits from their church folk because of the 'Colour Bar'.

Rev Huite was most thankful for the help given him by several helpers – Norman Magula, from Mbolompo; Samuel Ndzungu from Qelana, who unfortunately was one of those who had to work in Cape Town – 'he is full of love and zeal for the Lord', said Mr Sliep; Mrs P. Mzeleni, from Esisadweni, and Evangelist Simon Langa, also from Qelana, who was doing good work but was getting old and needed the help of a younger man ... Mr Sliep felt there was a great need for three young evangelists in Transkei – one for Idutywa, one for the Tsitsa Basin (Mqokelweni), and one for the other districts. However, he wrote of two young men whom he hoped would be evangelists in his area one day. One was George Mtukuli who had already started to work with Mr Sliep although he was only 20 years of age and had not received any training. The other man was Moses Baleka of whom we shall hear more later. Sadly, at Mqokelweni, there were divisions in the congregation which, according to some, were caused by the fact that some of the people were Xhosas and some were Fingoes. The Slieps felt that at that time the Transkei people were spiritually 'just babes' compared with the members of our churches in the Ciskei. They did not know about the doctrine and government of the Church, and the young people were hardly considered by their elders when it came to spiritual matters, yet in reality their knowledge of the Scriptures and their relationship to their Saviour were often much more intelligent than in the case of their parents.

There seemed to be a great deal of superstition in the treatment of the Sacraments. In former times a newly-born child was gently rocked to and fro over a smoking fire in order that no evil spirit take hold of the child. Now if the child was brought instead to be baptised, everything would be all right! The missionary needed to go more often to visit the churches – but found it impossible to go more than once in eight weeks. What was to be done?

The work among the women and girls had been maintained, and the Annual Women's Convention in 1949 had been held in Transkei at Esisadweni and was *'quite a success'*. Some of the girls at Gqunu, up in the hills, were particularly keen to learn skills in knitting and embroidery.

Rev & Mrs McCracken in the Burnshill District

With the Andrews now looking after the Pirie District and the Slieps looking after Transkei, the McCrackens had taken over the leadership in the Burnshill District.

A Comprehensive Overview

Mr McCracken's official Report for 1947 was very detailed as he had time to investigate all aspects of the Field's work, and the Foreign Mission Committee was greatly indebted to Mr McCracken for such a comprehensive overview of the work. They were also encouraged by the growing partnership in the work on the part of both the Irish Evangelical Church and the Free Presbyterian Church of Australia.

In his Report he touched on the social life of the African people. He pointed out that while there was much that was destructive of good social and community life, the church provides 'a common fellowship and means of co-operation, which are thoroughly relished by the people and have no counterpart in heathen practice.' The Africans were becoming increasingly politicised, as the Union Government was becoming more racially divisive, moving Africans to locations that were decided upon by the government regardless of the wishes of the Africans themselves. The understandable resultant anti-white feeling made no distinction between friend or foe, missionary or not.

Concluding the First Term

After more than five busy years on the field, the McCrackens were due for home leave. Before they left there were three encouragements.

An Evangelist, Mr Thomas Solwandle, a fully trained man, was appointed to the Burnshill District where the McCrackens worked. This man was described as 'a very interesting and eloquent preacher of the Gospel.' He conducted missions with encouraging results in the churches in the Burnshill District. No doubt Mr and Mrs McCracken felt relief as they set out for Belfast leaving the work in capable African hands, for alongside Evangelist Solwandle was Mr Buti Njana 'this lovable character' from Amatole Basin, Mr Edward Nyamza of Ngqumeya and Mr John Zuzani of Burnshill itself.

Then a short time before he left, on 10 December 1949, the church which he had been building at Gqumahashe, near Alice and the University of Fort Hare in his district, was completed. Mr McCracken had been travelling the 30 miles from his home to see to the building most days since August 1st. The day of its formal opening was a highlight for the area. Under lowering skies, Miss Carrie Ross, descendant of the original Ross family of missionaries performed the opening ceremony. It was to this area that the first member of that family, Rev John Ross, came when he arrived from Scotland and it was there he established his first mission field in 1823. Now, a century and a quarter later, this fine church was opened by one of his granddaughters. The people filed in thankfully as the thunderstorm broke overhead.

A further joy was that a 'memorable' Annual Convention of the Women's Christian Association was held in the new church at Gqumahashe from 13–15 January 1950 a few weeks before the McCrackens left on leave. A specially chartered bus brought over 30 people from the Transkei, while 55 came by bus from the outlying stations of the Burnshill District. A lorry conveyed the

Pirie people from Alice station to the church. The theme of the Convention was 'The Love of God'. One of the speakers was the African poet Rev J.J. Jolobe, B.A., who later translated the Psalms into Xhosa metre, the Psalter which is still in use today.

At the end of this Convention an unexpected presentation took place. Mr and Mrs McCracken had looked after the Free Church people of Transkei as well as their own during the time that they waited for their own minister, Mr Sliep and his wife to arrive from Scotland. Now the Transkei folks wanted to acknowledge this help and to express their thanks for it. Mrs Zokufa, Vice-President of the Transkeian W.C.A. then presented Mr and Mrs McCracken with a Royal Stewart travelling rug as an 'appreciation of your untiring services to us'.

Home Leave

They sailed from East London on 24 February 1950 and arrived home in Belfast on 22 March for a well earned home leave. As they left they looked back on five years of service in which "over 400 children and adults were baptised in the name of the Lord, and numerous souls were pointed to the Saviour, including quite a number of heathen people".

Mr McCracken concluded that Report to the Missions Committee:

> We have been gloriously happy in the carrying out of our commission, and have proved the truth of Christ's words: "Lo I am with you always even to the end of the world." We have known joy unspeakable as men and women came from darkness into light and from the power of Satan unto God.

Well – praise the Lord!

SOME FIELD MATTERS

Politics in 1949

The context in which missionaries were working was becoming increasingly difficult from a political point of view. The *Monthly*

Record of January 1949 made a strong criticism of the way the Nationalist Government under Dr Malan was prepared to "keep South Africa for the Whites at all costs". Such a policy "was bound to create for itself fierce hatreds within its own borders and strong criticism outside". The article went on:

> The present Government in South Africa must appear to all sane men to be pursuing a suicidal policy based on no higher motive than fear. And the more stringent and unjust its repressive measures the more cause it has to fear! It is all very strange coming from a section of the community composed largely of good Dutch Protestants and Presbyterians who still find a large place for the Christian faith and ethics in their lives. But stranger still is it that this policy of repression should be carried out in the name of Christianity as interpreted by the Dutch Reformed Church.

As the apartheid policy of the Nationalist Government gathered momentum the *Monthly Record* in an editorial in January 1950 spoke of its being unworthy of a Christian nation. Dr Andrews wrote of the barriers to the progress of the Black people being erected by the Government, witnessed by their withdrawing of training facilities for Black artisans and grants for schools among other things.

The high hopes that Rev Zokobe Taho would be in Scotland for the Assembly of 1950 were again dashed as the 'Colour Bar' went into operation and his passage on a ship was again refused. Dr Andrews adds bitterly, "As a clerk in a shipping office was led to confess it would have been easier to secure accommodation for a wild beast than for this Christian gentleman."

The impact of drought

The devastating drought in the later years of this decade, the 1940s, described as the worst in living memory, resulted in many more men having to leave home and look for work in the cities or the mines. This impacted on both church attendance, but of course most of all on family life in the rural districts of Ciskei and Transkei.

Steady work

And so, in the midst of difficulties, the work went on steadily. Each of the three missionaries and their wives reported diligence in all aspects of the work – church services, funerals, weddings, Sunday School work, Kirk Sessions and Deacons' Courts ... And there were encouragements, people coming to faith, sometimes discarding their red blankets, sometimes no doubt suffering abuse at home for doing so.

ON REFLECTION

- Mr McCracken was not the first to recognise the need to train African men as Evangelists and Pastors but he was the first one to actually do something about it in framing a course for some of the Evangelists to study.

- The Reports of the Deputies who visited South Africa contained several very pertinent recommendations, some of which were not acted upon. The recommendation to concentrate on the larger congregations and work out from them, even if this meant stopping services in very small congregations, would have made for more effective use of the limited manpower resources available.

- A comment by Rev Professor Finlayson had always to be borne in mind: *"The missionary was not there to stay indefinitely or relieve the Christian community of the burden that rightly belonged to them as Christians: he was there to establish, organise, instruct and foster a Christian Church which should shoulder its own burdens and recognise its responsibilities to the regions beyond ......"*

8

A Memorial Sandwich
1951–1960

A s 1951 opened, a brand new church at Mdisa in memory of the Gregor Macleods was opened too. And as the decade closed, a big new church at Whiteville was opened – this time in memory of Mr Dewar. In between there were busy and industrious years for the missionaries. In letters, articles and reports to Scotland, Ireland and Australia they kept the sending Churches well informed of the joys and sorrows, the need for prayer and the 'rejoice with me' over the answers. The church schools were eventually taken over by the Government. It was a period in which South Africa itself was engulfed in a lot of racial unrest, the precursor of the really bloody struggle that was to come before a 'new dispensation' was ushered in four decades later. The African lion was beginning to stir.

The Opening of the Macleod Memorial Church at Mdisa

Early in 1951 the church building at Mdisa, Knox District, was completed. It was to be a lasting memorial to the lives of Gregor and Elizabeth Macleod, lost at sea in 1942. It was Rev Joe McCracken's idea to have their memorial in the form of a church building in the Pirie District, and Rev Duncan Leitch had turned the first turf in 1947, but various problems had later been encountered. The actual building took only three months to complete, and now at last it was ready. The McCrackens were still on home leave at the time of the opening of the church. About 600 people gathered for this event from all over the Free Church in South Africa. Among the guests was Mr Albert Sliep, brother of Huite, at that time working as an accountant in Umtata, but later to follow in his brother's footsteps and become an ordained missionary in the Burnshill District and in Transkei.

Dr Campbell Andrews invited Miss Caroline Ross to carry out the opening ceremony of the new church. In his address at the opening of the church, Dr Andrews said, "This church is a memorial, then, of a devotion to Christ which was unto death. It is a grateful and loving tribute of many in South Africa and Scotland whose hearts have been touched by the grace of God and moved by the death of His servants. May it be, in the experience of many, *'none other than the house of God and the gate of Heaven'.*"

A memorial tablet was set up on the wall of the church where it still stands with the following inscription:

To the Glory of God
This Church was erected in 1950
With the gifts of many people in Scotland and South Africa,
In memory of REV GREGOR MACLEOD,
Missionary of The Free Church of Scotland,
And of his wife, ELIZABETH MACDONALD.
They lost their lives at sea on 7th December, 1942,
When, responding to the call of God,
They were on their way to South Africa,
To serve a people whom they loved but did not live to see.
"He sent from above; he took me;
He drew me out of many waters"

PSALM xviii: 16

On the Lord's Day following the opening, 18 February 1951, Rev Huite Sliep, Transkei, preached at a moving communion service in the church. At this service, of the eleven new members who sat at the Lord's Table for the first time, two were formerly 'red' heathen women "who had delighted the Session with their rare insight into Christian truth and experience when examined earlier in the month". Ten of the new members were from Mdisa itself. Dr Andrews wrote that: 'The prayer of our Evangelist Mr Kobo at the close of the service seemed to gather up all the blessing received at all the services.' In summing up thoughts on the whole occasion, Dr Andrews said, 'A delightful, spiritual atmosphere prevailed throughout the meetings. The response of the people on this occasion far surpassed my expectations.'

CHURCH LIFE – THE MCCRACKENS IN BURNSHILL

It was all go on the mission field. Rev Joe and Mrs Helen McCracken and Anne sailed back to South Africa in late March after their home leave, arriving in April 1951. They had taken 247 meetings around Scotland and Ireland and these certainly raised the profile of the missionary work in South Africa. On their return they went to live in the small town of Alice from where they resumed the oversight of the Burnshill District.

Three Schools to Manage

This work included the management of three schools. Mr McCracken wrote of a visit he paid to the school at Mzantsi:

> Leaving this morning at 8.20 to visit our Mzantsi School I went via Burnshill and the Boma Pass. Passing through this winding narrow road, beset on one side by towering hills and on the other by the Keiskamma River, my thoughts travelled back over the blood-stained pages of the district's history, to a scene, one hundred years ago, when the native warriors, urged on by their chief, Sandile, massacred the unsuspecting (Scottish) soldiers of the 74th Highland Regiment, under the command of Colonel Mackinnon, when on their way to Keiskamma Hoek. Indeed, as one travels through this district, the stones which mark the resting place of many a gallant Scottish soldier testify to the necessity for the Gospel of grace and peace in these days ... What the sword of the soldier could not accomplish, the sword of the Spirit did.
>
> On arrival at the school, started and made possible by the generosity of the Scottish people, yea, by some, who, no doubt, are descendants of those early soldiers who laid down their lives on African soil, I found

seventy-four children present, some of them, no doubt, descendants of the wild Xhosas who shot, hacked and stabbed to death the members of the 74th Highland regiment. Such are the paradoxes of life.

The Principal of Mzantsi School was Mr Gladwell Mfikile, who served the church well and long over the years. His assistant was Miss Pearl Fikela, who later became the wife of Mr Harold Magodla and together as a team they became pillars of the church in the Knox District.

At Mzantsi, Mr McCracken was asked to help in a case where fire had mysteriously destroyed two huts at one home. The distraught family had even consulted witchdoctors but to no avail. It was subsequently found that a 'weak-minded' child belonging to the family had been the arsonist. While visiting the school at Amatole Basin Mr McCracken heard of another case involving witchdoctors. A charge was levelled against a leading woman member of the church alleging that she had used witchcraft to bring about the death of a young girl. The ensuing discussion was illuminating for the missionary, who took the opportunity of setting before the people the teaching of the Word of God. The charge proved to be unfounded and the member was cleared of all guilt.

After 45 years of 'toil, sweat, blood and tears' the goal of Government recognition had at last been reached in the school at Amatole Basin.

The story of two men

At about the same time as Mr McCracken was visiting his schools and doing much other worthy work, his wife Helen wrote about two men who were well known to her.

One was the son of a very godly elder of the Free Church. The elder had died and the son, now a young man, went to train as a carpenter at a Missionary Institution. On his return home it was evident he had lost his faith and was, in the words of Miss Carrie Ross, 'reverting to heathenism'. His faith had been undermined at the Institution where he was studying and where he was led to question the veracity and authority of Scripture. His life became a mess, he began to drink, his wife left him. He had gone far away from his father's lifestyle and beliefs.

(By God's grace, however, some years later, that young prodigal did return and became a faithful member in one of the congregations of the church.)

The other man professed faith in Christ in a church service when, the missionary suspected, he was under the influence of drink. However, his subsequent life testified to a deep and saving change that had taken place in his life. 'This man was a real joy to us', said Mrs McCracken. Just a week after the McCrackens arrived back from home leave in 1951 this man died, having testified to the end to the saving power of Christ. 'One wonders how this poor sin-sick, drunken one would have fared, if instead of having been pointed to the One who is able to save to the uttermost he, like the other man, had been told that he was not a fallen creature, that he must be good and do good and all would be well.'

The McCrackens alone

During 1953, Mr McCracken was alone on the mission field, as both the Andrews and Slieps were on home leave. During this time Mrs Andrews had to undergo a serious operation, which had to have a number of months of treatment, so it was May 1954 before they returned to South Africa. Happily she made a good recovery.

The New Church at Ngqumeya

One of the places in the Burnshill District which Mr McCracken looked after was Ngqumeya. There was not yet a church there but there were hopes of building one. 1953 was a year of great rains which was good for the crops but bad for travel, with muddy roads making it difficult (and Rev Joe did 13000 miles that year), and hindered church building. One Sunday a young man of 25 was going up to Ngqumeya to help in the church service. He asked the way from some local boys, but they beat him up with their knobkerries and he died. This place was often the scene of these knobkerrie fights, which usually took place on a Sunday after a night of drinking.

It was on 17 December 1955 that the church at Ngqumeya finally got finished and was opened for worship.

Rev Joseph McCracken, like Rev Alexander Dewar, was elected a Fellow of the Royal Geographical Society. No doubt his increasing knowledge of African customs and practices and his filming of some of them helped to gain him this honour.

The Mnyameni Convention

Mrs McCracken was particularly diligent in her work with the women and girls. She went from place to place taking meetings, quarterly meetings and sometimes hosting the Annual Convention for the whole church, when up to 450 people attended.

At Mnyameni (in 1955) the whole village became involved in the preparations for the Convention. The road to the village had been repaired. The Headman had forbidden any abakweta (circumcision) or marriage ceremonies to be held for a certain time prior to the Convention so that full attention would be given to getting the place ready for the influx of visitors expected at this annual gathering of our church people. The church building itself had also received a very thorough 'spring-clean'. It was, of course, the Women's Convention but increasingly men also attended and took a full part in some of the proceedings. In reporting on the Convention, Mrs McCracken wrote that, "one after another testified to blessing received, mentioning the address, verse or thought that remained with them. We rejoiced because the Spirit of God had been at work applying the Word to the hearts of the people".

Quarterly meetings could go on all night, and at one such she tells us that at the hilltop village of Amatole Basin in their district of Burnshill she had addressed the first meeting, and then, from 3.30 to 8.30 p.m. she had visited homes in the location. The evening service got under way at 8.30 and about 12.30 a.m. she called on the Evangelist Mr Solwandle to pray. "How long he prayed I do not know, for the next thing I was conscious of was a voice speaking as from a great distance and saying, 'I have finished, Mfundisikazi (minister's wife)'. I awoke with a start! Fearing a repetition I resorted to the back seat of the car where I stayed until sunrise." The meeting finished at 7.00 a.m.

An Mnyameni Communion

An account Mrs McCracken wrote of a Mnyameni Communion service gives a flavour of the worthy woman she was:

Rising about 6.30 a.m. in order to make ready lunches, flasks etc for the day, we were ready and on our way by 8.20 a.m. It was a lovely spring morning, the sky was cloudless, and everything looked fresh and green after the rain. The wild peach trees in full bloom were a pretty sight ...

As soon as the bell was rung, the people filed into the church and in a few minutes every seat was occupied ... After the opening exercises 18 infants were baptised. Three of the mothers were attired in their wedding dresses as they were presenting their first-born for baptism ... Several of the young men present were fathers of the children and as they stood beside their believing wives, the missionary made the most of his opportunity by presenting the Gospel to them.

After a break of about twenty minutes the second service commenced ... Six teenage girls and one woman were received into membership on profession of faith, two of the girls were also baptised. The case of the woman received is an interesting one as she was a 'Red' (heathen) who professed faith about a year ago at evangelistic meetings. She had been married according to tribal custom and in order to be received into full membership had to have Christian marriage. Her husband, a 'Red', had refused to submit to this when approached by both the evangelist and elder. This meant a special journey for the missionary to their little hut perched just below the crest of the mountain. After an earnest talk he consented for his wife's sake and arrangements were then made, and later the marriage was performed.

Words fail to describe what one feels on sitting down with those of another colour and nation uniting with them in fellowship around the Lord's Table, rejoicing in His dying yet undying love; reminding us of that time when the redeemed of every kindred and tongue and people and nation shall unitedly enjoy His presence for ever.

On the homeward journey we watched the sun sink in a cloudless sky leaving behind it a rich glow in the west which was reflected in pink tints on the mountains we had left.

Eunice, Biblewoman

For some time the thought of the usefulness of a Biblewoman in the district to work among the women and girls had been taking root. The people now felt strong enough to support one, and felt it would be an incentive to the members to support one of their own people. A woman named Eunice, from Whiteville church, was laid upon their hearts. She had had a little training at a Bible School, and was willing 'to try'. So she began her work. Mrs McCracken explains:

(Eunice) left home on a Tuesday travelling on foot, and then sometimes by bus or train to the appointed church. Wednesday was spent visiting the sick and aged members of the church, especially those of the Association, and a meeting for the girls was held the same afternoon. On Thursday morning more visiting was done, followed by the usual weekly meeting of the Women's Association. Friday morning usually saw her on the journey homewards ... Towards the end of the year she had to rest, and has since given birth to a baby boy. Her husband is now student-evangelist and this is an ideal combination.

CHURCH LIFE – THE ANDREWS IN PIRIE

Medical Work

Dr Andrews continued to get requests to set up clinics from the many African villages some miles from King William's Town, requests he was unable to fulfil. He did conduct clinics at Dyafta, Tyusha, Pirie, Mngqesha, Knox and Mdisa. This last clinic was to close, however, as it was fairly near a clinic run under the auspices of the Mt Coke Mission Hospital. T.B. continued to be prevalent as did eye problems among other common diseases. The house in which they lived at 14 Frere Street, King William's Town was bought (it had previously been rented), the Australian church paying half the cost of the house. Dr Andrews later got permission to set up a clinic on part of the property. Little Jamie Andrews was born on 29 June, 1951, a brother for Elspeth.

Dr Andrews was very keen to set up a hospital for T.B. patients and travelled to Durban to investigate the possibilities for such a venture to be started in the Ciskei. However, the Foreign Missions Committee felt it could not back such a proposal as both the setting up costs of £15,000 and the estimated running costs were well beyond the means of the church. There was encouragement in two generous gifts from Mrs Margaret Gillies, Australia, which provided £500 towards the proposed building of a new church and clinic at Tyusha. More funds were to follow.

An Office-Bearers' Conference

A special conference for office-bearers was held in the new church at Mdisa in the Pirie District and all the missionaries took part in this. They felt that it was a good experience for both leaders and men, and they felt that after this conference they had a better knowledge of one another and a better understanding of the customs and problems of 'native life'. The need for this type of conference was apparent when one realises that elders had a heavy responsibility in their congregations. It was they who had to prepare and train those who wanted to become members of the church.

The Kirk Session of the Pirie District made it a rule that no child born out of wedlock was to receive baptism, as an infant, even though the mother should afterwards profess repentance and be admitted or restored to full membership. It was also decided that no unmarried girl who had a child would be admitted to full membership until she was properly married. Such rules were an attempt to deal with the prevalence of immorality and superstition attached to the sacrament of baptism, but they also raised many other problems.

Candidates for membership

The missionaries and pastors often worried about the lack of knowledge of some of those who became members in the church and the spiritual state of the people continued to weigh heavily on the missionaries' hearts. This was a sad reflection on an area that had had a Gospel witness for over a hundred years, but it does testify to the real lack of regular pastoral oversight in nearly all the congregations – and that not just in the Free Church?

Yet sometimes men in the Kirk Sessions received real encouragement as they examined candidates. Dr Andrews, Pirie District, wrote:

"People professing faith in Christ are registered as candidates and undergo a period of instruction under local office-bearers. The instruction is intended to give them a knowledge of the catechism and of the Gospel of John." This is the sort of thing that happened:

> Ella ... comes from Mdisa. She is eighteen years old, reached Standard 2 at school and has been a Christian for one year. She is questioned:
> "What led you to be a Christian?" "I found I was a sinner."
> "What did you do about this?" "I prayed in the name of Christ."
> "What did Christ do for sinners?" "He died for them."
> "Do you believe that He died for you?" "I believe."
> "Who made you?" "God."

"For what purpose did God make you?" "For his glory."

"Is there a Saviour from sin?" "Yes."

"Who is he?" "Jesus."

"Who can change the heart of a sinner?" "The Holy Spirit only."

After some further questions, all well answered, the elders agreed Ella should be admitted. She was a regular attender at worship and lived an upright life.

Nonayiti ... of Mdisa is fifty years old, has no schooling and was converted little over a year ago.

"What led you to become a Christian?" "I feared that if I died I would have nothing to bring to God. When God found that I was alive He gave me sickness. I asked while in bed that God would not let me die while still a sinner. When I got better I went to the church and was shown the right way by the preachers. Now God is waiting for me to bear fruit."

"What did you do about your sins?" "I asked forgiveness of God and asked God to cleanse my heart and make me new."

Subsequent questions showed an almost perfect knowledge of the Catechism.

Nolast of Tyusha, another converted Red, of forty-five years, quite illiterate, has been a Christian for three years.

"What made you want to be a Christian?" "I wanted to be subject to Christ."

"What awakened you?" "A preaching."

"What do you remember about the sermon?" "The elder said I should come to the wagon of Christ and be on it."

While her knowledge of the Catechism was weak she seemed clearly to understand that Christ had died for her sins and that only through him could she be saved.

CHURCH LIFE – THE SLIEPS IN TRANSKEI

Travelling Teachers

Up in Transkei, Rev Huite and Mrs Helen Sliep were soldiering on. They too were burdened by the 'lack of knowledge of the most simple aspects of Christian truth' among those who were applying for membership. They felt that this was really due to lack of instruction. The candidates could often recite page after page of the catechism, but they were very hazy about their conversion or their relationship to the Saviour. With the great distances and difficulty in travel it was not easy to manage regular classes for instruction in all the villages. A Vacation Bible School was held at Esidwadweni with twenty or thirty mostly young people attending, and at the same place a Convention was held. The theme of the meetings was 'The Person and Work of Christ'. During intervals in the meetings evangelistic work was done among the homesteads around the church. Many 'red' people were visited and a cordial invitation into their homes was received, 'and they listened with deep respect to the Gospel'. 'Evangelist-on-trial' Moses Baleka and deacon Oliver Ndzungu helped with this Convention.

At Gqunu and Mqokolweni and at Esidwadweni the Slieps spent some afternoons with the young people and encouraged them to distribute portions of Scripture throughout the villages. They were very willing to do this, and the hope was that there was a desire in their hearts to follow the Lord.

It was worrying that six of the elders in Mr Sliep's district could neither read nor write yet they took their turn at preaching in the various congregations. One member said of these men, "They come to the church with empty buckets."

So the Slieps spent long periods in the various congregations preaching and teaching, and at times they had help from the Ciskei, e.g. Evangelist Kobo held special meetings at Qelana and Mbolompo.

A Visit to Gqunu

Mr Sliep tells of one of their visits to Gqunu – a village set high up on a hillside inaccessible by car. The Slieps set out for the three-mile climb to Gqunu. "Three girls come to meet us and volunteer to carry our luggage – a case of books, a can of water and some blankets, for we have arranged to stay for the week-end."

It is already hot; soon the perspiration is running down our faces and our clothes feel sticky and wet. But we take it easy, and here and there we stop for a little rest, and admire the beautiful scenery around us. Down below flows the Tina river and round about are the hills, some of them breath-taking in their ruggedness. Here and there on our way up we pass the huts of the Africans. Most of them are Reds. They wear a blanket round their bodies, many of them have faces mutilated by big scars in order to frighten off the evil spirits. Whenever possible we have a word with them, and tell them of Jesus the Good Shepherd who came to save them from their sins and the power of evil spirits. Some promise to come to the church and to the special services.

At last we arrive at the church. What a welcome awaits us there! The service this day takes the form of a school when all join the class. Young and old enjoy being taught from the Bible, and at Gqunu the maxim holds good that what the people need and want is not so much preaching but teaching.

The young converts are doing well. The oldest of their number, Miss Emma Mcapazele, sets them a good example ...

Lately there have been coming to the services quite a number of men and the husbands of our women-members have also shown an interest in the church. This is clearly an answer to prayer, because we made that the burden of our petitions, that the Lord would cause the men to have an interest in the things of God. As far as Gqunu is concerned we see the beginning of a definite answer.

That was on Friday. On Saturday Mrs Sliep taught the women and girls knitting and sewing and in the evening a Gospel service was held at the home of a Red family. The meeting lasted all night. Unsurprisingly the services the following morning started a bit late.

Strange Providences

Gqunu was on a mountain top. Mqokolweni was in a valley some miles away. Sadly for a time there, divisions had spoiled the fellowship, but Mr Sliep thanked the Lord that there was now a different spirit among the people from the one which usually prevailed. Indeed at the last communion he had attended there were about forty communicants and a brotherly fellowship among the office-bearers. More reason for praise and thanks!

Meantime Mrs Sliep had been paying the fees of a promising student evangelist called Moses Horatio Baleka at Union Bible Institute in Natal. During his summer holidays he helped in the various Transkei congregations. The Young Men's and Young Women's Christian Associations were launched in a number of congregations, so things were looking up a bit in the Sliep's corner of the woods.

However there were strange providences ahead. One of their best men, Mr John Xabadiya, was ordained and inducted as an Evangelist. He was a really spiritually minded man. Every morning in his prayers he kept John 3:16 in the front of his mind. He took no salary for being an Evangelist but worked hard for the Lord. At one time he was ministering with Evangelist Nenemba in a mostly heathen village near his home when his wife came to see him to say that his brother's village wanted him to come and explain the Gospel to them. Mr Nenemba offered to go, but it was John Xabadiya who was wanted. So after an all night meeting he set off on his bicycle and arrived home, feeling a bit weak and asked his wife to make him some tea. He threw down his jacket on the bed in a small hut they used for sleeping and eating, and sat down in a chair to rest. Just then a bolt of lightning hit the hut, killing John instantly and setting fire to the furniture. How sad – not for dear John who went straight home to heaven, but for those left how inexpressibly sad, as lightning was considered to be a curse, and one struck must not have a normal funeral. However, John's funeral was a Christian one and a testimony to his faith. Some people there, including his own brother and sister confessed that it was through John that they had come to faith in Christ. So even his funeral was a testimony to God who brings us from darkness to his marvellous light.

Just at the beginning of that year, 1957, the oldest of the Deacons, on his way home from special meetings held with Mr Sliep at Gqunu, was drowned as his horse stumbled attempting to cross a swiftly running river. Drowning was also considered to be a curse and a body had to be buried on the river bank or wherever it was found.

We can not understand such providences, but we have a Sovereign God who does understand why, and we can trust Him.

The End of Church Schools

In South Africa, originally and for many years the Churches and missionary societies were the sole providers of education for the Black population of the country.

Gradually the Government began to give some financial support by way of grants for teachers' salaries. By 1951 Dr Andrews reported that,

> Today a kind of partnership exists between Missions and the Government. Roughly, it can be said that the Missions provide the buildings, the personnel and the supervision required, and the Government provides funds and some equipment. This is particularly true of rural schools. However in some urban schools, both Primary and Secondary, the Department of Education has recently contributed the buildings and equipment ... Of the 2257 Native schools of all kinds in the Cape in September 1948, 2152 were Mission schools. In these Mission schools the Department pays the salaries of most of the teachers and remits half the cost of books

as well as the whole cost of whatever equipment it approves for the schools.

Commenting on the place of the schools in the life of the people, Dr Andrews wrote:

> There are many parents in our district whose efforts for the education of their children show the same spirit as that shown by many parents in the Scottish Highlands. Many of these parents are themselves Reds. The father of our esteemed Zokobe Taho, himself a red man, saw to it that all his children were educated, and the results of his care are today seen to the third and fourth generation. Our schools may well be the 'gate of the Kingdom of Heaven' to many heathen children who first come under the Word of God in the school Scripture lessons.

(Salaries ranged from £10 a month for recently appointed unmarried female teachers to over £30 per month for male principal teachers with families)

The 1954 Act

But then in 1954 an Act was passed in the South African Parliament which took control of the mission schools and passed them into the hands of the Department of Native Affairs and local school committees and boards. Good Christian instruction was included in the curriculum, but these Bantu children were compelled to study three languages – their mother tongue (Xhosa, Zulu etc), English and Afrikaans.

An Inspector of Native Schools in the area said, "Somewhat in the tradition of the land from which so many local missionaries have come, we produce in this area, not so much crops and animals, but education for export ... teachers, nurses, clerks, interpreters, and that growing host of urban workers, store-men, lorry drivers, factory hands etc. who for the last decade or so have been transforming South Africa from a rural to an industrial country ... The churches deserve the gratitude of the country and especially of the African people."

Tribute should also be paid to the men and women who served so well in the church schools down through the years. Many were elders in the church and helped the missionaries with interpretation and in other ways.

Presbytery Resolutions on Education

When the mission schools had to be handed over to the Government, the newly re-established Presbytery of the South African Free Church issued a robust response to the policy regarding the education of the Black people. Here is part of that response:

> The Presbytery view with grave concern the implication of statements made by the Minister and Secretary for Native Affairs which suggest that the chief, one would be almost justified in saying the sole, purpose of the policy is to 'equip the African to meet the demand which economic life of South Africa will impose upon him.'... It is realised that the 'economic life' mentioned is obviously determined by and directed almost entirely towards the interests of the European population of South Africa ...
>
> The Minister's assumption that the Bantu have no part in the spiritual, economic and political benefits of the civilised community of South Africa i.e. the European, is to be deplored. It suggests that civilisation as well as democracy in South Africa is for 'Europeans only'.

THE WORSENING POLITICAL SITUATION

Apartheid Arrives

The politics of the nation however, were going from bad to worse. In 1950 Field Marshal Smuts had died. His policies in dealing with the Black people were felt to be much more enlightened than those being pursued by the Nationalist Government which had come into power. Already plans were afoot to remove Europeans from Native areas and Natives from European areas. In spite of promises to develop the Native areas industrially and in other ways the scheme aroused much resentment among the African people. Apartheid had arrived.

The Effect on the Church

Already plans were afoot in the Black community to organise a 'sit down strike' as one effort working for the overthrow of White domination. The Nationalist Party speakers tended to quote Scripture in support of their views of Bantu subjection to European domination. This was repugnant to many Whites as well as Blacks. It was not surprising that politics in some African Christian churches and sects tended to be preached from the pulpit more than the Gospel, and so the people's souls were even more starved of the truth and nourishment of God's Word. At the same time it was unfortunate that the teaching of agitators among the African people had become anti-Christian. Missionaries were represented as the agents of industrialists and imperialists whose aim was to exploit the Native for the enrichment of the European. They were opposed to all Christian teaching and all Christian Churches, African and European.

Later, further restrictions were placed on the work of the churches when it was decreed that, "Under no circumstances shall any non-native personnel be accommodated on a Mission church site."

Naturally the missionaries felt increasingly frustrated by these policies. If they spoke out about apartheid, they were branded as communists; if they kept quiet, they felt they were selling their own souls. Dr Andrews thought that the day of the field missionary in South Africa was fast running out, and in view of that there was a real urgency to give themselves over to prayer asking God to enable the missionaries to utilise to the full "the years that remain". Rev Huite Sliep, also worried by the political situation, stressed the urgency to make the African church virtually independent of the Church at home.

But it was to be a further twenty long years before that vision came to be.

Dr Andrews' Statement on the Mission's Stand

Dr Andrews said, "Our own Mission, because it is Calvinist, stands almost alone in condemning the repression and advocating the uplift of the Bantu. Such a testimony is needed in this land at this hour." Dr Andrews was referring to the fact that in South Africa the policy of repression of the Bantu was regarded as originating in Calvinism, whereas a more liberal policy was associated with Arminianism or humanism.

URBAN CHURCH PLANTS

East London

Many African men especially were flocking into the cities to look for work.

A congregation was established in East London in 1950 to cater for the increasing number of people moving to work in that city. The townships growing around the city were becoming heavily congested creating a health hazard which produced an incidence of tuberculosis rated the highest in South Africa, if not in the world. This came about because housing and other amenities did not keep pace with the numbers who flocked there for employment. Dr Andrews wrote, "The congestion, filth and squalor of the principal location in East London has to be seen to be believed." A congregation, under the leadership of Elders Siyalana from Rankin and Mngaza from Mdisa was formed and up to 70 people attended some of the Sunday services which were held at first in a fairly small room of a house and then in a garage, an overflow spilling on to the pavements in both places. There was obviously a dire need for better accommodation, and soon plans came to fruition in the township of Duncan Village, East London. A church belonging to the Baptist Missionary Society became available for sale and was bought for the Free Church. The money was raised by great efforts by the Africans themselves. However, a completely new phenomenon arose in connection with this church – for the first time Free Church missionaries had to contend with hostility to them and to their work.

The Riot

On 9 November 1952, Dr Andrews was in this East London township called Duncan Village when a very serious riot broke out. He tells the story:

> On 7 November the Minister of Justice had invoked the Riotous Assemblies Act and placed a ban on all public meetings in this area. On Sabbath, 9 November, the police entered Duncan Village and applied the ban by endeavouring to break up a political meeting being held there under the guise of a prayer meeting and thereby precipitated a riot. Non-European casualties were considerable as the police used firearms including stenguns. Firing continued well into the night. Two Europeans found in the location were savagely mutilated and killed by the rioters. One of them a Roman Catholic nun and doctor who had served the people of the place for several years was then burnt in her car. The only other European in the place when the trouble began was myself who, along with Mr Taho and Mr Kobo, had been conducting services there and holding a congregational meeting to discuss final plans for the opening of the church. The place was in turmoil when we came out of the church just before five o'clock, and Elder Mngaza said to Mr Taho, "Get the missionary away quickly." Fortunately the way out of the Location toward King William's Town led away from the scene of the fighting, and, although I had to drive slowly through crowded streets for nearly half a mile, the Lord opened a way for us and we passed safely through ... During the riot a number of churches, schools and other buildings were burnt, and attempts were afterwards made on other churches. Our church, however, thank God, was not touched. As Elder Mngaza said in connection with the whole incident and their safety, *"Jesus Christ, Umfundisi, Jesus Christ."*

As a result of the riots the actual opening of the new church building in Duncan Village, East London, was very low-key. Dr Andrews was advised not to go into the township and Rev Mashologu of the Baptist Mission Church presided at the service on 22 November 1952. Further events in connection with the opening were actually held at Knox Church when the people gathered for a special service on Saturday 6 December, bringing with them their gifts for the purchase of the church. This was the last united gathering of the Pirie District before Dr Andrews and family left for their home leave in Australia. They were farewelled with a monetary gift to, as it was put, "buy bread to eat on the way".

Port Elizabeth and Somerset East

Another tentative attempt at establishing a congregation in a city township was taken by Mr McCracken. He had visited Port Elizabeth at the request of several Free Church people there and it was decided to constitute a congregation in the New Brighton location there. The people met in a house once a month and at other times they met at Korsten Village which adjoins New Brighton. There were 36 members registered with the congregation, and this soon rose to 70. A site for a building had been acquired and further developments were now awaited. Because people regularly came and went between their work in Port Elizabeth and their home area up in the mountains, it was difficult to judge numbers.

Death of Miss Carrie Ross

Miss Caroline Ross had remained a stalwart friend and wise counsellor to all connected with the Free Church's work in South Africa. It was said that nobody knew the Bantu better than she did. Mr McCracken, who lived near her at Mngqesha for some years, said of her: "Many a problem was solved by her wise advice; many a direction given that proved wise; many a puzzling custom made clear by her understanding, and many quiet words of encouragement uttered when the way was rough." But on 31 October 1954 Miss Ross died at a good old age and she was buried at Pirie.

Mrs Lex Colville Arrives

On Monday July 4 1955 Mrs Lex Colville arrived in South Africa. She came out from Australia following the death of her husband and her father, both of whom she had nursed on her father's farm near Maclean, NSW. Mrs Colville, having heard from Dr Andrews of the great need for more workers, had tried to get some young men to go and help him, with no response. Then she thought, "Why not go yourself?" She was 53 years old. She asked Dr Andrews if he thought she could be useful. When the reply came that she could, she applied to the Australian Church to be sent as a missionary. To her disappointment she was not accepted as they thought she was too old, but in other ways they considered her suitable for missionary work. So she booked her passage, paid for everything herself, and left for South Africa – in a voluntary capacity.

"May I come and live with you?"

On the Tuesday after her arrival, she went with Dr Andrews out to a village called Mngqesha, where he had a medical clinic. They had dinner with an elderly lady called Miss Margaret Erskine, herself a great-granddaughter of Rev John Ross. (Her mother was the daughter of Dr Bryce Ross).

On the second Tuesday, Lex again accompanied Dr Andrews, and again they visited Miss Erskine. Lex looked around at the rolling hills and the many African houses dotting them, and at the lonely old lady supplying the lunch. She dropped a bombshell into her quiet life – "May I come and live with you?" she said. Miss Erskine took a week to think about this proposition. Next Tuesday, Lex wondered what answer she would receive. "Yes, all right, you may come and live here," she said. So Lex moved in and "rescued her from becoming a hermit"! They lived happily together for over twenty years. When Miss Erskine died, she left the home they then lived in in King William's Town to Lex, who in turn left it to the Mission for a house for missionaries.

Available and useful

Lex made herself useful in all sorts of ways. She helped in the Women's and Girls work, helped Dr Andrews in his clinics, acted as an ambulance many times taking people from the villages in to hospital, and even acted as a hearse on one occasion!

Many times in later years she also carted bags of cement and building materials too.

She made a valiant attempt at learning the difficult Xhosa language, and could understand most of what was said to her, but for her teaching she employed an interpreter. In the early days, Lex had the help of Miss Erskine's cook, Maryanne, as interpreter, as she spoke good English.

Mrs Ruby Andrews had four children to look after, and found it almost impossible to travel around the women of the congregations taking Thursday meetings and Girls' meetings, and so Lex took on most of her duties. Ruby was very grateful. Later on, when Mrs Pat Sliep had little children in a similar situation in the Burnshill District, Lex helped her out also, as well as taking lots of meetings of her own.

When Lex came to South Africa in 1955 she found conditions very poor. Most men were away in the cities at work in the mines or in factories. There was not much health care except that done by church workers. There were no schools except church schools. TB raged. People would spit on floors and crawling children would pick up the germs. There were problems with babycare – flies abounded, gastroenteritis in summer and chest infections in winter took their toll. But in the mid-50s new drugs were developed, mobile x-ray units travelled in the rural areas, and the incidence of disease went down.

She would buy vegetables at the market and sell them very cheaply out in the villages. Oranges were a great favourite as she gave them out at her children's meetings. She saw this as a way of improving the health of the children.

Attendance at the girls' meetings on Wednesday afternoons increased, sometimes up to 80 attending. Clothes which she was sent from friends in Australia and elsewhere were distributed, or sold for a tiny sum, at the Women's meetings and her gratitude went out to the many friends who sent them. There were drought conditions that year and many of the men from the area had to go to the mines to earn a living. Children succumbed to 'summer diarrhoea' due to the bad water and there were deaths among the little ones because of this.

Very soon Mrs Colville was given a Xhosa name – **Nomaka** – 'the meek one'. It is by this name she was always known thereafter.

AT DENOMINATIONAL LEVEL

"Come over and Help Us"

In the early part of the year 1952 Revs McCracken and Sliep went, at the request of the Church of Scotland Presbytery of Matatiele, far to the north of our mission in Transkei, to see if the Free Church would assume responsibility for the oversight of that Presbytery. This request had been made without any reference to the Foreign Missions Committee of the Church who, when informed of this, said the matter should have first been referred to them. However, the matter was passed from at the April meeting of the Committee. Looking back one feels sorry that the matter was dealt with in that way but realistically it would probably have been one burden too many for our over taxed missionaries anyway.

In later years there was an approach by the Bantu Presbyterian Church (now the Reformed Presbyterian Church) with a view to closer co-operation, and from the Free Reformed Churches in Holland, but both came to nothing.

The Young Men's Christian Association

For many years the Women's Christian Association and the Girls Christian Association of the church had been up and running. In common with many other denominations the Free Church women and girls had their uniforms which they wore on special occasions and of which they were very proud. Now a Young Men's Christian Association of the church was started in September 1951. This

Association does much good in motivating the men of the Church (the term 'young' is elastic!) to evangelism and more zealous Christian living.

The Presbytery of Kaffraria functions again at last

In 1954 the General Assembly of the Free Church of Scotland authorised the resuscitation of the Presbytery of Kaffraria. Somehow it had ceased to function away back in Mr Dewar's time. Its re-birth was made possible through the passing of Acts in both the Free Church of Scotland and the Free Presbyterian Church of Australia allowing for the ministers of either church to be eligible to accept a call in the other church. So Dr Andrews took his place alongside Revs McCracken and Sliep as fellow Presbyters. At the first meeting on June 4, 1954, Mr McCracken was appointed Moderator, Mr Sliep the Clerk, and Mr Zokobe Taho the Presbytery Officer (Interpreter). Elders from the three Districts were appointed: Mr Andrew Zokufa, Transkei; Mr Hamilton Tsewu, Burnshill; and Mr K. Kobo, Pirie. So began an important new phase in the work.

Reformed Bible School Needed

Interestingly, at this time Mr McCracken saw the need for a Bible School with a Reformed emphasis that would train evangelists and pastors of all denominations for the work of preaching the Gospel of the grace of God among the African people. He said, "We cannot say whether the Free Church of Scotland will be privileged to operate such a Bible School." He was the first of our missionaries to raise this question to address a situation which he saw from the outset of his ministry in South Africa, namely, getting Africans to proclaim the Good News of Jesus to their fellow Africans. He lived long enough to see the Dimbaza (later Dumisani) Bible School fulfil his vision. Meantime he was thankful to see the new church building opened at Ngqumeya, as was Dr Andrews at Dyafta, and a new church and clinic was to go ahead at Tyusha – these last two projects made possible by the kindness of Australian friends.

New African ministers

Another landmark event in the year of 1955 was the ordination and induction of **Mr Zokobe Taho** to be the assistant minister in the Pirie District, an honour so well deserved after many years of intelligent and devoted service. It was a recognition of the status he already had in the minds of his own people. About 400 people attended the service. Rev Joe McCracken preached from Philippians 2:25. From this he said Mr Taho was a 'brother', a 'fellow-labourer', a 'fellow-soldier', a 'messenger' and 'he that ministered to my wants' – teacher, interpreter, guide to the churches, and counsellor to the missionary. Dr Andrews then addressed the congregation from the last two verses of the same chapter: *"Welcome him in the Lord with great joy, and honour men like him, because he almost died for the work of Christ, risking his life to make up for the help you could not give me."* This was true. Mr Taho had ridden many miles to Dyafta to preach, coming back in severe cold and rain, and had almost died as a result.

Mr Moses Baleka was ordained and inducted as Assistant Pastor in the Transkei District, having successfully completed his theological course in a Bible College in Natal. In an article telling something of the story of Mr Baleka, Mrs Lex Colville wrote: "Moses Horatius ... What hopes had the parents when they planned that name?" Whatever hopes the parents had we do not know; the Free Church had great hopes for him but, as so very often was the case, these hopes were dashed when he, like many another Xhosa pastor, left the church for another denomination. He did come back again, and again, but eventually severed his connection with our church. This was a great pity for he was a good man and worked well with Rev Huite Sliep. However, as a married man with little children the stipend paid to him by the Free Church was completely unrealistic; it was less than half what he had been earning as a waiter in a hotel.

On 8 June 1957 the Presbytery accepted **Rev L.L. Miza** as a student-pastor and those congregations he had under his supervision were accepted as congregations of the Free Church. This was confirmed by the General Assembly of the Free Church of

Scotland in 1958. Rev Miza was to continue his theological studies under the supervision of the Presbytery. Most of his congregations were small, mainly on farms or in similar situations in areas some twenty miles from Port Elizabeth, and also in Somerset East. Altogether there were about 275 people admitted from these congregations. Rev Miza was allowed to have another job as well in the meantime in order to support his young family.

Then began the waiting game. The main group of people who had been accepted into the Free Church belonged to Somerset East. Although the black, coloured and white people had lived there together for years, now, under apartheid, they had to be segregated into separate locations. This meant it was a long and tedious process to get a site for a church in the new black township. The process of getting Rev Miza recognised as a minister of the Free Church was even more tedious. Mr McCracken asked the Foreign Missions Committee in Scotland repeatedly for a decision on the matter of the work in Port Elizabeth district, on Mr Miza's position and if financial and other help would be available to build up the work. Time after time the decision was put off. Eventually in November 1959 it was reported to them that Rev Miza had left the Free Church in Port Elizabeth and a section of the people there had gone with him.

Miss Erskine's gift of a farm

Towards the end of 1958 Miss Madge Erskine made the gift of a farm at Mngqesha to the Church, and wanted it to be used for the welfare of the African people. Dr Andrews had advised her it would be better to sell the farm and use the money for the purpose she intended, and with this the Foreign Missions Committee concurred. The farm was sold, the proceeds banked with the Church's law agents, and the interest was used for various good causes in the Church. Miss Erskine and Lex later moved to a farm nearer King William's Town and a friend, Mrs Eagleson, visiting from Australia was impressed by what she saw there of Miss Margaret (Madge) Erskine with whom Mrs Colville lived: "Her farm is called Buffalo Farm. It might be more aptly retitled Benevolent Farm, for

Miss Erskine conducts it, if the truth be known, as a missionary enterprise. She will take in Africans who are ill or impoverished and restore them. And she also attends to their souls. How could we ever forget her morning 'family' worship with close on twenty souls gathered to sing Psalms, pray and hear a short lesson? It is not only the Africans who receive of her bounty, for she has been generous over the decades to our missionaries also."

Encouragements

There were many encouraging things along the way. Mr Sliep mentioned a 'goodly number of young converts who needed much prayer'. And Mr McCracken, reflecting on the ten years since he had arrived on the field, could compare the situation favourably. There were 13 more churches, 3 European missionaries, one more Black pastor and five more evangelists. There was a number of young men now who served as elders and deacons.

It had been a decade of hard work, but of rewards; of disappointments and encouragements; of the death of many of the old stalwart men and women of faith, but of the new birth of babes in Christ all over the mission field, and the business now was to nurture them. Mrs Colville had a roll of 302 girls on her books and 9 of these girls had been admitted to membership of the church. At Ebulembu she said that 15 women and 12 men had been converted, which was most encouraging as this place was then largely a heathen location. In Transkei a good number of young people, between the ages of 18 to 25 had come forward to join the church.

Some excellent men, such as Mr Wilfred Vumindaba, Mr Timothy Mdledle and Mr P. Nenemba had begun work as evangelists, and would serve the church for many long years. An application to serve as a missionary had been received from Mr Albert Sliep, brother of Huite, and he was off to Scotland to train at the Free Church College.

New churches had been toiled over brick by brick but were now opened – at Tyusha and Kowana, at Tabase in Transkei ('after a nine year battle'), at Fort White in Ciskei and finally in 1959 the Alexander Dewar Memorial Church at Whiteville.

The Opening of the Dewar Memorial Church at Whiteville

This took place on 28 February 1959. There were some poignant memorials to folk who had been vitally interested in the mission in the past. The pulpit was a gift from Mrs McCracken's family in memory of her mother who had died just before they arrived on furlough in 1956. The large bell hanging outside the church was sent in memory of Mrs Fraser, Dumbarton, Scotland, whose son David followed the bell to the mission field many years later. There was an inscribed Bible on the pulpit sent by the Ministers' Wives Fellowship in Glasgow in memory of Mrs Gibson of Govanhill (another ardent supporter of mission work). Dr Rex Dewar, the elder son of Mr Dewar and his sister Margaret gave the church a fine communion vessel and plate, and a big contribution towards the cost of the building came from Mrs Dewar and Iain, who were unable to be there because of illness.

The church door was 'officially' opened by Dr Dewar, who was accompanied by his wife and his sister. He gave an address outlining details of his father's life and work. He described how he accompanied his father to the centres around where this new church was built. Usually the services were held in the homes of the people. The African people were kindly and hospitable, happy and prosperous. There were plenty of mealies and kaffir corn, sheep and cattle. Life was pleasant and on the whole easy. Time mattered little. "Never could I forget," he said, "the communion services at Pirie when out in the open air hundreds used to gather to worship. For 50 years my father laboured to help the people, to bring justice and righteousness in your midst. No more fitting memorial could he have than a sanctuary where the Word of God is read and the people can be taught to apply the eternal words to the way of living. Set your heart on your church life," he continued, "make it the centre of your thoughts, your meeting place where guidance will be given you, bring in your friends and above all bring in your children." He also paid tribute to his mother who had been such an intrepid and intelligent co-worker with his father before being tragically killed in East London.

It must have been a strange but encouraging experience for brother and sister to come back to the scenes of their childhood, and to see that their father's lifework had not been in vain. There was still a Free Church, maybe not flourishing, maybe struggling, but still witnessing and bringing new souls to birth and slowly growing in love and knowledge of the Lord.

A QUARTET OF CAMEOS

Here we meet four African Christians who featured in the life of the church during the 1950s.

Mr Wilmot Nqebe

The Nqebe family were from Middledrift but moved to Whiteville. Wilmot went, like many others from the area, to work in Port Elizabeth and there he fell into bad company and bad living. This took a toll on his health and he returned to his home. One night he had a vivid dream in which he felt himself hemmed in, on the one hand by a dense forest and on the other by a raging sea. However in front of him there was a beautiful city, full of light and freedom. He found (in his dream) that he could only progress towards the city with great difficulty along a narrow path. Eventually he woke up and recognised that God had been speaking to him through the dream. He got to his knees and yielded his heart to the Lord. In due time Wilmot became a member of the church and was a living witness to the Lord's saving grace. His TB developed and he was hospitalised; there he evangelised other patients, formed a prayer meeting and gave out literature which the missionaries had passed to him. Mrs McCracken said that God blessed these efforts to many souls. When he came out of hospital he became a part-time evangelist and took great care in preparing candidates for membership. His illness progressed and one day he visited his friends bidding them goodbye and telling them God was calling him home and, after the visits, he went to his house, lay on his bed and passed into the Lord's presence. As Mrs McCracken wrote of him, "Wilmot was a young man and young in the faith, but the saving change wrought in his life was very evident and he matured quickly for glory."

Mr Wynne Dakada

Rev Joseph McCracken told his story:

"Mr Dakada was born in the year 1880 at Batrice, near Port Elizabeth. He did not qualify as a teacher, but had a good education to which he added the practical knowledge of carpentry. After serving our schools at Knox and Mdisa for about six years he was transferred to Emnyameni in 1919. It was here that he gave the best years to our Mission School. The Rev Alex. Dewar and others have testified to the great help afforded them by Mr Dakada. Many times have we enjoyed the hospitality of his home …

"Mr Dakada was a man of commanding presence, suffused with a genial personality, with something very tender about him, … which led some people, even from his own family, to take advantage of this side of his character and which gave him a sore heart and many secret tears. For some years past he suffered from ill-health, but when we went to Emnyameni in 1948 for an intensive evangelistic campaign, which involved walking up and down the mountains each day for over ten days, and interpreting every message of the missionary, he declared at the end of the campaign that he felt better than when it started!

"At the beginning of 1954 his health deteriorated, and after a period in hospital it was evident to his friends that his condition was serious. In April when we called on him we found him in the valley of the shadow. We sang the 23rd Psalm, read from 2 Corinthians 5, and passed a few comments on certain verses in the chapter, and then commended God's servant into the loving hands of the Good Shepherd of the sheep. Before leaving we asked about his faith in Christ, and he replied in Xhosa that his faith was very, very much in Christ. We shook hands assuring him that we would meet in the land that is fairer than day. To this he assented. He passed away the following day.

"Mrs Dakada has told us of the conversation that passed between them on the day that he died, and all of it was shot through with a confident faith. At one stage he had been very quiet. When asked if there was anything on his mind he replied: "No, all is well for I am going home." Truly, "Blessed are the dead who die in the Lord."

Nosense

Mrs Lex Colville tells the story of this Xhosa lady with what to our ears may be a strange sounding name. The first two letters of the name are just the equivalent of 'Mrs'. Maybe the remainder of her name was more true than perhaps her household had anticipated!

Mrs Colville wrote:

> I first met Nosense as she was sitting in the sunshine beside the fence of her cattle kraal. I was seeking a place in this heathen location of Gwaba to tell the 'Good News,' as the Xhosas call the Gospel. In this location there are two headmen, one the official one, the other, his elder brother, who has been deposed by the Government because in a quarrel, he shot one man dead and blinded another. Although deposed officially, he still rules the location. I had received permission from both these men to visit there. Nosense readily gave consent for me to use her hut, and those that were sitting with her formed the nucleus of a congregation. Before long others, including some men, had come in until there were about twenty present, all heathen. Mary Anne, my interpreter, and I were well embarked on the story of Adam and Eve and how sin first came into the world, when the old headman stormed in in a great rage. He called Nosense up before him and soundly berated her for allowing me to hold the meeting there. Mary Anne would not let me speak. However, he quietened down and told me to proceed. Mary Anne's voice was trembling and mine wasn't too steady as we called on the Lord in prayer, then took up the story again. The headman went to sleep. He was drunk.

Next time I met Nosense was in the TB hospital, where she was in the bed next to Mrs Kobo, our Evangelist's wife, whom I had gone to visit. I started meetings in this ward until a group of Africans started to come on Sunday afternoons and they helped Nosense spiritually. She eagerly listened to the Gospel and accepted it. "The preacher asked those who loved the Lord to stand up," she told me, "so I stood up because I love Him." At one time it looked as if she were dying in the hospital. The Christians there held a prayer meeting, and from then on she improved, so much so that she was able to return home. I believe the Lord sent her home as a light and a witness in that dark place. Nothing further could be done for her in the hospital because the disease was too far advanced. I was able to supply her with European clothes, so she discarded the red blankets of the heathen, which itself was a witness to her conversion.

Sunday by Sunday for some months I visited there in her home, instructing her in the faith. Many heard the Gospel because they came to listen too. She could not read herself, so I used to read the Scriptures telling of the heavenly home and the longing of God's people for His house. She always regretted that she was unable to attend God's house on earth because she was too weak, but Christians who heard her pray said there was no doubt she was a believer. In the hospital she learnt the Xhosa version of the hymn, "Rock of Ages" and Psalm 42. The latter is even more plaintive and poignant in Xhosa than in English. A few hours before she died she and I sang it through together. She smiled sweetly as we shook hands and said "Goodbye", with the words "Kulungile" (It's all right). Two of her daughters profess conversion, but her husband says he is still "outside". He remarked that he noticed she was praying a lot when she told him she had become a Christian. After the funeral I was able to give the Gospel message to about forty heathen women in her hut. I pray that she may be one of many from Gwaba who will praise Him throughout eternity.

(To add a P.S. to that story – Mrs Colville continued to hold services in that village and in due time a congregation grew up and a church was built – with much help from her. About 2003, the people extended their church.)

Mr Andrew Zokufa

In 1958 Rev G.N.M. Collins and Mrs Collins visited South Africa and one of those whom they met was Andrew Zokufa, an elder in the Tabase congregation, Transkei. Dr Collins wrote the following tribute to Mr Zokufa when he learned of his death in 1960:

Andrew Zokufa was no ordinary man. Of powerful build, he had followed the trade of blacksmith for many years, and commended his faith by honest workmanship and Christian character. He impressed us as being an unusually intelligent man. He spoke English well, and was an interesting conversationalist. Our missionaries bear witness to his unfailing helpfulness in all the work of the Mission, and to the impression that his Christian life made upon his neighbours. For long he had desired to see a church building erected at Tabase, and had given all possible help with the unnecessarily tiresome preliminaries to such an undertaking. But when, at last, a beginning was made with the work it looked as if Andrew was not to be spared to see the building for which he had prayed and laboured. He was suddenly stricken down with a serious illness from which recovery seemed impossible.

Andrew had just one remaining favour to crave of his Lord before taking his departure to be with Christ; it was that his life might be spared just long enough to see the church finished and opened. His prayer was granted. The morning we called to say "Goodbye" to him, we found him sitting in the warm sunshine in front of his hut, looking across to where the workmen were putting the finishing touches to the new Church building. His head and feet were bare, and his shirt-sleeves were rolled up to reveal massive arms that still suggested great muscular strength. It is not exaggeration to say that his face was radiant.

We suggested to him that, now that the Church was about to be opened, he would be saying with Simeon, "Lord now lettest Thou Thy servant depart in peace" and he smiled and nodded acquiescence. As we said our farewells, we spoke of the pleasure we had had from meeting him. "But we shall meet again," he replied, "and when we do Jesus will be there also."

That is our last memory of a singularly attractive man. His heart's desire was given him, and he has left behind him a memory that will, we believe, be a blessing to others.

To meet African Christians like Andrew Zokufa is to realise that the final answer to criticism of Foreign Mission enterprise has been given by the Holy Spirit in the transfigured lives of such subjects of grace.

On Reflection:

Sorrow and thanksgiving are often mingled in our life's experience. So it was during the decade we have just looked at in the African Church's story as the two memorial churches at Mdisa and Whiteville remind us. In the Lord's goodness both these churches, born out of such different circumstances, continue to be platforms from which the Gospel of grace is proclaimed to new generations of African people.

1. A recurring complaint over the years has been the lack of not just Biblical knowledge among those coming forward for membership of the church, but a sad lack of spiritual application of Bible truth. The church itself must

bear much responsibility for this as it has not provided adequate pastoral oversight and regular doctrinal preaching to teach the people sufficiently.

2. The work of the Gospel in urban areas presented the Free Church with new opportunities but also with many problems and dangers. It is a fact of mission, however, that if any mission is going to succeed in rural environments it has also to succeed in the urban areas, in strategic centres, as we see in the ministry of the Apostle Paul. We have struggled with this in South Africa just as much as we have in Scotland.

3. The church's work in South Africa, both in the rural areas and, increasingly, in the urban areas, was being carried out as the tensions created by the Government's *apartheid* policies were coming more and more to the surface, making it more and more dangerous in certain places. How grateful we are that our church people did not turn against the missionaries in those times! It is also to the credit of the missionaries that they continued their work without demur, because they loved their people whom the Lord had called them to serve.

9

A Decade of Developments 1960–1969

POLITICAL INSTABILITY

The work in the churches was played out against a backdrop of political instability. Dark clouds were building up and the air was heavy with the threat of stormy change. The independence of many of the countries in the continent of Africa was having profound effects on the country at its southern tip – South Africa. Christianity seemed to be losing ground. There was a growth of sects claiming to be Christian but which were syncretistic, i.e. having relics of the old tribal religions such as veneration of the ancestral spirits and so on. Several were also anti-White (like the *Poqo* movement).

A dictionary definition of *Poqo* speaks of it as "*a religious denomination that refuses to have anything to do with the white man*". However, it was political in its formation, possibly financed by the Communists, and its aim was to overthrow and expel the white man from the country. It was similar to many of the 'liberation' movements current throughout Africa at the time – part of the "winds of change" sweeping the continent.

In his Report on the work in 1960 Dr Andrews wrote of the situation in Africa generally where, South of the Sahara, the continent was in ferment. About South Africa in particular he wrote:

> In South Africa this year we have had our Sharpeville and Langa (two separate riots which were violently quelled), our attempted assassination of the Prime

Minister (Dr Verwoerd) and grave unrest in Pondoland (North Transkei).

While he noted some improvements for the development of the African people he went on to say:

> But for the Bantu and non-European generally there remain, with little prospect of removal in the near future, grievous and galling restrictions. They lack freedom of speech in criticising or opposing the government. They lack freedom of movement in search of employment. They lack freedom to strike in bargaining for better conditions of work and of living. Their limited vote and representation in Parliament is a mockery to them. And how long they will tolerate these conditions in the light of changes elsewhere is difficult to determine. Whether they will seek alleviation by passive resistance or by active violence is also uncertain.
>
> But for their needs in present circumstances of subjection, and for their greater needs through spiritual servitude, the Gospel of our Lord Jesus provides the answer. That we shall continue to hold forth while opportunity remains.

Reflecting on the continuation of the work in South Africa, Dr Andrews said, "Work in town and city locations will become dangerous for European missionaries, and is likely to become more difficult in rural areas. In anticipation of future developments in South Africa our most urgent need is for devoted and able African pastors and evangelists to lead the indigenous church when the work of the European field missionary comes to an end, as soon it must." But how many years would it be before this hope became a reality?

"In the hands of the Africans themselves"

Again in 1963 in its Report to the General Assembly the Missions Board reiterated the need for the church in South Africa to be in the hands of the Africans themselves. "It becomes increasingly clear that the future of the Church in South Africa must lie with the people of the land. The Mission is served by excellent native Evangelists, Elders and Deacons, but there is need for many more such men and of improved facilities for their education and training so that they may meet the needs of a people more critical as they become more sophisticated. The older people may be satisfied with the *status quo* but the young are susceptible to influences that arouse prejudice against non-African Pastors and leaders." Problems encountered by Mr McCracken in Port Elizabeth and comments by Mr Sliep about Transkei bore out Dr Andrews' words.

The 'Republic of South Africa'

In 1961 South Africa became a Republic and was separated from the Commonwealth. This led to some uncertainty as to the future of our missionary work there and also increased the tension among the Black people in their attitudes towards the Nationalist Party that ran the Government. The uprisings in other African nations were giving cause for alarm, especially the tragedy in the Congo in 1960.

Transkei troubles

The Transkei was also experiencing change as the South African Government was granting it a certain amount of autonomy in running its own affairs. This led to African evangelists sometimes being taunted as being the white men's servants. In response to this the Board "felt that this should stimulate endeavours of the mission to secure and train men of suitable quality for the full pastorate. Only so would they win the respect of their own people". Dr Andrews was asked to consult the Presbytery and report on the best way to do this. Mr McCracken was to be asked about this as well.

Rev Huite Sliep, who was living and working in Transkei, spoke to the 1966 Assembly while on leave in Scotland of this new political situation in Transkei with the granting of semi-independence to the territory. He said that one of the outcomes of this independence was the more open practice of the old non-Christian rites. "Christianity and the witch-doctor cult have gone hand in hand," he said. He wondered how long there would be any scope for proper missionary work as done by our church, or how long we still had left to consolidate our own work in such a way that our people would be able to continue as a part of the mother church. "The only thing we can say is that the time is short." He put in a plea for another missionary in Transkei to help consolidate and build up the work.

On a more sinister note, Mr Sliep told of violent men creating terror at Sidwadweni, one of the congregations in his care. Church families had been bereaved due to the violence and church property was damaged. In referring to Pondoland, Transkei, Mr McCracken wrote : "On one of our journeys we passed through the troubled area and actually saw hundreds of native huts on fire. We questioned some of those fleeing from their homes, but they seemed very unwilling to say anything about what was happening. Many lives have been lost. Some say these troubles are reprisals for cattle stealing, while others affirm that certain of the Pondos have rebelled against the new Government law of the Bantu Authorities Act. Probably both are mixed up in the people's minds."

SO – WHAT STANDS OUT FOR MISSION AND MISSIONARIES IN THIS DECADE OF THE SIXTIES?

The McCrackens in the Sixties

The McCrackens had moved to the village of Keiskammahoek which was a more convenient base for their work in the Burnshill District. Mr McCracken had the help of three part-time evangelists and one full-time evangelist in his work. They were Mr Wilfred Vumindaba, Mr Timothy Mdledle, Mr Alfred Mtshwane, and Mr Sydwell Matakane (full-time). In later years Mr Vumindaba trained at Decoligny Dutch Reformed Training College and became a minister in our church. Mr Mdledle and Mr Matakane (newly recruited in 1960), continued as Evangelists for very many years. Mr Mtshwane had come to help in the Free Church from the Bantu Presbyterian Church and he returned to that denomination with the good wishes of the Free Church folk who appreciated his ministry very much. Mr

Matakane, the full-time evangelist, was a young man from a family that over the generations have served the Lord faithfully and are still doing so. He was given a bicycle so that as well as evangelising in his own area he could go the fifteen miles to the people who met regularly under a tree at a place which became known as Umqwashu, the Xhosa name for the milkwood tree under which they met.

And thereby hangs an interesting story:

Umqwashu

Umqwashu was situated beside the road that ran between Alice and Grahamstown. It was an area of large European-owned farms in dry scrub country suitable for the rearing of cattle. The African workers on these farms had their families with them. Mr McCracken said that for "as long back as they can remember it has been their custom to meet, weather permitting, on certain Sundays of the month, under a big tree at the side of the road to worship UThixo (the name for God in the Xhosa Bible) of whose character and person they had but a very scanty knowledge. The other weekends they spent at beer-drinks. Throughout the years they were not once visited by a missionary." Sometimes as many as 70 people gathered under the tree. Eventually this meeting was brought to Mr McCracken's attention and he began to visit the people as often as he could and encouraged the evangelist to do the same. Other people responded to the message of the Gospel and eventually, with the co-operation of the farmers in the area a site was procured for a church and a simple building was erected which came to be used both as a church and a school. The building was officially opened on 16th December 1961.

In other areas of Mr McCracken's District he undertook intensive distribution of Gospel literature involving some of the girls and the three evangelists to spread the Word to as many people as possible in the various villages. Evangelistic meetings were held in conjunction with the literature campaign.

Port Elizabeth and Somerset East

The McCrackens were also overseeing the developing work in both one of the Port Elizabeth city townships and in Somerset

East township 100 miles away. The new and fragile congregations were keen to have a place of their own in which to worship, but finance was a problem among other things. Rev Joe spoke of the chequered career of the Port Elizabeth congregation "which, if related in detail, would tell of crippling frustrations, bitter disappointments, disheartening setbacks and enervating misunderstandings". Well, after all that they were certainly survivors and surely deserved their celebration and new building! For eventually permission was given for a building to be erected in Kwazakhele township, Port Elizabeth. This was an area with a population of between 20,000 and 30,000 so there was plenty of scope for evangelism, although "there were new church buildings springing up everywhere, but alas, in many of them there will not be the Gospel of Grace preached". With much thankfulness, a 'hall' was opened there in February 1962. Now the work could begin to develop, and it still continues today.

Home leave and a visit to America

The McCrackens were due to go on home leave in 1962 but delayed this in order to oversee the work in Transkei while the Rev Huite Slieps were on their leave. So from February to December 1963 the McCrackens were on furlough, leaving daughter Anne behind to continue her schooling, boarding in the school for those months. During his furlough, Rev Joe was pleased to be appointed a Free Church delegate to the Reformed Ecumenical Synod meeting in America. They returned to South Africa in December with, as Mrs McCracken said at their farewell meeting in Glasgow on 17 December, "a sense of urgency blended with a greater fullness of joy in the Lord to whom they were committed and a stronger faith in His wisdom".

Resuming work and changing districts

When Dr Andrews departed for Australia for some years, in order to complete the education of his children, the McCrackens were asked to leave the Burnshill District, where they had laboured for twenty happy years, and to work in the Pirie District instead. So

Mr McCracken was inducted to that charge on 10 January 1965. Looking back over his years in the Burnshill District he compared the state of that district with what it had been when he came to it at the beginning of his time in South Africa in 1944. Then it had five churches and was the weakest district in the church. In '64 there were ten churches and three preaching stations. Having to oversee the work at Port Elizabeth and Somerset East, the latter with seven out-stations, had certainly kept the missionary busy. As well as the usual pastoral duties, the overseeing of building projects and the like, there was also the promotion of a scheme to supply nutritious food products at cheap prices to the people. The women's and girls' work proceeded under Mrs McCracken's direction and altogether there were twelve Women's Christian Association meetings in the Burnshill District.

"An African Church in the making"

Meanwhile on the same day as Mr McCracken took over responsibility for Pirie District, Rev Albert Sliep was inducted to the now vacant district of Burnshill.

Joe was not long in settling in to his new district. Shortly after his 'transfer' to the Pirie District Mr McCracken produced an excellent little booklet, *An African Church in the Making*, giving an overview of the church's work in South Africa, and copies of these were distributed to ministers in the church in Scotland. This was one of a series designed by the Board to inform the home church of the various mission fields served by the church's missionaries.

Joe's boys' classes

Not long after his move to Pirie District, Rev Joe started after-school Bible Classes for boys in four of the villages: Mdisa, Mxaxo, Rankin and Dyafta. This was in addition to the girls' classes held by Mrs McCracken. Sunday School classes were being held in some of the congregations but, in spite of an increase, following a very helpful paper on the subject given by Mr Bryce Taho to a conference for Sunday School teachers, there was a falling away again because of a lack of really committed teachers. However, the Bible Classes were the means of reversing the trend. Vacation Bible Schools also produced increased numbers in the churches where these were held. A year later Mr McCracken could report that over 500 boys were enrolled and at each place these boys were encouraged to attend by office-bearers of the church who were teachers in the schools concerned.

Candidates' classes

In those villages where Mr McCracken held Boys' Classes he also held Candidates' Classes. One of the highlights near the end of 1967 for Mr McCracken was the Communion Service in his District when ten candidates were received into membership, four people restored to membership, twenty-one children were baptised and six elders and five deacons were ordained to office. Quite a day for thanksgiving! Some days later an Office-Bearers Conference was held and over the days of the Conference those present discussed the subject of Evangelism. From reports this was an excellent time of learning and of fellowship. About half the number attending were from the Dutch Reformed Church.

Some Key Concerns

While these things were encouraging, there were other things which worried the missionaries. The high incidence of immorality among the African young people, which led to many teenage pregnancies was a constant source of worry to both the missionaries and to the church as a whole. Also, the increasing number of funerals which were being held on the Lord's Day was having a detrimental effect on church attendances, so much so that Mr McCracken refused to conduct funeral services on Sundays where it was not essential for the funeral to be held on that day. The introduction of the possibility of 'keeping the body on ice' meant that a funeral could be postponed until a large number of friends and relatives could gather from far and near and so Sundays came increasingly to be a suitable day for the funeral.

First contacts with the Gereformeerde Kerk

In January 1967 Rev Joe was appointed as the Free Church of Scotland's delegate to the Synod of the Gereformeerde Kerk of South Africa at Potchefstroom. This denomination was the smallest of the three main Afrikaans Reformed Churches. It was politically conservative but theologically close to the Free Church and was a Psalm-singing church. This was the first official visit by an English-speaking delegate to the Synod in over 100 years. Mr McCracken stressed to the Synod that the indigenous Free Church that was being encouraged would need the fellowship and support of the other African Reformed Churches. He urged closer co-operation in the light of the recommendations of the Reformed Ecumenical Synod, which urged that fellow members of the R E S working in the same area should endeavour to co-operate in every way possible. While these contacts were fairly formal at that particular time they became much more meaningful in later years as the Gereformeerde Kerk began to develop some mission work in the same area in which the Free Church was operating.

The Pirie District is split up

It was decided to split the Pirie District into two, one half to be called the Knox District. So following consultations with the Kirk Session, the Presbytery and the Missions Board, it was agreed that the following congregations would constitute the new **Knox District:** Knox (Xukwane), Izihlahla, Mngqesha, Mdisa, Mxaxo, Gwaba, Ebulembu and Ngcamngeni.

The Pirie District would now be comprised of the congregations of Pirie, Dyafta, Tyusha, Rankin, Ginsberg, Ndevana, Kowana and Mdantsane. A new church at Pirie, called the Ross-Erskine Memorial Church was opened on 29 June and the new church at Mdantsane was opened on 9 November 1968.

Rev Joe McCracken continued to look after the 'new' Pirie District while Rev Bryce Taho became minister of the Knox District.

The Andrews in the sixties

Actually, the Andrews family spent only half of the Sixties in South Africa. From 1964 until 1970 they were in Australia for the education of their family.

But in the years 1960–64 Dr Andrews was very active in the work and very acceptable to the people. When they knew he was to go back to Australia, the Foreign Missions Board received a petition signed by 1054 people asking that he should stay.

A new church in Mxaxo

In 1960 Dr Andrews helped to build the Arthur Allen Memorial Church in Mxaxo, 7 miles west of King William's Town. This was a church in which Dr Andrews had a special interest as Arthur Allen had been a close friend of his in Australia. Large sums to help with the building came from Australia. It was officially opened on 1 October 1960.

The congregation at Mxaxo had an interesting history which Dr Andrews outlined in his article on the opening of the church there:

> The congregation is comprised mostly of Fingoes who moved from the vicinity of Mngqesha about 1914 and settled among the AmaToise, a Xhosa tribal group, which had shown until then, and largely still does show great resistance to the Gospel. Two names stand out in the memory of the people and were several times mentioned at the opening of the new church, Mabosholo and Siswana. The latter, it was said, taught the people how to plough, but the former taught them the way to God ... I learned in the Session some years ago how Mabosholo rather dramatically interrupted the first heathen funeral he attended at Mxaxo, protested against burying a human being like an animal, and had Scripture reading and prayer. Thereafter, no funeral was conducted without him. The church which began in his house later developed into a small congregation which worshipped in the temporary building erected in the days of Rev Dewar. The church became known and is still known as Mabosholo's Church, not only because it was built on his kraal site, but also because he fostered and ministered to it.

It was interesting that at the opening of the Mxaxo Church people from the new Somerset East congregation joined the large number from other parts of the church. It was good to see that this new congregation was being integrated into the larger church family.

As far as the medical work was concerned, Dr Andrews had closed the clinics at Knox and Pirie, (Government clinics were nearby) but he opened one at Donington, sometimes called Izeleni, which was quite near to the Rankin church.

Dr Andrews oversaw the building of a new church at Izihlahla, in a settlement that was formed some fifty years previously by people from Cwaru and Mngqesha. As so often in the Pirie District in particular, Evangelist Kobo was left to conduct evangelistic services and the Lord always blessed his ministry, especially among the heathen people.

At the General Assembly in Scotland in 1964

Dr Andrews visited Scotland in 1964 and at the General Assembly that year he was received and warmly thanked for his missionary service in South Africa ... He was greatly loved and respected and his pastoral and medical care were much appreciated. "No church was ever served by a better missionary." The petition with 1054 signatures received from the Pirie District as mentioned, asked him to stay, but he did not change his mind.

Dr Andrews said that he was not keen on an accelerated move to an indigenous church – the pressure for such was political; our own church people still preferred White to Black ministers. Within the present resources of the Church he did not see a noticeable expansion of the work. He did not see scope for an expansion in urban areas beyond existing work.

The Zakobe Taho Memorial Church at Rankin

The whole Church was saddened when Rev Zokobe Taho died on 18 June 1962. "The loss sustained by our South African Mission in the passing of this good man is hard to over-estimate. Not even the missionaries on the field can yet assess the greatness of their loss or give expression in words to their sense of gratitude to the Lord for the labours of His faithful servant. For Taho was a man apart, and he can have no successors." (From a tribute by the Foreign Missions Board).

Dr Andrews, who knew him so well and appreciated him so very much, wrote, "So there has passed from our midst a man, gentle, hospitable, courteous, loyal and faithful, such as one rarely sees. His contribution to the present strength, stability and unity of our scattered congregations in South Africa can never fully be assessed. He has proved to be one of God's choice gifts to the Christian Church in this land, and his passing has impoverished his people and country."

One of the last big tasks of Dr Andrews' time in the Pirie District was to oversee the building of the new church at Rankin (or Cwencwe, to give it its Xhosa name) and he must have been very happy that the name given to the church was the *Zokobe Taho Memorial Church*. At the opening service on 31 October 1964 Dr Andrews said, "It was one of the crowning joys to 15 years service in South Africa to be able to see this new church completed and to have a hand in erecting a permanent memorial to a humble and devoted servant of God to whom he (Dr Andrews) acknowledges a great debt of gratitude for advice, encouragement and help."

Farewell

On Saturday 7 November 1964 there was an official farewell to the Andrews family when the Africans expressed their appreciation and on 9 November the Andrews sailed for Australia. The departure of Dr Andrews brought the Free Church's medical work in South Africa to an end. The Government's medical services were becoming more effective, the number of clinics in rural areas was increasing so there was not the same urgency for the church to sponsor its own medical work as there had been in the past.

So as the Andrews sailed back to Australia they left behind a people truly sad at heart, no doubt thinking they would never see each other again.

However, as the decade ends, the good news was filtering through that Dr and Mrs Andrews were coming *back* – and this they did in 1970.

The Huite Slieps in the sixties

Highs and lows

The Sixties for the Huite Slieps were a bit of a roller coaster ride. There were highs like the accepted application of Huite's brother Albert to be a missionary in South Africa also, and then his arrival with his young bride Pat in 1962, and there were lows like the fact that Huite and Helen had to spend part of their last term in South Africa living in a room in a hotel. Why? Because the area in which they used to live was designated as an area for 'coloured' or 'black' people and whites moved out. The Board never could quite make up its mind about whether to build another manse so the Slieps stayed on and on in this 'hotel'. Eventually Rev Huite moved back to Scotland at the end of 1970.

However, during much of the decade, with the exception of two furloughs in Scotland in 1961 and 1966, Rev Huite continued his work in his widely scattered parish in Transkei. Mr Sliep's love for the people and his fervent desire to preach the Gospel were always severely tested by the journeys he had to take to get to his congregations and his rather adventurous relationship with his motor car. However, he was, more than most, conscious of the need to have the church firmly in the hands of the Africans themselves and of the need to give adequate remuneration to the Evangelists and Pastors who were needed to do the work. He always paid warm tribute to the men who were co-workers with him in the Gospel.

One bright spot was the re-opening on June 9, 1962, of the church building at Ngcingwane which was extensively renovated. Rev Huite Sliep commented rather ruefully that, with being involved with so much building work, the home church might be thinking they have sent out amateur builders rather than missionaries!

Many times by letter and in person to the Foreign Missions Board Rev Huite stressed the fact that many of the congregations had poor and very dilapidated buildings in his area of Transkei. The people themselves were so poor they just could not contribute enough to give the evangelists a proper salary. He wrote about the way the church collected its funds. "The so-called 'Ticket' system leaves much to be desired. It conveys so easily to the mind of the African that the means of grace are to be bought with money. A set amount payable per month causes sometimes hardship to the very poor and at the same time does not induce the better off African to give more ... The whole of the financial aspect of the work needs to be overhauled, and much tact and wisdom and patience is called for."

Semi-independence for Transkei

In 1963 the Government pressed ahead with granting a large measure of autonomy to a locally elected administration centred in Umtata, Transkei. It was under this new political situation that the transference of some areas from white to coloured and black zones took place and the manse of the Slieps was sold.

Mr Sliep reported that there had been sporadic outbursts of violence in Transkei. After partial independence was given to Transkei, the power lay with the traditional chiefs and Mr Sliep reported that there was a returning to traditional tribal ways. The work of the evangelists was difficult and they were taunted as being the 'tools of the white man'.

W.C.A. Convention and Office-Bearers Conferences in Transkei

In 1967 the W.C.A. Convention was held at Sidwadweni, Transkei, something they had been hoping to do for a very long time. After fairly familiar problems with muddy roads a gathering of about 250 folk enjoyed the Convention. It was only after all the visitors had gone that Mr Sliep was told that on the Saturday night of the Convention two of the evangelists and two young women were attacked and beaten while on their way to get fuel for the lamps. Thankfully no serious injuries resulted.

Mr Sliep now had the help of Mr Thyson Nkwelo who was working full-time as an evangelist in the Transkei. Mrs Nkwelo was very active in the women's side of the work. Mr Nkwelo later became a minister in Transkei for many years.

When Office-Bearers' Conferences were held it was usual to invite men from the Dutch Reformed Church and good fellowship was enjoyed. At the end of March 1968, in Cicira, Transkei, another Office-Bearers Conference was held. "There were heresies at this Conference," said Mr Sliep. Then he said the heresies were specially invited, and after "having introduced them, analysed them, and evaluated them by the standards of the Scriptures and our own Confessions, they were dealt with as they deserved and without ceremony thrown out by the neck – lock, stock and barrel!" This was a conference for office-bearers to teach these men the danger to the church posed by Jehovah's Witnesses, Seventh Day Adventists, Zionists (one of the African Independent Churches), and Roman Catholicism. All of these were active in the areas where the Free Church ministered, and such a conference was timely to point out those elements that were really a denial of Gospel grace.

At this time drought was making life very difficult for the people, with huge loss of cattle, crops withered to nothing and previously green and fresh hills looking like desert country.

The congregation of Gqunu had a very special place in Mr Sliep's heart, in spite of the stiff climb to get there. He asked the people, "Why have you put this church further away since the last time we were here?"! And they cheerfully replied, "Umfundisi umdala" – "The minister is old"!

Mr Hamilton Mcapazele of Gqunu

One of the men there in Gqunu was Hamilton Mcapazele, whose father had been an elder in the congregation. Mr Sliep tells the story:

> Before his conversion he got mixed up with a terrorist organisation called the '*Poqo Movement*'. This movement had been responsible for the massacre of five Europeans, just 30 miles from Umtata, some years ago. That Hamilton ever actually took part in the movement we cannot say. There was, however,

sufficient evidence that he was associated with it. He served a prison sentence of five years. While in prison he got gloriously converted, and desired with heart and soul to follow the Lord. A kindly Christian benefactor who visited him in prison made it possible for him to follow a correspondence course with the University of South Africa. One of the main subjects he took was Systematic Theology. After his release from prison he was given a banning order for another five years, prohibiting him from leaving his home, attending any gathering, and further restrictions ... What a joy it was to meet this trophy of Grace! We found him a deep spiritual Christian with a fast growing knowledge of Scripture.

Looking back

In his Report for 1969, Rev Huite Sliep looked back over his period of missionary service which was due to come to a close at the end of 1970. He said that the take-over of the schools by the Government was one of the biggest changes experienced in his years on the mission. The change was not for the good in that Christian teaching was no longer given the emphasis it had been given in the past. Yet he acknowledged that the church could benefit from a better educated membership which would eventually lead to a better equipped leadership to develop the indigenous church. He noted the benefits that had come about in the instruction of the candidates for membership now that the Catechism and Confession of Faith had been made available in Xhosa. He paid tribute to the ministry of Evangelist Thyson Nkwelo and to Mrs Nkwelo for her work among the women of the Transkei District.

THE ARRIVAL OF ALBERT AND PAT SLIEP IN 1962

Rev Albert Sliep was the new boy on the block in the early '60s. He was a younger brother of Huite. He had lived in South Africa for a number of years, working as an accountant and also serving as Chief of the Boy Scouts in Transkei. Early in the eventful

Inverness

year of 1962 he was accepted as a missionary for South Africa, having completed his course at the Free Church College. In July he married Pat Maclaren and they were 'farewelled' at a meeting in Inverness on 20 July 1962. The occasion was also the farewell meeting for two medical missionaries for India, Dr Anne Urquhart and Nurse Flora Macleod. It must have been a real encouragement to the home church to see four fine young people dedicating their lives to the service of the Lord on our mission fields. Albert and Pat Sliep sailed for South Africa on 16 August 1962 and Mr Sliep's ordination took place on 10 November that year.

Preparation and induction

For the following two years the Slieps were busy with language study (under the direction of Dr Andrews) and with looking after the various districts of the church when the other missionaries were on home leave. Because of this Albert was given a thorough introduction to almost every area of the church's work and it was a good preparation for his own district work in time to come. In common with the views of the other missionaries, and perhaps because of his 'peripatetic' ministry over this period, he wrote, "Training of office-bearers and other leaders will have to have priority. This must, however, go hand in hand with pastoral care of each individual member and adherent of our church."

While South Africa was not new to Albert, it was to Pat Sliep and she wrote of her first impressions of the country, the vastness of the land, the scarcity of cars on the roads and the friendliness of the people. "Many of the things in South Africa are still strange to me," she wrote, "but as the first impressions are good ones, I expect I will soon be completely at home here." This is typical of Pat – accepting, cheerful and enthusiastic. The Slieps were completely at home in South Africa and stayed there from 1962 until 2007 when they returned to the U.K.

The Slieps in the Burnshill District

On 10 January 1965 Rev Albert Sliep was inducted to the charge of the Burnshill District. On the same day Rev Joe McCracken was inducted to the Pirie District left vacant after Dr Andrews had gone back to Australia. When he became the missionary in the Burnshill District, Albert also assumed the oversight of the work in Port Elizabeth and Somerset East. The people in Port Elizabeth already had their building up and running and the loan provided by the Board was paid off. On 20 March 1965 a temporary building in Somerset East was officially opened – a building that had, quite literally, taken only one day to erect. It was a wooden prefabricated building but a meeting place nonetheless and the people were thrilled. On the Lord's Day three services were held and during the week two prayer meetings, the Women's Christian Association met on Thursdays and attempts were being made to start a Sunday School. There were already over 100 members in the congregation, and they obviously just enjoyed being together as a family of God.

Work in the Burnshill District also absorbed the Sleeps' time. When baby Mary and later Wilma were born, Pat had her hands full, and Mrs Colville gladly helped out with women's work. Albert said that "Everywhere we go we always receive a warm welcome and find a friendly people." However he also found much formal Christianity and a very low spiritual level in the majority of places, both among ordinary members and among office-bearers. This situation was true in many of the denominations. He said, "It is very disheartening to find this after so many years of Mission work in this country."

As well as Burnshill District and Port Elizabeth and Somerset East, Albert had the oversight of Transkei during 1966 while his brother Huite and his wife Helen were on home leave in Scotland. When Albert sent his Report for 1966 to the Board he gave it the title 'The Care of all the Churches'! He said he felt like a Bishop in the Anglican Church as he went his rounds conducting Communion services, baptisms, admissions to membership and so on. He said 'We have covered many miles'.

He was still discouraged by the lack of knowledge of the Scriptures and the lack of spiritual understanding of members and even leaders. He put this down to the fact that many could not read, and that African Christians as a whole were disinclined to break completely with heathenism. But maybe the clue was in the fact of his travelling many thousands of miles. The situation has come about just because there was no continuity of teaching, no week by week help given to those who had to preach. Missionaries had to spread themselves so thinly as they endeavoured to nurture people in small groups miles apart. Congregations only received a visit from a missionary every few weeks, and most of the week by week preachers had no training at all apart from this visit.

Sadness and rejoicing

As in every pastoral situation there was sadness and rejoicing in the Slieps' patch.

One particularly sad event occurred at Gqumahashe where a young Christian man, Simon Fana lived. A violent storm had burst just as people were leaving the church. Simon lived near the church so he ran to his home and almost as soon as he entered he was struck down and died instantly.

Another strange but happier event took place at Geju. There an elderly lady, Nosayizi Mnqaba, who had been a witch-doctor, called for the Evangelist to visit her. She had had a dream. In the dream she was told to give five shillings to the church. She did this. Then she had another dream and sent for the Evangelist again. This dream was more worrying for her. She saw a woman dressed in heathen clothes – her sister – and in her dream she was led to a house and to a room that was full of beads. In this she recognised her sins which she now wanted to confess. As the Evangelist prayed with her and spoke to her from Acts chapter 16, the evil spirit that had been possessing her left her and she accepted Jesus Christ as her Saviour. Praise God that people from both these families are still serving the Lord in the Church today.

Home Leave in 1968

Rev Albert and Pat Sliep, Mary and Wilma were back in UK for a time in 1968. They did good deputation work, and Albert addressed the General Assembly that year. He mentioned his worries about the "lamentable ignorance of the Word among the people", fearing that church affiliation had become merely a part of civilised life. He stressed his feeling that the areas assigned to each missionary were far too large. So he was especially pleased to hear that Rev and Mrs Angus Alex Macdonald were now on the way to join the Mission in South Africa. During their time away Mrs Colville was conducting the meetings for women and girls and this was much appreciated. The Slieps returned to South Africa by boat arriving on 1 September 1968.

Back in South Africa

Albert and Pat Sliep developed some new ventures after their return. Two camps for boys were held, one in January 1969 attended by 29 boys, and one in December when 32 boys attended. A camp for girls was held in July with 30 girls attending. All the camps were held at Lovedale Mission and much blessing attended all of them. Leaders at the camps were from Free Church members along with helpers from the Evangeli Xhosa Bible School at Kentani, in Transkei. Several of the church's evangelists trained at this Bible School, including the two evangelists working in the congregations around Keiskammahoek in the Burnshill District, Mr Oggie Mgidi and Mr Archie Makapela. Two other men from the District, Evangelist Sydwell Matakane and Mr Ayliff Madlokazi hoped to attend that Bible School also.

During the year Mr Sliep had put much effort into organising Sunday Schools and training Sunday School teachers so that Sunday Schools had become well established in most of the Burnshill District congregations. Efforts were in hand also to promote classes for the teaching of illiterate adults to read and write. Help was being given in this work by an American society, 'Evangelism through Literacy Campaign'.

More connections with the Gereformeerde Kerk

In 1969 Mr Sliep mentioned having been to Potchefstroom in connection with the centenary celebrations of the University and Theological College of the Gereformeerde Kerk. He said, "There are very good opportunities for co-operation and mutual help, including the training of our African ministers. This Church has become very missionary minded and its mission work has expanded greatly during the last decade. There is a great eagerness to assist and work together for the expansion of a Reformed witness among the African people. The services of their well-equipped and well-staffed Theological College for African Ministers at Hammanskraal in the Northern Transvaal are now at our disposal. It includes facilities for Matriculation for University entrance, a three year B.A. degree course and a four year Theological Course."

So began a partnership which resulted in a joint Dimbaza Bible School in which a Xhosa congregation of the Gereformeerde Kerk worshipped on the Lord's Day and later Dumisani Theological Institute, in part of which the Kerk still worships.

ARRIVAL OF REV ANGUS ALEX AND MRS HELEN MACDONALD

Rev Angus Alex Macdonald had applied to the Missions Board to go as a missionary to South Africa in February 1964. But after many visa and health trials and tribulations it was only on 8 June 1968 that he and Helen and baby Anna arrived in East London by boat. After ten days in King William's Town with the McCrackens they went to live in Somerset East. The Somerset East and Port Elizabeth congregations were to be Mr Macdonald's responsibility. Faced with the task before him he said, "I feel like one who sits at the controls of a car for the first time and is afraid that the whole thing is going to move off and leave the road!"

Mr Macdonald was ordained and inducted to the charge of Somerset East and Port Elizabeth on 13 and 14 July 1968.

Somerset East and Port Elizabeth

Earlier, while the Albert Slieps were looking after these congregations, Mrs Pat Sliep described the two places like this:

Somerset East is a fair sized farming town with a very good Secondary School. Many churches of different denominations serve the Europeans. The African location is next to the European part and most of the African churches have been erected in a row along the main road. Our Free Church is the first in the line. It's a temporary building, only a hut, but our people are proud of it for it's their own and they no longer have to hire the community centre for their services. The congregation consists for a large part of domestic servants who work in the town and of farm servants and labourers from the many farms in the area. This congregation has a large percentage of men on the roll (40 men, 84 women). It's a church that can be built up by a resident minister. As well as services in the church, services are also held on several farms in the area.

Port Elizabeth is some 120 miles from Somerset East. The African location (where our church is) is huge and is a wicked place. If you want to think what the location is like, just think of rows and rows of British pre-fabs (they're not really pre-fabs but that's what they look like, but smaller). Think of people (swarms of them); think of donkeys, cows, goats, horses, dogs, cars, busses and bicycles; and children everywhere. Think of them all on the roads either going somewhere or aimlessly standing about. Think of all that and then you have a rough idea of the Port Elizabeth location. Inside the church you'll find the usual friendly warm-hearted Free Church people.

So this was the challenge facing Rev Angus Alex and Helen Macdonald as they found a mission house and started out on missionary life in Somerset East.

Angus had to begin with Xhosa language study. For this purpose he studied at Rhodes University, Grahamstown, during the week and came back to Somerset East at weekends. Mr Macdonald had much encouragement during those early times in his new congregations with some new members in both Somerset East and Port Elizabeth. In the former he had an early morning prayer meeting and a Psalmody class as well (he was hoping to get the folk singing 'Stornoway'!)

Add also Cape Town

Earlier in the year 1968 Rev Joseph and Mrs Harman from Australia visited the South African field. Mr Harman was the Convener of the Missions Committee of the Presbyterian Church of Eastern Australia for several years and had a great deal to do with facilitating the service of Australian missionaries in all the mission fields of the Free Church. In South Africa he visited all the districts starting with Transkei, as he had been met at Durban by Rev Huite and Mrs Sliep.

During this visit Mr McCracken accompanied the Harmans to Cape Town where he and Rev Bryce Taho met with a group of Free Church people in Langa township and as a result a new Preaching Station was set up there on 4 and 5 May (1968). It was decided that Rev Angus Alex Macdonald would assume responsibility for the work in due course. So Angus added Cape Town to the care of the two churches in Port Elizabeth and Somerset East. Cape Town was over 400 miles west of Somerset East so it was a long way to visit these scattered parishioners. Nevertheless Angus continued to look after the Cape Town congregation for many years even after he had moved to King William's Town in the mid 1970s

Mrs Lex Colville in the sixties

From the base at Mngqesha, where she shared a home with Miss Madge Erskine, Mrs Lex Colville became a sort of Biblewoman. She and Maryanne, the cook who spoke good English, would set off together in Lex's car or pickup truck, and in time she developed a routine for her days:

On **Mondays** she took patients from the outlying areas in to King William's Town to the Amatole Hospital for TB patients there. TB was, and is still rife in the area.

On **Tuesdays** she was 'at home' in Mngqesha where she helped Dr Andrews with his weekly clinic there – writing out names and helping in other ways. After the school came out, she had a meeting for the young people, and the building would be packed.

Some of these children had started a prayer meeting during their break times. The effect on the school was most marked but not only in the school. The children heard that a local trader, a white man, was ill with cancer and the children decided to go and pray with him. Mrs Colville wrote: "He is a person who hasn't been particularly nice to the natives. The Scripture of Isaiah 59:1–2 was read. 'Behold the Lord's hand is not shortened that it cannot save: neither his ear heavy that it cannot hear, but your iniquities have separated between you and your God, and your sins have hid his face from you, that He will not hear.' When the children prayed they asked God to heal the trader, but if it were not His will, He should forgive his sins and take him to be with Himself. One of their favourite choruses was, 'If you believe and I believe then Africa will be saved'." In 1964 Mrs Colville had 585 names on her book, 134 in Mngqesha alone.

On **Wednesdays** she took Girls' Meetings in different villages in rotation, at first for Ruby Andrews, then for Pat Sliep, but latterly in the little churches she had founded herself. For her Girls' meetings and children's meetings she always bought a sack of oranges or apples from a shop in the King William's Town market owned by Indians. She felt the children needed the goodness of the fruit.

On **Thursdays** it was the turn of the Women's Meetings – the W.C.A. (Women's Christian Association). Again, dressed in her blue and white uniform as a member of the Association, she rotated among them, teaching long and earnestly, sometimes using flannelgraphs. Occasionally, when friends from Scotland or Australia had sent her some parcels of clothes, she would have a sale, taking care that everyone got the full benefit of the message first – especially those who had only come for the sale! She found it better to make a small charge rather than to have a free-for-all scramble!

On **Fridays** she also took patients in her bakkie (pick-up truck) to Grey Hospital in King William's Town or to Mt Coke Hospital eight miles further on. In later years, she used to take Friday as her 'day off'. But it didn't last long. She got to know people in a very poor village. They had been shifted there by the Government from other areas and were in desperate conditions. They asked her to come and teach them. She said she would do this as an extra – just specially for the Lord!

On **Sundays** Lex was helped by Mr T.T. Nocanda. She had two meetings – one before lunch, and one after. Mr Nocanda took a Candidates Class and conducted the church service. He was an elder of Mdisa Free Church, Knox District, and Principal of Mdisa Primary School , near Dimbaza.

Unique ministry to the 'red' villages

In the 1960s Mrs Colville developed a special and unique ministry among a group known as 'red people' because they wore blankets of the colour of red ochre. This ministry came about in this way:

> One day after Lex had got established in Mngqesha, an evangelist came by Miss Erskine's house and asked Lex if she would like to come to an evangelistic meeting. Yes, she would. On the way they met a group of 'red' women resting from carrying heavy bundles of wood which they had been carrying on their heads from the forest. "Oh, let's stop and talk to them," suggested Lex. "Oh no," responded the evangelist, "we only talk to the Christians." Lex said, "No, I want to talk to them." So she approached them and they received her in quite a friendly way. "Do you know about God?" "Yes." "Do you know about his son Jesus?" "Yes." "Do you know He is coming again?" "No." "May I come and tell you about Him?" "Yes." So she went to their village and faithfully taught these women, and the work grew and expanded and some were truly converted.

Bulembu

The name of this village was Bulembu. At first they met in the house of a woman called Nowam. When the numbers got too large for Nowam's house, a woman called Nowenjini came to Lex and offered her home. Lex said:

From the way Nowenjini listened very carefully to the message from God, I believe she accepted it in her heart. We cannot read the heart, but she professed with her mouth Jesus as Lord. Nowenjini gave me what no other woman who has turned from heathen ways has ever given me, though I have asked for it a number of times. She gave me the hair necklace which is made from the tail hairs of the cow ... which accompanies the bride to her new home. The women believe it keeps sickness away and will cure illnesses, so you often see it being worn when they are not well. When I found her wearing it a couple of years ago, I asked for it and she replied as all others have done, 'It came from the kraal, it must go back to the kraal.' I explained to her that that meant she was still trusting in it, still believing in that heathen charm. So then she took it off and gave it to me and that is one of my treasures. When the Lord gave her an abundant harvest so that there was not room for it and the meeting in her house, she arranged another place for us where we have been meeting until recently, when a vacant house was lent to us. The man who lent this house, July, was a heathen, but after Nowenjini's funeral he came to me and said he wanted to be a Christian.

There grew up a warm love between Nowenjini and me, and I'm sorry that I shall see her no more here, but I could not wish it otherwise, because towards the end of her life she was suffering so much. When the great day dawns and the shadows flee away, I believe we shall meet again.

Lex and Teacher Nocanda went there many times on the Lord's Day, Teacher Nocanda taking the service. Lex used to take a Bible Study there on Friday mornings. Later, a church was built there at Bulembu, and Evangelist Bethwell Siswana was in charge of the building project. The Knox District Session asked Lex to come to a meeting with them and they then said they wanted the church to be named after her husband, who had died before Lex came to

South Africa. So it was dedicated to the memory of Lex's husband, Andrew – "The Andrew Colville Memorial Church". The door was opened on 26 June 1969 by Nowam Noge who was the lady who first invited Lex to use her home as a venue for services. There is still a good congregation there. Sometimes, many years later, it was the turn of Bulembu to host the district Communion and it would be packed. All the officebearers sat in rows under the benign photo of Andrew Colville smiling down at them, and sometimes we wondered if he were seeing from above and was glad at what the Lord had helped Lex to do there!

Happenings at Gwaba

Bulembu was just the start. Gradually, Lex got a foothold in other villages where many 'red' people lived. She held meetings next in Gwaba. She described it as 'a very heathen place'. Already they had chased an evangelist out of Gwaba, but Lex said she thought being a woman helped them not to throw her out! At village get-togethers, the men gathered round a barrel of beer, and normally no women went near. But Lex preached to them, and they always thanked her politely. No doubt her curly white hair under a squashed hat gave her an air of elderliness which commanded respect!

A witchdoctor's umvumiso at Gwaba

One Sunday at Gwaba Mrs Colville came across an *umvumiso*. An *umvumiso* means that the household had called in a witchdoctor to ask where the seat of a sickness was and who had bewitched the persons concerned – in this case causing the women of the home to be without children. During such a ceremony all those present cry out 'Siyavuma' ('we agree') in response to the witchdoctor's assertions. Lex takes up the story:

> What a retinue was there! The central figure was a huge woman, tall and well formed, her scanty clothing covered with a white bead garment, wearing a brown skin headdress, also decorated with beads. Her body was glistening with perspiration as she vibrated all over with her stamping dance. Her breath came out with a

swishing sound. Circling round the centre pole of the hut were five others – two men and three women, while a man of the party tapped a drum. All were clothed in white and blue beads, one man wearing them like a curtain over his face. They had been called down from Transkei.

Suddenly the drumming stopped and the dancing ceased, and the woman witchdoctor made her pronouncement. She spoke in short sharp sentences, and at every pause the listeners clapped their hands, shouting 'Siyavuma! Siyavuma!' (We agree) The hut was full of people ... Two men were seated in front of the others. These were the chief enquirers. I noticed the intent look on the faces of those present as they listened to the pronouncement. The witch-doctor was declaring that the sickness and barrenness of the women of the household was due to the fact that a girl of the family had become a witchdoctor but had not been trained properly, and would have to undergo further training by a competent witchdoctor. This girl they took with them on their return to Transkei.

A sheep and a white goat had been sacrificed to placate the spirits. These people still believe that 'without the shedding of blood there is no remission of sin'. How sad that they won't believe in the sacrifice of the Lamb of God! ... This ceremony made me realise what little progress the kingdom of God has made in Gwaba. At our meeting there were 25 people, and I suppose nearly 100 at the devil's.

However, in the providence of God, Mrs Colville's evangelism in Gwaba was not in vain. A new church was opened there on 28 May 1966, and the local chief, Toise, was present at the occasion.

Two brothers became Christians in Gwaba – Nelson and Wilson Mtishe. They were a great help in the church which was born there. However Nelson became very sick with TB. One night he said, "Who is that standing there in white?" And then he passed on to glory, where no doubt he met with his Lord. Wilson went on to become an esteemed elder there, organising the extension of the little church after some years. His wife was for many years a Biblewoman. They died within weeks of each other in 2007.

False marriage and true

Lex told the story of a woman from Gwaba and her daughter (who had been showing signs of true conversion) in two parts in *From the Frontiers* magazine:

She wrote:

> On Friday the girl was busy grinding corn between two stones when her mother called to her. "Nosine wants you to write a letter for her." Taking a paper and pencil, she went towards Nosine's house. As she neared the house, a group of men sprang out. Rough hands grabbed her and dragged her screaming across the veldt, through the valley and into a village beyond. There she was thrown into a hut and locked in. This is a heathen marriage custom ... When I (Lex) arrived at the house in Gwaba to hold a meeting on the following Lord's Day, the woman informed me that her daughter had been carried off in this manner ... During the week information came that she had run away and nobody knew where she was. A week later, after a rainy night, I wondered if I would reach Pirie for the Girls' Meeting on account of the bad road. All went well until about a mile from the village the truck stuck in some black slippery mud. A boy and some young children came to help and as I straightened up after laying some hessian under the back wheels, there was the girl herself standing beside me. Her face was swollen by weeping and she was wearing ragged clothes. She had run away from her new home ... and spoke of the Lord's protection and guidance during this journey and expressed the belief that He would still keep her. "But why did you run away?" "The man

was not right in his head and he's like a horse." "Well, your mother told me to tell you to come home and they will not force you to go to him." That brought another burst of tears, (as she knew her brothers might do so). "Are you praying?" I asked her. "Yes, see that donga (ditch) over there? That's where I go to pray."

Well, eventually after many trials this girl was able to come home. But what about a husband for her? There were no Christian men in her village. Lex agreed with her mother that she would pray for a Christian husband for her. Her mother would check with Lex, "Nomaka, are you still praying?" "Yes." Then one day she told Lex a secret – a Christian man had asked for her daughter in marriage. "What church does he belong to?" "The Free Church of course!" At a Girls meeting this girl always stood out from the others in the Bible Quiz for her good answers, so one of the mothers chose her as a wife for her son. They were married very happily for very many years, had three sons and three daughters and were a great help to the church.

NoElse's funeral at Gwaba

At one time Mrs Lex Colville was taking a meeting in a home in Gwaba, and one woman, NoElse, came to follow Jesus and she, too, became a pillar in the church which was later formed there. Many years later, some years after Lex had returned to Australia to look after her sister, she returned with the Andrews and a friend for a three-month holiday in 1982.

It was then that NoElse died, and Lex and her friends, Dr and Mrs Andrews and Miss June Harris, were able to attend her funeral. Let Miss June Harris tell the story:

> I have a very clear picture of a funeral at Gwaba one Saturday (27 November 1982). It was the funeral of NoElse Vukubi, and Lex took me into a little rondavel where the coffin was and where all the women had gathered and sang, and one woman spoke in what seemed an 'excited sounding voice' or very worked up. Lex seemed so at home in there with them all and

so natural whereas to me it seemed eerie. Then some men came in and carried the coffin out and everyone followed it in single file right round to where the service was to be held. Rev Bryce Taho read and prayed and two or three men spoke, followed by Lex, Campbell Andrews and Rev Taho. This lasted from about noon to after two o'clock, when Campbell and I went home, but Lex stayed after the actual burial and till the end of the funeral meal. What struck me was how 'at one' she was with the people, and the stamina she had to stay so long. It was the end of the day by the time she came home to King William's Town.

Ngcamngeni

After Gwaba, Lex started meetings also in **Ngcamngeni**. There the going was hard. At one time, doors that had once been opened to her suddenly became closed as the people had gone back to the beer-drinks so popular with the heathen people, both men and women. The services had been conducted there in the house of the Headman who had three wives, NoAmen, NoPlan and NoPayieti! But Lex persevered and was allowed to come back to teach the people. She tells the story:

> On Sabbath morning we visit Ngcamngeni. Early in the year there seemed some opposition to my speaking at the beer-drinks and if I were given permission some left rather than listen. For some time Sunday beer-drinks were forbidden by the headman as they got rather out of hand, so people went off to other locations where beer could be obtained. However, in the last few months they almost seem to welcome me and on the last occasion one of the men rose and made a speech thanking me and telling me not to be frightened to come to them, that they would welcome me and listen to what I had to say.

Again in later years a little white and blue church was also built at Ngcamngeni.

Mamata

Another largely heathen village nearby was **Mamata**. In Mamata Lex had a cruel disappointment. She was holding regular teaching meetings, and "had just reached Noah", when objections from a neighbouring church caused the stoppage of her work. Lex wept as she explained the disappointment to Rev Bryce Taho. His heart was sore as he saw how much she loved his people. For quite a long time she was excluded from Mamata. But at last she was allowed back to continue her work, teaching in a round hut (holding a surprisingly large audience, including many children). The hut often smelled of smoke from the fire which would burn in the middle of the floor when the hut was not in use as a church and which blackened the thatch above. There was a bench or two for the visitors, and the rest of the congregation sat on sleeping mats on the floor. The door was a 'stable door' style, halved in the middle. When closed, it kept out the hens and chickens and dogs, but mostly it was open for fresh air and the nearest person to the door chased out intruders! After the meeting was over, a little offering of pullets' eggs or some corn cobs was warmly received by Lex, who understood that it stood for friendship and was a considerable sacrifice from folk so poor.

After having been one of their best customers for many years, an Indian family from whom Lex used to buy sacks of oranges for the children in her meetings, donated money for the Mamata church as it was being built, which Lex used to purchase a proper bell, instead of a piece of iron banging on a tin lid. To her joy, members of the Indian family attended the church opening. Sometimes, at the time of an Indian feast, they donated sacks of oranges or some sweets to Lex for her children's work. She tried so hard to tell the Indians of the Saviour, but saw no change in her time. But the church bell still rouses the people of that village to come to the House of God.

Bebula

The last village which Lex pioneered for Jesus was **Bebula.** It was up on a hill, and in the earlier days was reached by a muddy track which could halt even Lex's sturdy vehicle. She dreaded going there on wet days, but only rarely could she be persuaded to stay at home on 'Bebula day'. She would go and try (and by this time she was over seventy years old). When the last muddy curve in the road had been reached, there was the village straggling on the brow of the hill which had a strange outcrop of flat rocks, almost like an ancient Roman road. So Lex went the length of the village sounding her horn as a church bell, turned on the flat rocks and came back to the hut which was offering hospitality for the meeting. Sometimes the lady whose house it was, was still preparing it by smearing it with fresh watery cow dung, but she would wipe her hands on her apron and come to give a warm welcome. After some time (for a new outlook on time had to be learned in Africa) people would gather and the meeting would begin. Now, in that place too, there is an attractive church building.

Tensions in the work

At times Rev Joe McCracken questioned some aspects of Lex's work, especially in her distribution of free fruit, and he suggested that she might be removed from the field. This hurt Lex deeply but she continued to do what she could until the matter was resolved. In considering the matter the Board's decision was as follows: "The Board resolved that (while) they have no official responsibility for Mrs Colville's work they are grateful for it, hope it will continue, and suggest that the Kirk Sessions of Pirie and Knox accord her official recognition if this will help her activities within their bounds." When the matter was resolved, there was no animosity between Lex and Mr McCracken and the two Kirk Sessions affirmed her in her work.

A visitor friend of Mrs Colville's from Australia, Mrs A.B. Richards said, "Quite frankly I don't know how to describe how hard she (Lex) works. Her love, sympathy and understanding of these people is only equalled by her boundless energy. Never is she too tired to 'just make another visit, take a few clothes to a new mother, leave some oranges for children in a needy home or pray with the bereaved'. That she is loved by all is never in doubt, she is their guide, philosopher and friend. They come with their troubles and trials and always she sends them away happier. Her love for them is maternal and she makes them understand that Christ is her first interest for them, and they must get their priorities right." So Lex went on her way and the Lord blessed her by adding to the church those that were being saved.

WHAT WAS NEW FOR THE CHURCH DURING THE SIXTIES?

First fully trained minister of the Free Church in South Africa

Although Rev Zokobe Taho had been an excellent minister for many years in the Free Church, he became a minister because of his obvious gifts and as an exception. He never had a District of his own.

In 1964 the Church had the joy of receiving its first candidate for training for the ministry in **Bryce Taho**, grandson of Rev Zokobe. In February of that year he began his training in Decoligny College of the Dutch Reformed Church in Umtata. His grandfather and his grandmother had both died two years before, but perhaps they knew of his plans before they went to be with the Lord.

When his training was completed, Mr Taho was called to the Knox District and he was ordained and inducted to the District at Knox on 6 and 7 July, 1968. This was a great day for the Church in South Africa.

Dr Andrews had been watching with pleasure and much prayer Bryce's good progress through his theological studies and was there in spirit on 6 July as he was ordained and inducted. He sent a fatherly letter from Australia to the young minister, much as Paul would have sent to Timothy:

> Yours will not be an easy task for many reasons. Of the ministry of the Gospel the Apostle Paul said, "Who is sufficient for these things?" He recognised that special grace was needed and had been given him "to preach among the Gentiles the unsearchable riches of Christ". He came to realise that in his weakness and insufficiency Christ Himself would say to him, "My grace is sufficient for thee, and my strength is made perfect in thy weakness."

It was because of these experiences that he was able to write, "Our sufficiency is of God" and "I can do all things through Christ who strengtheneth me ..."

Your task will not be made any the lighter because of the special circumstances which will be yours. You will be ministering to your own people, many of whom have known you as a child, and as a young man you will be leading older men, never an easy thing among so conservative a people as the AmaXhosa. Moreover, you will be pioneering a great change in the work of the area among our people in that you will be taking over the work which has for so long been done by the European missionary. For these things you will need at all times the enabling grace of the Lord Jesus, and I am sure you will be seeking it at every time of special difficulty. Let the Word be your guide for its principles are right and true and apply to every situation. Let the Holy Spirit's voice be heard in the conflict of the thoughts within you, "This is the way, walk in it." Let the counsel of men of good sense and spiritual judgment and charitable outlook influence you. Avoid the suggestions of the hot tempered, hasty, unforgiving and grudge-bearing people who delight in strife ..."And the servant of the Lord must not strive; but be gentle unto all men, apt to teach, patient, in meekness instructing those who oppose themselves ..." 1 Timothy 1: 24 ...

Please convey to your Mother and all members of your family my greetings and good wishes upon this very important day in your family history. The prayers and longings of your grandfather are this day answered. God bless you.

The Xhosa translation of the Psalter is finished and in use

Up to now the Free Church had been using the Presbyterian Praise Book (Ama-Culo Ase-Rabe), a Hymnbook but which had a small selection of the Psalms in metre, because there was no complete translation of the Psalter. However, work had been progressing on getting a Xhosa Psalter prepared for publication. Rev James Jolobe was revising the earlier translation of the Psalms into metre made by Rev John Knox Bokwe and Mr William Kobe Ntsikana (Gaba) and he was also modifying some of the metres and setting all the Psalms in the new orthography.

At last in 1965 the long-awaited Psalm book was published (in Xhosa **Incwadi Yeendumiso**). An edition of 5000 copies was produced. Interest in using the Psalm book was expressed by the Gereformeerde Kerk (which was a Psalm-singing church and which had recently begun work among the Xhosa-speaking people).

It took our people quite some time to get used to the exclusive Psalmody that was now being introduced. It had been hoped to produce a tune-book in sol-fa to help match tunes with the Psalms but this has not (yet!) materialised. A revised version of the Psalm book was published in 2007.

The Free Church starts new work in some towns and cities

Up until the 1960s the Free Church work was mainly in country villages in Ciskei and Transkei. But during the 1960s as people migrated from the country to the townships in the cities, many Free Church people were among them. No doubt they missed their church, and Free Church people began to gather together in their new environments. Gradually Free Churches were formed, places of worship were found and eventually churches were built. So by the end of the decade, there were Free Church communities or churches formed in Port Elizabeth, Somerset East, East London (first in Duncan Village and later moved to Mdantsane), in Langa Township in Cape Town and in Ginsberg and Zwelitsha (near King William's Town).

Our work has never been so strong in the cities and towns, but that is where now so many people live, and that is where Paul would no doubt have advised us to concentrate our efforts. From these centres, Xhosa people would go out with the Gospel into all the other areas. So it was a good development in the sixties that saw the testimony and Gospel preaching of the Free Church moving into the populated areas of the cities. But because Xhosa pastors were so much more acceptable in those areas than White missionaries, it became all the more imperative that the Church should produce and train its own ministers and send them forth to their own people. For this, we have to wait until the end of the next decade.

ON REFLECTION

From all that was happening during the 1960s there are five main issues which stand out:

- This decade was a time of core development in the Church: Rev Bryce Taho's ordination, new missionaries, new churches, Boys' Bible Classes and Girls' Meetings, the new Xhosa psalmbook, urban development.

- The political backdrop against which the church had to function: this was becoming more radicalised, more unsettled and in many ways more ungodly.

- The ministry of Mrs Lex Colville, the sole 'single' lady missionary on the field bore much spiritual fruit. While not officially seconded by the Foreign Missions Board she conducted her work under the Sessions of the Districts and was always encouraged by them.

- There were increasing opportunities for co-operation in ministry with both the Dutch Reformed Church and especially the Gereformeerde Kerk. While the missionaries were positive in their reaction to this, the African brethren were much more hesitant and so little happened apart from neighbourly fellowship.

- The frustration of large distances to be travelled, too many congregations to be looked after and the limitations imposed by the scarcity of both language proficiency and well-trained African leaders must have made it very difficult for the missionaries to feel they were providing the best service for the people.

10

All Change 1970–1979

Sometimes in life things go on as if there will never be anything different, then suddenly it is 'all change'. Something like that happened in the South African mission in this decade.

Changes in missionary personnel

By the mid 1970s most of the men and women who had held the fort for so long had retired, leaving only two missionary families and three African pastors. Then soon others came and the work went on.

Changes in the Church

The independence of the Church, the subject of many discussions through the years, finally took a big step closer in 1976 with the setting up of the semi-autonomous Free Church in South Africa. There were many choices to be made as to how the new Church would function.

The political situation changed too

The political situation too began to boil and after the Soweto Riots, Johannesburg, of 1976, nothing was the same again. On October 26 of that year Transkei was granted its independence.

Dimbaza Bible School was started

And the Bible School which had been hoped for many years was finally opened in 1979.

It was a momentous decade.

CHANGES IN MISSIONARY PERSONNEL

The Huite Slieps leave for Scotland

The first of the missionaries to go was Rev Huite Sliep. He and Mrs Sliep left for Scotland in mid-August 1970.

At meetings on July 19 and 20 a large congregation gathered at Esidwadweni to say thank you and farewell to the Slieps, twenty-two years after a gathering at the same place had welcomed them. Dr Andrews was present and described the occasion: "Feeling references were made to deeds long since done and words long since spoken, and perhaps forgotten by the missionaries, yet remembered and treasured by those to whom they had brought blessing. Evangelist Nkwelo in particular stressed Mr Sliep's deep and sympathetic grasp of the circumstances and of the ways of thinking and acting of the African people." Along with the kind words of many there were also their gifts, demonstrating the 'riches of their generosity'.

Dr Andrews ended his remarks by saying, "... As Rev Huite and Mrs Helen Sliep leave these shores they will find flashing before their eyes the well remembered features of their African friends, and there will long resound in their ears the echo of their farewells – 'Hambani kakuhle' – 'Go Well'."

In February 1971 Rev Huite and Helen Sliep became minister and wife of the Rothesay congregation in Scotland where they ministered faithfully until retirement in June 1979. Mrs Helen Sliep died in December 1980. Later Huite went to the island of Coll, where he was in 'Resident Supply' but was in effect the minister. He married Miss Annie Jessie Maclean in September 1981 and stayed in Coll until his death in 2007.

The McCrackens retire

Rev Joe and Mrs Helen McCracken worked on in the Pirie District. The after-school Boys' Classes continued at Pirie, Rankin, Tyusha and Dyafta. The Principals of the schools in those places cooperated and greatly helped Rev Joe in that work. He told of one young man who had gone astray and then came to faith in the Lord Jesus and who eventually became an elder in the church. On the day he was being received into membership Joe said to him, "This is a great day for you, being received into the church. Your mother would have rejoiced to see this day." The man replied, "I have prayed for this day since I was a child; it was always my desire to be a Christian but I went astray. You know all about me – the drink and all the other nonsense I went after, but now God has given me a new heart and I don't want to be a Christian only on the outside, I want to be one from the heart. *I want to be pure!*"

So things went on until 1973 when Joe had a heart attack while supervising the building of a new church at Ndevana. He recovered well from this, but intimated that he would retire at the end of August 1974. He and Mrs McCracken came to Scotland and Ireland for some months before returning to South Africa to begin their retirement there. They were able to attend the General Assembly of 1974 in Edinburgh, but as Joe was not too well, his wife, Helen, read his farewell speech on his behalf. He said: "On this very day thirty years ago I was received into the Free Church of Scotland with a view to becoming the Superintendent of the Church's South African Mission Field." Mr McCracken went on to describe his thoughts as he now came to lay down his missionary task. There were the contrasts between what confronted Mrs McCracken and himself thirty years ago and what pertained in 1974, changes which have helped people to a better standard of living, to the church being better organised and growing, and to self-government being implemented in both Transkei and Ciskei. He spoke warmly of many of the men and women with whom they had come in contact over the years, people who 'showed by their changed lives that they had been born again of the Spirit.' He ended his address with this appeal to the young men of the Free Church of Scotland: "Surely, surely there are young men whose hearts have been touched by divine grace who will hear the Call of God in the Command of God – *Go ye into all the world and preach the Gospel to every creature.*"

Before returning to South Africa the McCrackens had two farewell meetings, one in Belfast and one in Glasgow. Then back in South Africa they were the guests of honour at a special gathering at Dyafta Church on 31 August. There, representatives of the whole Free Church in South Africa met to acknowledge formally the long and devoted service of the McCrackens. Fellow missionaries, elders (many of them teachers whose careers got off the ground under Mr McCracken when he was responsible for the Church's schools), ladies of the W.C.A. bringing gifts … all paid tribute to their faithful and fruitful work. At one time or another Mrs McCracken had been President of all the District W.C.A.s, and showed a true quality of leadership. In graphic Xhosa fashion, one of the elders likened Mr McCracken to a good old ox who ploughed a straight furrow and insisted that the other oxen keep a straight course!

On the following day a special service was held at which Mr McCracken preached. The ministry of Mr McCracken had impacted on every part of the South African field. To begin with, when he came to South Africa in 1944, he had no missionary colleague (as Mr Dewar had died before he arrived) and he had to find his way in a completely new environment. "Everything was in a state of chaos," he said. "The church had lost many places of witness. But, in the goodness of God, the number of congregations had grown from 22 places in 1944 to 44 in 1973."

After all the excitement of his retirement 'parties' it must have seemed a bit of an anti-climax for Mr McCracken to have to continue in charge of the Pirie District until the end of the year when Rev Angus Macdonald was inducted as its minister on 21 December. Joe and Helen McCracken moved from the manse at 14 Frere Street to a house of their own a short distance away in Wodehouse Street. After some years they moved to East London to be nearer a hospital and their home was a Bethel to many of us as we came to the city for hospital appointments or other business. Joe died in East London on 13 November 1987. Helen moved back to a retirement complex in King William's Town. Although later severely incapacitated by a stroke, she remained vitally interested in the work of the missionaries and of the Church. Yet her heart was in her heavenly home and at last she arrived there on 3 March 2007, aged almost 97.

The Andrews retire to Australia

Dr Campbell Andrews and his wife Ruby had been in Australia for the education of their children since November 1964. But in 1970 they returned without the children to South Africa, with a work permit to allow Dr Andrews to work as a medical missionary, the permit to run for one year. One lady who was visiting the field recorded that, "There is great joy in all the Churches at the news that Dr and Mrs Andrews are returning to South Africa. The people do not look on Dr Andrews only as a missionary and Doctor, but as a tried and trusted friend, and so many told of their great grief when he left and the joy of his expected arrival." On 18 March they arrived.

Medical work

Arrangements had been made for Dr Andrews to work at the Mount Coke (Methodist) Mission Hospital, some eight miles from King William's Town. The fares and other expenses for the Andrews were paid by their church in Australia and he and Mrs Andrews stayed in a doctor's house at the hospital. Dr Andrews undertook preaching engagements whenever he could and was always welcomed as a wise and good messenger of the Gospel. He chose not to become a member of the Presbytery of Kaffraria but was always associated with the Presbytery whenever he was able to attend although he was not responsible for looking after any of the Districts on a long-term basis. He did serve as interim-moderator of the Pirie District and the Burnshill District while their missionaries were on furlough. Dr Andrews felt that since he was then 61 years of age, it would be unwise to try to initiate new medical work in any of the Districts. Mt Coke Hospital served an area in which many of our people lived, it had a spiritual and evangelical witness, and it urgently needed medical personnel, so he saw his most effective role in serving there.

Retirement

Dr Campbell and Mrs Ruby Andrews retired in mid-1975, after paying a three-month visit to Scotland and attending the General

Assembly there that year. He was interviewed by the Foreign Missions Board and thanked for his years of service to the Church in South Africa. He made two important points at this interview:

One was to note the increasing powers being devolved to the Ciskei Government which had a bearing not only on medical work but in other areas as well.

And secondly, he said it was necessary to press ahead with speed with the setting up of a more independent church 'as the people were getting used to it'. He advised that the Board should remain *in loco synodi* and that there must be a speedy resolution to the impasse which had arisen over the ordination of African ministers.

After their visit to Scotland the Andrews returned briefly to South Africa and then sailed for Australia on 2 July 1975. They had a long and fruitful retirement there.

Dr Andrews passed away on 23 January 1994, and his wife Ruby on 13 April 2002.

The Albert Slieps change from Ciskei to Transkei

Albert and Pat Sliep had been in the Burnshill District in Ciskei since mid-1965. They had nurtured each of their congregations, teaching the Word, holding camps for the young people, building up Sunday Schools in most of the places in the district.

Then when Albert's brother Huite left for retirement in 1970, Albert was appointed interim-Moderator of the Transkei district. This added burden, which he assumed cheerfully, was far too much for one man to carry. But, though overseeing the work of the twelve congregations of the Burnshill District and then the Transkei work, Albert and Pat were still able to continue to organise camps for boys and girls, training conferences for Sunday School teachers, the production and distribution of Christian literature and the holding of evangelistic campaigns. Albert Sliep said: "A great encouragement and joy has been the work amongst the young people in our camps ... we greatly rejoice to see the Holy Spirit working amongst these youngsters." One of the older girl campers wrote to say: "I was saved when I was at the camp. I used to think I had accepted Jesus as my Saviour but I was deceiving myself. When the Word of God was preached it got to me because I was a hypocrite."

A camp was held in Transkei as well, using the premises of the Bible School at Kentani.

Also a new bookshop was opened in Keiskammahoek, under Albert's guidance.

Slow change is happening

Mr Sliep had always been an encourager of the idea of the indigenous church.

He took up this theme when he addressed the General Assembly of the Free Church of Scotland during his leave in 1973:

> The task of the White missionary is changing but his work is not finished. He may be considered a temporary worker in a growing national indigenous church, specially at the moment when there is a growing awareness among the African people of their own identity as Black people and, partly as a result of the development of a Black Theology – a dangerous trend. It is good when, in our Free Church, there are those who are anxious to retain the services of the missionary to help and advise them. But it is up to the young church to decide how long the missionary should be there and in what capacity. Part of the findings of the recent Reformed Ecumenical Synod said, "It is stressed that financial support should not endanger the autonomy of any church," and "Members, office-bearers and ecclesiastical bodies shall refrain from every kind of domination, the one over the other, because Christ reigns supreme in His Church ...".
>
> The church in South Africa is not a dying Church, but a lively growing Church. She is an active member of the Church of Jesus Christ, busily engaged in evangelising among the back-sliders and indifferent ones.

The change to Transkei

It was agreed by the Church in Scotland and in South Africa that the Slieps should transfer from Burnshill to Umtata, where Albert would take responsibility for the work in Transkei which was not under the direction of Rev Thyson Nkwelo (who was minister of the Tabase District). They moved in early 1975.

About this time new congregations were being established in the Kentani area of Transkei which represented quite a geographical extension of the Free Church work.

In the year 2000 Albert wrote a letter remembering a time of storm during his time in Transkei.

> In the late seventies or early eighties the Transkei was hit by a terrific storm. Streams became raging rivers, homes destroyed completely or partly by heavy rains. Also some of our church buildings, those at Mqokelweni, Gqunu and Sidwadweni suffered damage. At that time we did not yet have a building at Nkanini – the people there met in the home of the Elder and later became a separate congregation and, encouraged by Evangelist Nenemba, put up their own building, the present one. At Tabase, where we met in the Elder's home, many homes were damaged. Through the Skogheim Convention I had come into contact with a Brethren congregation somewhere near London and approached them for financial help. World Vision helped with foodstuffs and with seeds. We made them up in parcels and took these to the congregations for distribution amongst the most needy families. We were also able to buy water tanks and encouraged the congregations to grow vegetables. We had then still enough funds left to help with the financing of a fence around some of the church grounds.
>
> In June 1978 Thomas Sliep was born, adding a new dimension to the home in Umtata where Mary and Wilma were attending secondary school.

The Macdonalds move to the Ciskei

The Macdonalds were continuing their good work in Somerset East, Port Elizabeth and Cape Town, none of them easy assignments and involving quite a lot of travel.

A highlight of the year 1971 was the opening of the new church in Somerset East. The building, one of the smartest in the Free Church at the time, was a tribute to the hard work and persistence of Rev Angus Macdonald. The church was given the name *The Donald Macleod Memorial Church*. This was in memory of Lewis-born missionary Rev Donald Macleod who died in 1878 at the age of thirty-eight years after just four years as a missionary among the amaXhosa. He is buried at Burnshill.

The Macdonald family were in Scotland on leave in March 1972. In May of that year Angus addressed the General Assembly. After giving a graphic picture of many of the problems in the South African church and social situation, especially for young Africans going to start work in the cities, such as he was familiar with in Cape Town, he ended his address with this appeal: "It is customary to appeal to those present to consider giving themselves to this work of the Lord. Well, there are various ways you can do this. You can emigrate to South Africa and take a secular job ... We commend to you South Africa ... Come as you are, not necessarily as a missionary, but as a Christian."

Then at the end of 1974 it was all change for the Macdonalds too. After Rev Joe McCracken's retiral, Angus Alex left Somerset East and went to be minister of the Pirie District. He was inducted there on 21 December, and remained in that district until his own retiral in 1997. During their time in Ciskei they lived in the house at 14 Frere Street, vacated by the McCrackens. However, Angus continued as interim moderator of the Cape Town congregation and also continued to look after Somerset East and Port Elizabeth as well as he could.

His own new district of Pirie was really split into three or even four different areas, each with its own distinct outlook. Nearer home were the four established congregations of Pirie, Dyafta, Rankin and Tyusha. A girls' camp held mostly by folk from these villages had 80 girls in attendance as well as leaders and cooks. On the way to East London was the newer congregation of Ndevana, high on a hill, with the new church which had been supervised by Joe McCracken. Down near the coast were the small outpost congregations of Vivi, Ngqinisa and Kowana. They were in heathen surroundings and included some new Christians. Then there were also the town and city congregations of Mdantsane, Zwelitsha and Ginsberg, which were quite a different matter altogether. The last two were outside King William's Town and Mdantsane was a large city township outside East London.

Angus says in his report for 1978: "By the courtesy of the school Principals, we were encouraged to visit the schools of the Pirie District, Dyafta, Tyusha and Rankin every week during the last school year." Helen also was most diligent and caring in looking after all the different groups of Women's Christian Associations in each congregation. She knew each woman by name and knew about her many problems in most cases too. So between looking after the spirituality of their flock and building and restoring church buildings, and bringing up a growing family – Anna, Fiona and John – Angus and Helen's time was more than full.

But with the start of the new decade, an even bigger and most ambitious project had to be undertaken on top of all the others – the Cape Town, Gugulethu, church building.

Mrs Lex Colville shares her home

Mrs Colville kept up her busy round of meetings for women and girls on almost every day of the week. In 1975 she visited Scotland and the General Assembly for the first time. Her address to the Assembly was illustrated by her wearing of traditional Xhosa dress first, then during a break she did a quick change and appeared again as a Christian Xhosa woman in the Free Church blue and white uniform! At this time she was a sprightly 73 year old.

She and Miss Erskine (with whom she had lived since coming to South Africa) had now moved to a house on Maitland Road, King William's Town. The farm where they had been living was considered unsafe for two elderly ladies to live in on their own. On January 9 1976 Miss Madge Erskine died. Lex wrote: "She had been my dear friend for over 21 years, the one who had shared her home with me for those many years. She was a constant support in my work for it was a work in which she had been concerned all her life and wanted to continue and expand – the growth in children's hearts of the kingdom of God. The constant care and provision she gave me extended beyond the grave as she bequeathed to me her house and its contents. So the year began with "mourning", but later it turned to "gladness". Rev W.D. Graham heard the call for help from the South African mission field and responded, leaving his charge in Edinburgh, and came with his family with the special call to train African Blacks as ministers and office-bearers in the church here. I was glad to share my home in King William's Town with them with happy results for me." Friends wondered if she were wise in this! But in the event all lived together very happily until her retirement to Australia in 1981.

THE GRAHAMS COME

Now, with the arrival of our family on the scene, we will need to switch to the first person at times (like the 'we' sections in Acts!)

For some time in the congregation of Buccleuch and Greyfriars in Edinburgh we had been praying for a new missionary to go to South Africa to replace one at least of those who had retired. Then when the way opened up, the Lord said "Go yourself"!

The application was accepted. The Board considered our sphere of service. They were to bear in mind that "in future the Board expect the general emphasis of missionary work to be in the direction of advising and aiding the church in up-building, specifically in regard to the operation of courts, and in the training of candidates for the ministry, and in general Christian education of church members – e.g. in the operation of Bible Schools". Our induction to the South African mission field took place on 16 June 1976 and we arrived there on 6 July. On the same plane travelled two Board delegates, Profs Fraser and Graham. After landing at Johannesburg they went to meet with representatives from the

Gereformeerde Kerk while we flew on to Durban to meet up with our colleagues, Black and White, who were attending the Evangelical and Reformed Conference nearby at Skogheim. The McCrackens were there, and Albert and Pat Sliep and family, Angus Macdonald and Lex Colville, with eleven of our Black colleagues, ministers or elders. We arrived at dusk, and after the evening meal, we met up with them outside under a tree, with a big moon and the different Southern Hemisphere stars looking down. The men formed a semi-circle and they sang the Xhosa National Anthem and Psalm 23 to us in Xhosa. We all shook hands then, and we tried out the little Xhosa we had learned before leaving Scotland – they found this very funny! We were Bill, Elizabeth, Anne (aged 8) and Ruth (aged 6). It was an unforgettable occasion.

"Missionaries please go home"

The following day we attended our first session of the Conference while the girls played with the other children on the trampolines. In the late afternoon session question time an African delegate (not a Free Church one!) stood up and made an impassioned speech saying, "**Missionaries go home**!" He said that while they really appreciated all that the missionaries had done for the Africans, as long as the white man and his money was there the Africans would rely on him and be lazy and would not support their own pastors, they would never grow up. "Missionaries, please untie the apron strings!" And we had just arrived! In conversation with our black colleagues attending the conference, they assured us that with only three black pastors, missionaries were certainly still needed in our situation ... for a time! But White and Black agreed that the role of the missionary must change.

Living with Lex

At the end of the Conference we took the long journey by road in Mrs Lex Colville's car to King William's Town. Everything was so new – African women carrying bundles of wood on their heads, picturesque round houses and, in Natal, fields and fields of sugar cane. There was room for us all in Lex's welcoming home. There was even a double garage, so our 'bakkie' (pick-up truck which was the means of transport used by all the missionaries) and Lex's big white Peugeot could be housed as well. There were three bedrooms and a big rambly garden. We learned more from living with Lex for almost five years than we would ever have learned any other way. She had such a solid, practical love for the Africans, and a good Australian sense of humour. Nothing was too much of a bother. At the beginning of the school year there would be a queue of parents asking for help in sending their children to school. If she could help, she would. She was keen to help us in our need to learn the Xhosa language, and had already engaged a teacher who came to teach us regularly. We were issued with Xhosa Bibles from which we had to read at family worship times, even though we didn't understand much at that stage! She encouraged us in all the projects we got involved in, and was a ready-made Granny to the children. In the early days we would accompany her on her travels and see her taking meetings and interacting so well with the people.

She had a great sense of adventure, and through her we went to places and saw things which even the elders in the church had never seen. She came home one day in a hurry and said, "There is a heathen wedding happening in Ncamngeni – hurry up and we'll go." It certainly was fascinating to see the old customs which have probably quite died out by now.

In the Burnshill District

The District assigned to us was the Burnshill District, left vacant when Albert Sliep went to Transkei. Joe McCracken showed us round – first by Keiskammahoek, the little town of bungalows and trees where John and Elizabeth Macdonald had lived so long before, and later the McCrackens and Slieps, and then up stony 'roads' to the higher villages of Geju, Mnyameni, Ngqumeya, Burnshill and Amatole Basin. It was a beautiful area of blue mountains, wide veld, aloe-clad hills, wild flowers, mud houses clustered along the sides of the mountains and lovely friendly people. Bill had a regular weekly plan of visiting the congregations on a set day each week. The people knew he would be at the church, and he had classes aimed at helping those who wanted to become members, or met with the elders, encouraged people to come with their pastoral problems, and so on. In the process a close bond was forged between pastor and congregations.

At Geju, two recently ordained elders said after a service when the sermon had been on the call of Abraham how the Lord had spoken to them and had brought them from sin to a true faith in the Lord Jesus Christ. Another man from the same place had just recently been converted after hearing the Gospel preached at a relative's funeral. Funerals are great evangelistic opportunities as they are well attended and many of the folk are non-churchgoers

By the end of 1976 the Macdonalds were due to go on leave till October of 1977, and we were looking after their eleven congregations as well as those of Burnshill. While it was hard work, nothing could have given us a better overview of much of the Church and of such different types of location and work.

THE ARRIVAL OF THE FRASERS

There were still more changes in the missionary personnel in this decade. In October 1977 Rev David Fraser and Marion arrived in Umtata with little Alexander. He turned one year old just a few days after their arrival. They arrived on the same day as the Macdonalds arrived back from home leave.

The Frasers stayed with the Slieps for a few days and then the Slieps left for home leave and the Frasers looked after their district of Embo in Transkei until they returned early in 1978, living in the manse at Umtata.

On the Slieps' return, it was decided that the Frasers should move to Butterworth, in Transkei, about half way between Umtata and King William's Town. A flat was found which was central and safe and they were soon well established there. David was to be the interim-moderator of the Ncgingwane and Kentani District which included the old church of Ngcingwane, built in the time of Mr Dewar. Other congregations were in heathen locations nearer the coast and there was ample scope for David's gift of evangelism in the villages there. Also at Kentani, down near the coast, was the

Evangeli Xhosa Bible School run by Harry and Gay Oosthuyzen, and Basil and Lorna Frew. The Frasers and the two Bible School families soon became firm friends and each supported the others in their evangelistic, teaching and, later, building efforts among the amaXhosa whom they all loved to serve.

On 15 March 1978 Donald Samuel Fraser came to join the family. He was born in King William's Town and counted himself fortunate in being born in "King Billy's Town!"

Welcome

Later in the year, on 27 May 1978 the Frasers had their official 'welcome' to the District. It was held at Ngcingwane Church. It was a wonderful welcome with many gifts from a people who had already come to love and respect their missionary and his family. Children from local schools came to sing, showing how rhythm is built into the African body. The Headman of the location, an elder in the congregation, brought words of welcome. Mr P. Mfaxa, Principal of one of the schools in Kentani and Session Clerk of the District, presided and in an interesting and perceptive speech stressed the problems of living as a Christian in a basically non-Christian environment. The Christian takes himself out of his traditional culture and this culture keeps pulling him back at every turn. He said that the minister, and especially the missionary, must develop a sympathetic and patient understanding of the problems arising from the situation. He gave a warm welcome to all the guests, and an especial welcome to 'the old crock of the Free Church, Mrs McCracken'! After her initial shock she was very patient and understanding and accepted it as the compliment it was meant to be!

The area in which David and Marion Fraser served was indeed a needy one, with multitudes of heathen people to be evangelised and Christians needing to be built up in their faith.

Butterworth started life in 1827 as a Methodist Mission Station by the river Cuwa. (The African name for Butterworth is 'iCuwa'). It developed into a busy, sprawling typically African town and attracted several industries because of the large population around it. Marion Fraser takes us with her to visit some rural congregations in their new parish:

> With your mind's eye follow me along a dusty road to Macibe situated among the hills about 16 miles from Butterworth. Our faithful group meet in the picturesque Tshaka home which was once graced by a saintly convert of the Kentane Bible School mission. When Mr Bani Tshaka was liberated from heathendom he opened his home to the early witness of the Free Church in that area. It was our privilege to share Sabbath worship with him in his neat mud hut before this 'living stone' was taken to adorn a temple not made with hands, eternal in the heavens. His funeral was attended by a large number of people who came from miles around ... Further into the hills we go to a place called Godidi; there a dear lady, whose Christian name is No-England, opens her large mud home for the services. As we make our way to the narrow doorway we are greeted by a variety of furry and feathered friends! ... The members there are weak in the faith and still under the influence of some heathen customs and practices ... At Ngcingwane, some 25 miles from Butterworth, the impressive stone church stands prominently among pine trees as though translated bodily from a Scottish highland setting. Here, if it were not for the exceptional faithfulness of the women the doors of witness would long ago have been closed ... But the door is already open. Ask that grace may be given us as we seek the hidden gems in the plains, hills and valleys of friendly Transkei.

CHANGES IN THE CHURCH

Between 1970 and 1976 the Church kept on with its work among men, women and children in towns and villages. It was still a Church under the wing of another Church many thousands of miles away in Scotland, but there was a sea-change, even during the early part of this decade.

For instance at the Women's Christian Association Convention of 1970, which was held in the Knox District where Rev Bryce Taho was the minister, for the first time the main speaker was an African man, Mr Matloba, the representative in the Cape and Orange Free State of the Sunday Schools Association. His addresses were practical, biblical and so obviously tuned to the situation on the ground as far as the place and Christian nurture of children was concerned in the African culture. Mr Matloba remarked on something he had seen following the slaughtering of an ox for meat for the Convention. He had seen the men enjoying freshly roasted titbits from the entrails and 'the boys hovering around like flies, being thrown a bit occasionally, as one would throw a piece to a dog.' His first address was entitled, *The Importance of a Child!*

With the progress towards self-government in mind the Office-Bearers' Conference in September 1970 dealt with *The Church – Its Structure and Action.*

The following year, 1971, (the 25th Anniversary of the Women's Christian Association) saw the business part of the Convention being taken over by the African ladies themselves with the appointment of Mrs Lottering from Somerset East as Secretary. Mrs McCracken wrote: "For the first time in the history of our Conventions we had an African woman speak to us – she was Mrs Moloi. Mrs Moloi's home language is Zulu, which might have presented a difficulty had she not been able to address us in perfect English, it being translated into Xhosa. In a masterful, outspoken way, she dealt with her subject , *The Promise of Power for Witnessing.* In African services one can always tell by the acclamations when a message is hitting the mark, and we were left in no doubt that the Spirit of God was doing His work in the hearts of the hearers."

While much was being discussed about the indigenisation of the Church it was easy to forget the fact that already so much of the Church's work was indeed being carried out by the African office-bearers themselves. A good example of this was Elder G. Pamla who had responsibility for the small congregation at Ndevana. He lived about an hour's walk away from the church. However, once a month he undertook to preach at Kowana, a round journey of over fifty miles by bicycle.

The area in which Kowana is situated was home to a large number of people and many of them were Red people, largely or totally ignorant of the Gospel. The Evangelist Mr Bright Nkonzombi had been a great witness for Christ in the area and his death was a severe blow to the ongoing work there. His widow, Mrs Olga Nkonzombi carried on a good work among the children. An evangelistic campaign was held in this area with the help of students from the Kentane Bible School. The students covered the district, holding informal house meetings, distributing literature and conducting services in the Kowana church each evening of the campaign. As well as the church at Kowana services are held at Vivi and Nqinisa in the same area.

Vacation Bible Schools were held in some of the congregations in the Knox District. As the subject of the programme in 1970 was *Jonah*, the children were taken to East London where many of them saw the sea for the first time. "Look at the white goats!" many of them called out as they saw the foaming waves rolling in. They were impressed by the size of the sea and of the ships being unloaded in the harbour.

Two new African ministers

On 28 October 1972 the Transkei District was divided into three separate districts: Embo, Tabase and Ngcingwane and on 28 December 1972 **Mr Thyson Nkwelo** was inducted to the Tabase District. Mr Nkwelo had been a great help to Rev Huite Sliep during his ministry in Transkei and it was a real encouragement to have him ordained and inducted to a congregation in his native Transkei. In writing about the Induction, Mrs Colville said, 'Mr Nkwelo is blessed by having a wife who is keenly interested in the work of our church. She has a commanding presence and is prepared to devote herself wholeheartedly to the work, in which she was already very active.'

In 1974 the Presbytery agreed to divide the Burnshill District into two districts. The congregations at Mnyameni, Geju, Ngqumeya, Amatole Basin and Burnshill formed one district, where Albert and Pat Sliep were working before their move to Transkei and it was still known as Burnshill, and the other congregations formed a new district which came to be called the Dewar District. In January 1976 **Rev Wilfred Vumindaba** became the minister of this district.

Church and Presbytery move towards Independence

Back in 1970, Rev Bryce Taho became the Clerk to the Presbytery of Kaffraria. A Central Fund was set up by the Presbytery into which all donations from the Foreign Missions Board in Scotland were paid for the salaries of the African ministers and evangelists.

In August 1971 the Presbytery of Kaffraria formed a Committee to draw up regulations for the training of men for the ministry. The members of the Board said in their report to the General Assembly of 1971, "There are two factors which must be underlined – provision of well-trained ministers and leaders (from) among the African brothers themselves (this is the first priority) and then provision financially for the church ... Meagre as their wages are, the Bantu Christians must be trained in more realistic and responsible giving. More and more responsibility must be given to the African eldership, and, as they take over, the work of the European missionary can be phased out. But this is a long-term view, how long no one can really say."

Meanwhile, in order to keep the matter going forward, the Board asked the Presbytery of Kaffraria to give urgent consideration to the proposed changes. Among the matters which were to be considered by the Presbytery were:

1. The phasing out of evangelists (their responsibilities being taken over by Kirk Sessions);

2. The re-structuring of the Church with regard to Kirk Sessions, Presbyteries and Church Courts;

3. The relation of the missionaries to the African Church, and

Assoc Presby
+ p 236

4. The financing of the Church, which, increasingly had to be from within the African Church itself.

The growing momentum on the part of the Board to work towards the independence of the African Church was partly due to the anomalous situation of African ministers who were trained according to rules set by the Presbytery of Kaffraria and not by the Free Church of Scotland, but yet the Presbytery was a Presbytery of the Free Church of Scotland. The Board Secretary said in 1973: "The present position has become impossible from the point of view of order so the Board had to place a stay on further African ordinations and inductions to the Free Church of Scotland." This was unfortunate as Rev Wilfred Vumindaba was just about to be inducted to the Burnshill District. In the end, he was only inducted in January 1976.

The Board was, however, experiencing a major policy change. In their report to the General Assembly in Edinburgh in 1973 the Board said: "We are not interested in setting up little Free Churches of Scotland in India, Africa or Peru. Each national church has its own local history, which may not be historically relevant elsewhere, though the Christian principles involved in its history are perennially and universally valid ... Such churches will be *sister* churches of the Free Church of Scotland, rather than *daughter* churches, albeit younger sisters."

In 1973 Rev Bryce Taho was granted leave of absence to pursue degree studies.

Board and Presbytery matters

In 1974, following much discussion, the Board decided on the following course of action: "The Presbytery of Kaffraria should be re-constituted an Associate Presbytery of the Free Church of Scotland, which would be in direct consultation with the Board, would approve regulations for the training of the ministry and would ordain men to the ministry of the African church."

During the year 1975 Rev Prof James Mackintosh was to make a private visit to South Africa and he was asked by the Board to visit the mission area and make his assessment of the situation to guide delegates who might go out at a later date.

He reported to the September meeting of the Board and, among other things, he said it was a great disadvantage that the missionaries did not learn Xhosa. He did see definite potential in the work and that the Church should continue to work and witness there.

The Board drew up new regulations for the secondment of missionaries to fit the impending changes in the Church in South Africa.

Relations with the Gereformeerde Kerk of South Africa

Further moves were made by the Gereformeerde Kerk in South Africa to have closer ties with the Free Church. Some areas of co-operation were put in place. There was joint editing of the magazine *Umthombo Wamandla* (Spring of Water), and participation in the African Ministers' Pension Fund, and in delegates from the Churches attending various meetings of Church courts. And in 1979, there was real co-operation in the setting up of Dimbaza Reformed Bible School.

The Free Church just before semi-independence

African ministers*:* There were now three African ministers serving in the Church – Rev B.M. Taho was minister of the Knox District, where his grandfather Zokobe had laboured as an elder and minister, Rev Thyson Nkwelo was ordained and inducted to the Tabase District in Transkei on 28 December 1972, and Rev Wilfred Vumindaba was ordained and inducted to the Dewar District (then called Burnshill No 2) on 24 January 1976.

Districts*:* There were ten Districts, three in Transkei, four in Ciskei and three congregations in Cape Province.

In **Transkei** there was:

Tabase District: minister Rev T. Nkwelo, with one Evangelist, Mr R. Xabadiya. The congregations were Cicira, Nothando, Qabata, Tabase, Mbolompo, Ngangelizwe (Umtata) and Qunu.

Embo District: minister Rev Albert Sliep. The Evangelist was Mr N.P. Nenemba, and the congregations were Mqokelweni,

Twenka (or Upper Mqokelweni), Gqunu, Esidwadweni, Nkanini and Ntshiqo.

Ngcingwane District: The District was vacant but the interim-moderator was Rev A. Sliep. (In 1978 Rev David Fraser became interim moderator of this district). Mr O.M. Mgidi was the Evangelist. The congregations were Ngcingwane, Upper Ngcingwane, and in the Kentani area, Macibe, Godidi, Ndlambe, Nqusi, Ncerana, Butterworth (the latter three were in the planning stages).

In **Ciskei,** there were the following Districts:

Burnshill: It was vacant with Rev Vumindaba as interim-moderator. (In 1976 Rev W.D. Graham became the interim-moderator). There were three evangelists: Mr A. Makapela, Mr A. Madlokazi and Mr T. Mdledle. The congregations were Mnyameni, Geju, Ngqumeya, Burnshill and Amatole Basin.

Dewar: where the minister was Rev W.T. Vumindaba, and Mr Sydwell Matakane was the evangelist. The congregations were Whiteville (Ngcamngeni), Fort White, Gqumahashe, Melani, Ncera, Umqwashu, Welcome Rock and Tweni (Naude's Hoek).

Knox: The minister was Rev B.M. Taho and Mr M.Z. Qusheka was the Evangelist. The congregations were Knox (Xukwane), Mdisa, Mxaxo, Mngqesha, Zihlahla, Gwaba, Bulembu, Ncamngeni, Mamata and Bebula.

Mrs Colville also worked in this district among the women and girls.

Pirie: The minister was Rev A.A. Macdonald. The evangelist was Mr E. Soka, and the congregations were Jafta, Tyusha, Rankin, Zwelitsha, Ginsberg, Pirie, Ndevana, Mdantsane and Vivi, Nqinisa and Kowana at the coast.

The three congregations in the **Cape Province** were: Somerset East, (Mr C. Takayi was the Evangelist), Port Elizabeth and Cape Town (Langa Township).

Rev A.A. Macdonald was the interim-moderator of all three congregations.

While services were conducted at all the places mentioned above, some of them were preaching stations only and not yet fully fledged congregations. However it certainly illustrates the unrealistic load each minister had as far as pastoral duties were concerned. This was especially true with regard to Cape Town, Somerset East and Port Elizabeth. With very few exceptions there was an elder who had responsibility for each congregation.

Happenings in the Church

Presbytery and Session meetings tell only one side of what is happening in a Church. The other side was the real work happening on the spot.

In one village where services were beginning many of the people were used to beerdrinks on Sundays. One man thanked the church for coming and suggested that they should put up a building there to shelter them from the wind! But more seriously, he said that although many of them were heathen they were turning and they wanted their children to know better ways. The door is wide open but while we can tell them so much, how much more effectively their own people can evangelise them.

In another largely heathen village in the Knox District, some of the Christian men said to Rev Bryce Taho that they regretted they had not been Christians all their lives – "so many wasted years". Speaking about the heathen practice of sacrificing to the ancestors they said: "We have made a break completely from such doings. You can't do those things and be a Christian." This was indeed a great encouragement for politically there was a marked impetus given to the traditional beliefs and cultural practices of the people at this time; this was part and parcel of trying to give a sense of national identity to the Xhosa people of the Ciskei homeland. There was no discrimination as to which customs were good and which were bad and the effect was to enhance heathenism at the expense of Christianity (considered the white man's religion, and, therefore, alien).

A glimpse of village life

One morning we attended the installation of a village headman. A letter went like this:

All the men of the place are gathered in a horse-shoe formation by the cattle kraal of the headman-to-be. The smoke of the fire for the feast to be held after is drifting among them all. They will be kippered.

We passed a white-clad witchdoctress on the road up, her white beads on her ankles and box of tricks on her head. We edged past an ox-wagon sledge, and lots of sheep and goats. Five horses have just dandered past the car. A horseman has just arrived and there are noisy greetings. Now Lex and Michael and Catherine Qusheka with baby Elizabeth have arrived too.

We were taken into a hut. It was cool and fresh in there. A heap of newly gathered corn cobs was on the floor for winter's use, along with sacks of watermelons, a calabash shell, two little black cooking pots, stacks of bread – big round loaves baked in black cooking pots, some sleeping mats ... The ceremony began. We joined the men down by the kraal where all important business takes place and were given seats to make the fourth side of a square. The installation of the new headman was performed by the magistrate from King William's Town. As the magistrate and the Chief of the district and other headmen approached the men of the village, they shouted out. The men replied encouragingly. As they came nearer they shouted again, and so on, until they too joined the group, taking their places at a table. Then newcomers arrived, they greeted their Chief, shouting his name "Ngczizwe". He acknowledged their greeting. There were many heathen 'red' women; some look very tall and stately in their red blankets. They were cooking, or smoking their pipes.

Although it was not a Christian occasion the proceedings opened with prayer and a hymn, and closed with the Benediction, all done by one of the men. During the ceremony, some of the school children filed along singing. The Magistrate made a speech,

Assoc Mestr

announced the Headman installed, shook hands with him, and that was that.

We were taken back to the rondavel and two men came and brought a large chunk of black meat straight roasted from the fire carried in on a branch, presented it with ceremony, laid it on the branch on the floor. We later learned that this was possibly a custom usually done for the officiating priest at a sacrifice! Before the men could get their penknives out to cut up the meat a hen and some chickens came to investigate and the chickens hopped onto the meat. A dish was found and a knife and it got cut up. It still tasted very good.

Independence – Almost

In 1976 the first of two steps was taken towards complete independence – an indigenous church – the Free Church in South Africa. This was why the two delegates from the Foreign Missions Board of the Free Church of Scotland, Profs James Fraser and Clement Graham, had come out to South Africa. They had joined with all the missionaries and eleven ministers and men of the South African church for the Reformed Conference at Skogheim. Then they travelled to King William's Town and they and the churches geared themselves up for an historic meeting at Whiteville on 24 July 1976 when the new Associate (semi-autonomous) Presbytery of the Free Church in South Africa would be inaugurated.

The new Free Church in South Africa is set up

The new semi-autonomous Free Church in South Africa was set up on Saturday 24 July at a meeting in the Alexander Dewar Church at Whiteville, about fifteen miles from King William's Town. A full congregation had gathered from Cape Town in the South and Transkei in the North, and all the Ciskei congregations in between. The church bell here had been sent from Scotland in memory of Mrs Fraser of Dumbarton, mother of Rev David Fraser whose application to become a missionary was before the Missions Board back in Scotland.

It was a day of glorious winter sunshine with blue skies from dawn to dusk, although both morning and evening were cold. The hills had their quiet blue look and the veld was brown, not green. The people sat on the grass grouped mostly from the village they came from. They were getting warmed by the sun, which Africans say is 'the poor man's blanket'. Nine three-legged pots were already being set on fires at the back of the church in which the food would be cooked. It takes a long time.

The last Presbytery of the old regime was held first. The business of this meeting was to prepare the way for the main meeting of the day – the establishing of the new Free Church in South Africa and the Associate Presbytery – the new 'Presbytery of Kaffraria.' *Kaffraria* was the old name for this region – the area of the Kaffirs, which was a term used of the black people by the whites who were coming up from the Cape. Originally the name was an Arabic term for people who were non-Moslem.

Following the meeting of the 'old' Presbytery, a General Meeting of ministers, office-bearers and members of the church, was convened. The singing was hearty as is usual in Africa, and the congregation seemed to sense the importance of the occasion – the setting up of what would become their own African Free Church, independent but still affectionately attached to the Scottish Free Church. The meeting opened with devotions, welcome was extended to the two delegates from Scotland, Profs Fraser and Graham, and to the new Graham missionary family. Rev Joe McCracken was asked to begin proceedings with a short talk on his long years of experience, and Bill Graham with a short talk on his inexperience but hopes. Prof James Fraser then preached and Prof Clement Graham spoke outlining the various steps that had led to this day. A Resolution approving the Agreement followed, instituting the Free Church in South Africa as an Associate Presbytery of the Free Church of Scotland. The documents were duly signed and that meeting came to an end with singing, praying and rejoicing.

After this service of independence the ministers and office-bearers were closeted for another hour of Presbytery – the first meeting of the Presbytery of the new ***Free Church in South***

Africa. The Presbytery appointed Rev B.M. Taho as its Moderator. Associated with the Presbytery on that occasion were Profs Fraser and Graham, Rev Joe McCracken and Elder W.M. Botha of the Gereformeerde Kerk. It was agreed to ask the Foreign Missions Board to appoint Rev Joe McCracken as an Assessor to the Presbytery. The missionaries were appointed interim-moderators of the districts in which they had been serving, and all mission-aries were to serve as missionary-advisers in the new set-up.

The Significance?

Well, what was the significance of that day? The answer was given in the address by the Secretary of the Foreign Missions Board, and delegate from the Scottish Church, Prof Clement Graham. He said:

> The change of name to the Free Church in South Africa is indicative of this. Some day we hope your growth and expansion will be such as to justify the name Free Church **of** South Africa. The change of status of the Presbytery of Kaffraria is to the same purpose ... It will be free to devote all its attention to the work which lies at the very doors of your Churches here. We are not breaking but strengthening ties so that we may be more useful in the service of our Lord. May God's blessing attend as we pray to God – "Establish the work of our hand upon us, yea the work of our hands establish thou it."

The Delegates report

Profs Fraser and Graham had more information to collect. During their stay in King William's Town they visited various places in the vicinity, including Mt Coke Hospital where Dr Andrews had worked. They had also visited the congregations in Transkei. Then they left for Cape Town, visiting Somerset East and Port Elizabeth on the way. Unfortunately, because of riots they were unable to attend the Communion Service planned for the Langa congregation in Cape Town. They did, however, attend most of the second half

ℬ ·school

of the Reformed Missions Conference of the Reformed Ecumenical Synod in Cape Town before their journey back to Scotland.

In their report to the Board of their visit to the South African Mission the delegates picked up on various points in the church and political situations. They obviously felt there were too many church buildings in small villages to the exclusion of work being done in centres like Umtata, Idutywa and Butterworth in Transkei. Having fewer churches but in places where there were stronger congregations and from which outreach work could be done was one of the proposals put forward by previous delegates but which was never acted upon. The need for more African ministers was another obvious point stressed by the delegates, as was the need for the people to give them greater financial support. So the question arose of the training of prospective ministers. "There is a need also to secure that the responsibility of theological training is not entrusted exclusively to other bodies ... The institution of a Bible School would seem somewhat ambitious at this stage – but some small beginning might be made using existing church buildings."

TWO MORE NEW CHURCHES

At Mamata, Knox District, Ciskei

In chapter 9 we told the story of how Mrs Lex Colville began holding meetings in Mamata. Eventually on 20 October 1977 a new church building was opened there.

It was called the *Robert Allan Memorial Church* as much money from Australia had been donated in his memory.

On the Lord's Day following the opening over 130 people attended the church, many of them heathen women in their red blankets. Some openly responded to the challenge of the Word of God expounded from the text, "... choose you this day whom you will serve ... but as for me and my house we will serve the Lord". Joshua 24: 15.

At Macibe, Transkei, Ngcingwane District

The village of Macibe where Mr Bani Tshaka, whose story Marion Fraser has told, had had his home was the site of the first new church which was built under David Fraser's direction. He described how he embarked on an 'impossible thing, building a church for nothing, or almost.' With materials appearing from all sorts of sources, Vocational College students doing some of the skilled work, four prisoners hired as labourers, old bus seats for pews and so on, the Macibe church was erected and opened with much rejoicing – a monument to faith and ingenuity! The opening took place on 24 November 1979 in the presence of the Moderator of the General Assembly of the Free Church of Scotland that year, Rev Murdo MacRitchie and his wife and "Scottish, American, Canadian, South African, German and even English guests!" as David Fraser put it in his account of the opening. He went on to describe how "the humble people of Macibe saw such an international gathering as they had never seen before with people from Ciskei and Transkei and all the 'international' guests. They all saw the results of the toil of many months, the fruit of many prayers and sacrifices and worries, brought to blessed fulfilment". Rev MacRitchie addressed the congregation as they gathered outside for the opening ceremony which was performed by Mrs Violet Tshaka, the widow of Mr Bani Tshaka. The church at Macibe was fitted with a metal spire and as it was set on a prominent high spot it was given the appropriate name of *Kwanikhanyiso* (the place of out-shining).

The role of the women in the Xhosa Church

Meanwhile, as the men in the Presbytery of Kaffraria and in the Foreign Missions Board and General Assembly meetings in Scotland discussed and determined the future independence of the South African Free Church, the women's work just continued much as it had done for decades. As in many churches in other countries, the women's work is very strong, and the churches acknowledge that it couldn't carry on without their able help.

In the church in South Africa, the women's work was very well organised. The meetings had three tiers – the ordinary Women's Christian Association meetings which met every Thursday afternoon; the Women's Quarterly Meeting, which took place as the name suggests once a quarter, and the Annual Women's Christian Association Convention.

The Thursday Weekly Women's Christian Association meeting

The time of most meetings was roughly at three o'clock in the afternoon, though it could be held in the morning or late in the afternoon. The women would have been working all morning in the home or the fields, and so it took some time to get water and get washed and dressed, and then to walk over the fields or roads to the church. So the time of starting was somewhat elastic, but nobody minded or looked at their watches. One went more by the height of the sun in the heavens. The women who attended were usually older. The young women had children to attend to, and they would have the supper ready when their mothers-in-law returned from the meeting. All efforts to encourage the younger women to attend bore little fruit.

There were two types of dress among the ladies. Most would be wearing the black skirt, white overblouse, a wide blue collar and a blue hat. They were therefore full members of both Church and W.C.A. But some were wearing a black skirt, white blouse with no collar and a black hat or doek. They were not yet installed as members of the Association. Why? We often wondered, as they were regular attenders of the meetings, though they sat at the back of the group. We were told they 'were not ready'. They were being closely watched, and if they fell short in some way, e.g. if their husbands had made them brew beer, they were 'not ready'.

The normal weekly meetings almost took the form of the old Scottish question meeting. After singing and prayer, the one whose turn it was to lead the meeting that day would give out a text, expound on it for a little, then give a turn to any, usually most, of the other ladies to add their comments. As one was winding down, the next lady who wanted to speak would start to sing and rise up to go to the front. Everyone took up the singing. Then she would begin. Sometimes one would pray instead of preach, always preceded by singing. They were a singing people.

If anyone in the local church was in trouble – sick, or bereaved for example – the group met in her home. Before a funeral, they would sit on the mat on the floor, empathising with her in her grief. And always, all present, joined often by women from other denominations in the village, would take a turn to preach.

The Quarterly Meeting

Once a quarter, except for the quarter of the Easter Convention, all the local W.C.A.s in a District met together. Until the 1980s, they met in the afternoon, had a business meeting, a service and a meal, then preached, prayed and sang all night, taking up a collection all the while. In the morning they went home again. But with a rise in crime, and a few brushes with the 'tsotsis' of the place in which they met who wanted to steal the collection, they stopped having all night meetings and met during the day instead. Possibly another contributing factor was that most women now slept on beds at home instead of sleeping mats, and an all-night church meeting was less attractive.

During the service, new women who were now 'ready' were dressed formally in their blue and white uniforms, and were exhorted to behave as a Free Church Christian woman should. At the business meeting everything was done in a very orderly way. Biblewomen were chosen; two people were chosen to visit homes where there had been a death; arrangements were made for a 'taking out' service for a woman who had been keeping inside for a set time following a death in the home; a new secretary or treasurer was chosen if needed; how to pay for a bus to the Convention might need to be discussed; and much more. Over all there was a real and practical caring for each other. Paul would have approved.

The Annual Convention of the WCA

Once a year, and it was the highlight of the year, all the WCAs came together for a Convention. Again until the 1970s, there was only one. After that Transkei and Ciskei have had their own conventions for two years, and then on the third year they all meet together – in Transkei one time, Ciskei the next.

Here is an account of a typical Convention. This one was held in Mnyameni, in the Burnshill District, in 1977.

The men of Mnyameni built a great bonfire for the women to provide red-hot ashes for the ten black cooking pots. In the pots, bread had been already baked, and samp, rice, meat and potatoes simmered to feed the hundreds of people sitting quietly on the grass. In one of the round huts are stacked more of these homemade round loaves, and in the corner lies all that remains of an ox and six sheep.

Dusk comes early now that April has come and summer is almost over. The voices are subdued in the glow of the fire, but a little while ago the praises could have been heard clear across the valley. After all have been fed, the lanterns in the church will be lit and will hiss and splutter, the bell will clang somewhat unmusically but effectively, and folk will begin to pour, or perhaps better squeeze, into the church again. It is a source of marvel as to how many people can get on to one seat in church. Soon they begin to sing – they sing while waiting for the service to begin, while waiting to file out at the end, and at any emergency or pause during the service too – the sopranos and altos of the women blending with the deep bass of the men.

For although it is a Women's Convention, there are men here too – both wise old grey-bearded fathers and alive and enthusiastic young men from the cities – they wouldn't miss the Convention for anything. They will cheerfully preach and sing all night too. There is a great sense of order and propriety in it all. And so much inborn oratory and deep passion in the speech or prayer of a little old woman with her stick from a far away village on the top of a hill.

In the squash of people, it gets hot and thirsty, so a woman will come in with a zinc bucket full of water with a mug floating on top. She will squeeze to the side of each row through the people standing in the aisles, and will kneel down. The nearest person takes the mug and fills it, slakes her thirst and passes it on. When all that row has drunk of the water, she will rise and go to kneel at the next.

The theme of this year's Convention was 'The Christian Way of Living'. The full church listened quietly to some excellent talks on how to pray, read the Bible, get guidance, be disciplined, deal with temptation, win others and live in fellowship with each other, and service for the Lord – from African and missionary speakers.

On the Saturday morning there was a minor crisis – the three big sacks of bread flour were already finished – also the maize and samp. A truck left for the village shop on the next hill, which didn't close for Easter. There was singing coming from a hut. Another church service? No. This was a witch-doctor gathering. A young witch-doctress came out with white beads around her ankles and her 'box of tricks' carried on her head. What a contrast! How sad that such superstition which couldn't help should be so near the source of true power, but never would the two meet.

The Convention closed with a Communion Service on Sunday – Easter Sunday. Black and white, Pirie and Knox, all were one in Christ Jesus around his Table. Serving bread and wine to so many people takes time, but always someone starts to hum a psalm tune – often to Psalm 40 – and everyone takes up the melody. It is one of the most moving sounds in the world. Someone reminded us all at the end, of the words of Jesus on 'the last great day of the feast' – *If any man thirst, let him come unto me and drink.* So in the strength of that water of life, each went to her own home again.

The Visit of Rev & Mrs MacRitchie, Moderator 1979

From 26 October to 2 December 1979, Rev Murdo MacRitchie, minister of Stornoway Free Church and Moderator of the General Assembly of that year, visited the South African Mission along with his wife. The visit turned out to be a real success with the visitors keen to participate to the full in as many events as were arranged for them, including the opening of the new church at Macibe, a Conference for Office-bearers and their wives at Dimbaza Bible School, the laying of the foundation stone of the church building in Cape Town and special services in Transkei and Ciskei and much else besides. They brought real encouragement wherever they went. The Presbytery of Kaffraria wrote to thank the Board for their visit and the happy memories it had left with all who had come in contact with them. On their return to Lewis, Mr MacRitchie promoted the work being done in the African Church and raised several thousands of pounds for that work during many meetings he addressed throughout the Island of Lewis.

Shortly before this visit an inaugural meeting of the Free Church Teachers' Association took place at Mxaxo. There were many good teachers in the schools and it was good for them to get together as there were difficult times ahead for them all.

CHANGES IN THE POLITICAL SITUATION

While the women were meeting together regularly, and the men were preaching and having Presbyteries, and the people were sowing and hoeing and living Christian lives at home or at work, in the background the political situation was changing.

Apartheid was practised in full force during the 1970s. At this time it was supported by many South African white church leaders, but it brought international disapproval on the country and the white churches. Laws were required to classify people racially – black, white, coloured, Chinese, Indian etc. Beaches were portioned out in this way, with the best sandy beach reserved for whites and the rocky bit at the end for blacks. Black people were not allowed officially to stay with whites even as guests, and vice versa. There were separate amenities and accommodation, and employment was racially unfair, some jobs being reserved for whites only. By the end of this decade, some of the notices in Post Offices and banks and on park benches were beginning to come down and there was more integration, but the pass laws which required blacks to show their employment pass at all times were still in force. Black homelands were being set up, so that blacks from the cities who had originally come from these parts of the country could be sent back if they were unemployed or retired. Only whites had the vote. There was virtually unlimited power with the police and courts to enforce all this and many blacks were imprisoned without trial, tortured and treated brutally. Little wonder there was simmering resentment which came to the fore at times during this decade.

Mass protests

The spirit of mass protest had seemed dormant in the 1960s, but it erupted in the 1970s. On 16 June 1976, 15,000 school children gathered in Soweto to protest against the ruling that Afrikaans as well as English was to be taught in all schools. Pupils and teachers pled with the authorities to no effect. The people did not like being taught in the 'language of the oppressor'. Suddenly, the police opened fire on the students, killing 13 year old Hector Pieterson and others. The students retaliated with sticks and stones. Two white men were stoned to death, and many black school students and school children were killed or wounded. It was a turning point. Life was never the same again. The date of 16 June was called 'Soweto Day' and was kept as a holiday in remembrance of this occasion. Riots and violence erupted all across the country. Mass funerals became rallying points. In our mission areas schools were set on fire, and Fort Hare University was set on fire, closed down, and re-opened many times. In Transkei 350 pupils were detained because they were rioting *against* Independence. They didn't want to be a tiny independent state, they wanted to be fully South African. In Alice primary school and many others the head-master's room was torched in an arson attempt. In Port Elizabeth, the big city location where Rev Angus Alex Macdonald looked after our congregation, white men's cars were being attacked, and no whites were allowed in the Cape Town townships so he put off his visits there at that time.

The ANC, (the African National Congress), the PAC, (the Pan African Congress) and the Communist Party were all banned, so the Black People's Convention tried to take their place as a voice for the Blacks but this too was soon to be stamped out. The BPC advocated the philosophy of Black Consciousness, in many ways similar to the views advocated by the Black Power movement in the USA. They wanted a non-racial society, but they did not want any white involvement in making this a reality. Heading the movement in South Africa was Steve Biko. Biko belonged to the Ginsberg Location in King William's Town. He had his offices in the building which now houses the Administration Offices of Dumisani Theological Institute. Without entering into a critique of the movement or of Biko himself, the events surrounding his eventual arrest and death in detention have to be utterly condemned. As was stated by the Truth and Reconciliation Commission, "his death was a gross human rights' violation". Biko died on 12 September 1977 and his funeral took place in King William's Town, attended by thousands but within some of the most stringent (if largely unseen) security measures mounted at that time. It passed off without incident in very heavy rain. His death, especially the manner of it, sent shock waves across the world and turned Steve Biko (who was 31years old) into an international 'symbol' of the struggle against apartheid. Throughout South Africa tensions were mounting and riots at schools and other places against Government institutions increased.

Yet in 'our' villages, we felt perfectly safe and met with almost unbroken friendliness and courtesy.

The Mission's Response

The missionaries were allowed into the country on work permits which required to be regularly renewed until they became permanent residents. Such permits could be withdrawn at any time, especially if missionaries became involved in political activities. They were watched closely for any overt political involvement. If there was anything of this nature in preaching or in support for the anti-apartheid movements, then their visa was simply not renewed and that was the end of their ministry in the South African mission. That was the choice at the time, and the Board advised all its members just not to get involved in politics.

The missionaries were warned by the people themselves to adhere to this also – "Umfundisi, no preaching of politics in the pulpit. We are of different (black) political allegiances in the congregations anyway and it is better to keep away from politics." So the missionaries kept their heads below the parapet and concentrated on building up the churches in the faith, in the meantime. In our own churches, there was complete integration from the beginning. Black and white sat together, ate together, worshipped and prayed together. This was unusual at the time in the rest of the South African Christian world. However we could not live in each other's areas. Eventually, in the 1980s, it was the churches which played a leading role in the anti-apartheid struggle.

The Independence of Transkei

One of the bones of contention of the apartheid period was the creation of several independent 'homelands'. On 26 October 1976 Transkei celebrated its Independence. The Presbytery which had met in Transkei on 18 September agreed to send appropriate messages to both the President of Transkei and his Prime Minister. The more militant black youth felt they wanted a non-racial country of South Africa, not small independent worthless countries. But the folk living in these states were mainly very happy to feel that they had a degree of independence from the white apartheid government next door. However, they were really not so independent in reality. But the mood on the day of independence was euphoric.

Albert Sliep wrote from Umtata, the capital, at the time:

> Many people trembled with fear at the thought of the 'day', because just before that time there had been a lot of trouble and arson in other parts of South Africa. Although there had been a few incidents in the Transkei, nothing very serious had taken place.

Many people gathered for prayer for the Transkei. We even prayed that the bottle-stores would be closed over Independence time. That prayer was answered. Umtata was 'dry' over Independence! In fact all our prayers were answered because the Transkei had a very peaceful Independence time with Black and White co-operating in everything. There was a very friendly spirit among all the thousands of people who had gathered at the Independence Stadium. Everything went off well without any hitches. Even the rain did not dampen our spirits. It rained for an hour in the beginning of the evening but during the actual Independence ceremonies, which was a very impressive time, the weather was perfect. The following evening was also a very pleasant one when we watched various magnificent gymnastic displays and great fire-works.

So now we no longer live in South Africa but in this new country, Transkei ... Please pray for Transkei. Doors are wide open for the Gospel.

DIMBAZA REFORMED BIBLE SCHOOL

At last, during this decade of change, the Free Church did get a Bible School of its own in which, eventually, to train pastors – but the development of this needs a chapter of its own.

ON REFLECTION

- This was a decade of change – changing workers, changes coming in the church, changes emerging in the political and social situation in the country; a demanding decade and heavy burdens had to be carried by too few people. Yet there was much for which to give thanks to God.

- The Report of the Delegates from the Missions Board in 1976 was ignored in one of its most important points (which echoed what previous Delegates had said) that there were too many small congregations in scattered communities to the exclusion of work in the major centres such as Umtata, Idutywa and Butterworth, from which evangelism and church planting work should emanate.

- No recognition was given to African ministers ordained by the Presbytery of Kaffraria as ministers of the Free Church of Scotland although such they were because the Presbytery was a Presbytery of the Free Church of Scotland. The whole business of the Presbytery's situation should have been resolved at the very beginning by not having the Presbytery of Kaffraria as an integral part of the Free Church of Scotland.

11

Dimbaza Reformed Bible School

Over and over again the need was stressed for a bible school to train men for the Free Church ministry in South Africa. In February 1979 this Bible School was opened, though not at first to tackle the full training of men for the ministry. It happened in this way.

Let's begin at the very beginning

At the meeting at Whiteville on July 24, 1976 to set up a semi-independent Free Church there was present an elder from the Gereformeerde Kerk, Dr W. (Barry) Botha. He was most inter-ested in what he heard expressed about the possibility of the Free Church starting a bible school. His own church had had the same idea. In fact they had the promise of land in Dimbaza on which they had intended to build a bible school but had given up that idea in favour of a small church. So Barry introduced himself, extended a welcome, his Church revised their ideas and discussions began. They now felt it would be a good idea to have a joint bible school with the Free Church – in a building which could be used for the Xhosa Gereformeerde Kerk services on Sundays. On 3 October 1977 a joint meeting of the local Gere-formeerde Kerk Missions Committee and a Special Committee of the Free Church in South Africa met 'to further plans for the establishment of a Bible School to be run as a joint venture by the participating Churches'. They discussed building plans, established a Committee to draw up a doctrinal basis for the operation of the proposed school, drew up a Form of Agreement regarding the functioning of the school and recommended Governors and Trustees for the oversight and finances of the school. An outline programme of the school's activities was presented and a committee appointed to oversee the courses to be run by the school. Rev W.D. Graham was appointed Instructor *ad interim* of the school's programme and later as Principal of the Bible School. The name of the school was to be **Dimbaza Reformed Bible School.** So they had covered a long distance in a short time.

In Scotland, the Foreign Missions Board said this news was possibly one of the most encouraging communications they had received in years. They were in agreement with all the measures being taken and encouraged all the missionaries to co-operate in the venture.

First steps

The project was launched on 27 March 1978 in the Gereformeerde Kerk of East London. Representatives of the four participating bodies in the Bible School – the Free Church in Southern Africa, the (Xhosa) Gereformeerde Kerk eMonti, the Free Church of Scotland (Foreign Missions Board) and the Gereformeerde Kerk East London – signed a Memorandum of Agreement. A Trust Fund was established with three Trustees, (although the role of the Trustees fell away fairly soon). Mr L.M. Jacobsz was appointed Treasurer, and remains so to this day! Reporters from the local newspaper attended this meeting and the photograph of the signing of the document setting up the Bible School appeared in the local paper, the *Daily Dispatch.*

The doctrinal basis of the school was, and continues to be at Dimbaza's successor, Dumisani, the Subordinate Standards of the Gereformeerde Kerk and the Free Church – The Belgic Confession, the Heidelberg Catechism, the Canons of Dort – and the Westminster Confession of Faith.

To get advice and to see what happened in other Reformed Bible Schools visits were undertaken to Potchefstroom, Pretoria, Hammanskraal and Johannesburg.

About Dimbaza

The name 'Dimbaza' was notorious throughout the Western world due to a film *'Last Grave in Dimbaza'* which exposed the apartheid policy of the South African government. The Government was determined to remove Black people from certain areas which were to be 'White only' and therefore many Black people of Xhosa origin were almost literally dumped in this place with no facilities and no family connections with most of the surrounding areas. Many of them didn't even speak Xhosa, but Afrikaans. Gradually housing and amenities improved and a large industrial estate was established on the edge of the township where factories made rubber boots, furniture, digital watches and such like, giving employment to many of the people in Dimbaza and the surrounding district. Dimbaza was about twelve miles from King William's Town on the Alice road, and was a fairly central location for Free Church people from the villages, although when the political situation became volatile the village people were afraid to come there.

So it was into a dusty road of this new town that the Dimbaza Reformed Bible School made its appearance. There was a factory in Keiskammahoek, a further half-hour away, which made basic wooden houses – a living room, kitchen and two bedrooms. Four of these houses put together under one roof formed a good Bible School. The 'two houses' in the middle had no room partitions so this made a big hall for use as a church building for the Gereformeerde people on Sundays and a good gathering place for conferences and meetings for the Bible School the rest of the time. The rooms of the 'houses' at either end were used as kitchen, storeroom, study, a small office for the typist and a library in which two translators and correctors worked.

Opening Day 1

By February 1979 everything was ready for opening. The Bible School was painted cream with a red zinc roof. Chairs were bought, and desks, bookcases, curtains and rugs, pots and pans, crockery and mugs, paper and typewriters. There were two main opening events.

On Friday 16 February there was a gathering of representatives from various churches who were interested in the ministry of the Bible School and of the Reformed faith in an African context. They came from faraway Potchefstroom and Hammanskraal, and from places nearer Dimbaza like Fort Hare University, as well as our own churches in the area. Prof B.J. Van der Walt of Potchefstroom had been a real encourager of the whole venture from the beginning and remained so for many years. He gave the inaugural lecture on that opening day.

Opening Day 2

Saturday 24 February was a hot and humid midsummer's day, only a little relieved by a later thunderstorm. The Bible School was officially opened with a Service of Thanksgiving which a large congregation of church people and friends both Black and White attended. Dimbaza could be a confusing place to get about if you didn't know your way so people holding arrows pointing to the Bible School were stationed at various junctions along the way. The last arrow was held by an elderly evangelist named Mr Soka, and his arrow was found to be pointing heavenwards! The sermon on that day was given by Rev David Fraser, Butterworth, Transkei, who was Moderator of the Presbytery of the Free Church in South Africa at that time. So, with the Bible School now officially up and running, everyone enjoyed a good meal before making their way home.

PERSONNEL

Rev Bryce Taho

Rev Bryce Taho was a wonderful first colleague in the Bible School. He was a quiet, wise man, declared 'brilliant' in interpretation. He was a most meticulous translator from English into Xhosa, and he knew his Xhosa people and their culture like few others. Although minister of the Knox District, he agreed to throw his weight into the work of the Bible School as lecturer, translator and writer of Correspondence Courses, and the hope was that he would be its Principal one day. He was a great help in the lectures and teaching in the many 'Teaching Days' or conferences held after the opening of the Bible School.

On April 28 1979, a few weeks after the Bible School opened, he graduated B.A. from Fort Hare University. When the Grahams went on home leave for three months from May to August that year, he undertook to look after the Bible School, working on translation and writing etc. However not long afterwards Rev Taho took a job with the Ciskei Government. He went on to do very well there and in subsequent jobs on Radio Xhosa, and as chaplain to the Defence Forces, he was known as a man of strict Christian principle and excellent preacher of the Word. In later years he was able to take up District work again in the Free Church areas and after retirement helped with lectures in the Bible School (Dumisani by this time).

Mr Theophilus Nocanda

Into this situation of bleak disappointment bounced one of the best colleagues anyone could have, and we came to look on him as a God-send. He was a newly retired teacher, Mr Temba Theophilus Nocanda, from the nearby village of Mdisa where he had been Principal of the school for many years. He was an elder and preacher in the Free Church, a cheery and very responsible man. He was helpful in whatever needed to be done and always keen to evangelise anyone who came his way, but he was especially good in his way of dealing with 'red' people who might be contacted.

So he took his place in Dimbaza, turning up for work each morning and setting to in translation, or helping with conferences there, speaking to passersby or dealing with some of the many callers who came to return their completed correspondence course lessons and get the next one. On one of the many days when we took the Bible School out to the people in the districts, he accompanied us, and took a full part in the programme.

His day-to-day knowledge of the Xhosa people was invaluable. He could be relied on to know what was the correct thing to do and what was not!

One day a school principal from the faraway town of Dordrecht (who was studying the Correspondence Courses) came into the Bible School. He had heard about it from Radio Xhosa, and wanted to know more. Teacher Nocanda spent a long time with him, taking him to his home, and explaining all about the Free Church and what it stood for. When the principal went back to Dordrecht, he passed on this information to a group of his friends. They had all been Roman Catholics, but were attracted by the Reformed teaching of the Free Church and the Bible School. So they extended an invitation to Bill Graham and Mr Nocanda to come up to Dordrecht (3 hours away by car) and to teach them more. When they arrived, they found an eager congregation gathered in the school, with a big 'Welcome' written on the blackboard.

This initial visit was followed by many more Teaching Days or weekends, as well as preaching and talking. Eventually at a meeting of the Presbytery on 19 June 1982 a request from 52 people from Dordrecht led to a congregation of the Free Church being established there. (Actually Mr McCracken had started a congregation in Dordrecht many years before but the people did not keep up their connection with the Free Church). In 1984 ten of the members attended the Annual W.C.A. Convention. They were thrilled and tape-recorded new psalm tunes to take back to the members who couldn't come.

At last, at the end of 1984, Mr Nocanda felt his powers were failing and the time had come for him to retire – again. This time he and his wife went back to his early roots in Whittlesea – a long way north from the Ciskei area, and we missed him sorely. In an interview before he left he was asked what he saw as the greatest need in the church at that time. His answer was, "Revival, coupled with instruction where new believers are taught the way of salvation and also taught about preserving the Lord's day for worship only (not for sport)."

Mr and Mrs Bunguza

But the Lord had his eye on the Dimbaza Bible School and when Teacher Nocanda departed, He provided a husband and wife team to translate and to help – Mr and Mrs Bunguza, both of whom were retired teachers. Mrs Bunguza had been active in translation work in the Bible School on her own since the end of 1979 when a second

Members of the Free Church Girls Christian Association

Young folk at Pirie

Food for the Convention?

Womens' Christian Association Convention at Tabase, Transkei

DIMBAZA

Signing the Agreement to set up the Dimbaza Reformed Bible School, 27th March 1978

Dimbaza Reformed Bible School, opened 24th February 1979

Bill Graham and Teacher Nocanda at Dimbaza

Mr and Mrs Bunguza translating and correcting books and courses

Book of Daily Bible Readings (in English)

Receiving Certificates Day at Dimbaza

DUMISANI

Dumisani Bible School (later Theological Institute) Opened 11th February 1987

Literature produced at Dumisani

Interior of Dumisani

Mrs Pearl Magodla at Lovedale College on its Reopening Day

A Biblewomen's Day at Dumisani

Study House, Dumisani

The first students to train for the ministry at Dumisani with Ian Glover (left) and Bill Graham

A Graduation Day at the end of the Century

Ken and Joan Cameron

*Kenny and Coleen
Macdonald*

Ian and Sandra Glover

Ian and Maryanne Wylie

David and Meg Miller

MISSIONARIES UP TO 2000 AD

Donald and Isobel Maciver

Douglas and Julia Campbell

Ronald and Morag Christie

Norman and Angela Reid

The Southern Presbytery at work

The first service in the new Free Church in Umtata, 10th December 2000

teacher was needed to cope with the translation and correction work. Now her husband was able to join her. The Bunguzas also lived quite nearby in Mngqesha, and had been staunch helpers in all the work of the congregation there. Mr Bunguza was an elder and preacher there too and Mrs Bunguza had a children's Bible Hour once a week. They, perhaps especially Mrs Bunguza, bore the brunt of the growing literature work and its need for accurate translation, and correction of correspondence courses as they went in and out.

A typist, a gardener and a caretaker-cleaner came to swell the ranks of the employees of the Bible School and it was a busy and happy place. For a time too a colporteur from the Gereformeerde Kerk came to take Christian books, Bibles and tracts around the town, factories and schools in the area. We had hoped to develop this work, but this did not happen. Perhaps the volatile political situation overtook these hopes too.

We also had **short term help** occasionally. Colin Drummond and Alasdair Macleod-Mair from Scotland and Elspeth Anderson from Australia, as well as some students on placement from the Gereformeerde Kerk Seminary in Potchefstroom came for between 1 to 6 months to help with varied work in the Bible School – collating, stapling, printing, folding, posting out, painting etc., and attending the Teaching Conferences held out in the Districts. And they also helped the other missionaries in their work as well.

ACTIVITIES OF THE BIBLE SCHOOL

Although the training of our own ministers was a long-term aspiration, in the short-term the aim was to give training to those in the Churches who were already preaching every week and teaching in the Sunday Schools and taking Women's and Girls' meetings. We did this in three ways:

1. Conferences and classes in the Bible School.

Following the opening, various short conferences and courses were held between the beginning of March and the middle of May. There were two courses for ministers and evangelists, and one for teachers who taught Religious Education, two for office-bearers and one each for young people and women. In addition a series of lectures for office-bearers was given in Transkei. Some students were coming to the Bible School for study help of one kind or another. The first lessons of the first Correspondence Course were being taken up and that work grew rapidly. In later years many more courses were held, refresher courses for ministers and evangelists, Day Conferences for office-bearers, or for Women's Groups from different denominations (sometimes ending with a cookery demonstration by Mrs Helen Macdonald), Sunday School Training Days to which teachers came from many denominations, Youth training or Choir competitions, Family Life conferences, and monthly Biblewomen's Days. The South African Free Church General Assembly sent a request to the Bible School that Bible-women should be trained there, and this became, and still is, a very interesting and worthwhile work.

On a Training Day, little groups of people would arrive as their buses came in, some quite early in the morning. First things first, so they had breakfast – a big mug of hot sweet tea and bread and jam were the favourites. Then after worship, a training session with interaction and participation from everyone, sometimes a report back on how things had gone since the last time we met, some more shared ideas and helpful books, and it was time for lunch. After good portions of meat stew, pumpkin, cabbage and potatoes and pudding there was sometimes another session or a slide show, closing worship, and then buses home to catch.

Sometimes these days were really well attended, sometimes there would be funerals in the districts or other events and we were left with lots of food and very few students. One never knew. It was best not to set hopes too high.

We held evening classes on Tuesdays in the early days but these had to be discontinued, especially when things got politically 'hot' and it was not safe to be about at night.

During 1980 Bill Graham was able to teach two double period lectures per week in Fort Hare University while the normal lecturer was on a 'sabbatical', as well as preaching at times in the evening church service there. This was an opportunity for which we were grateful, as very shortly after this the political troubles affected the University and it was closed for various periods. In addition Bill continued to look after first the Burnshill District and later the Knox District.

2. Teaching sessions out in the Districts

Because it could be a major exercise to leave home and get buses to Dimbaza, we very often took the Bible School out to the people. Up to Transkei, or down to Somerset East and Port Elizabeth, and in the nearer districts of Ciskei, we held Day Conferences or Weekend Teaching Courses for those already active in the church life of the area. These took the same form as those held in the Bible School, but the host congregation provided the food. Again, sometimes these were well attended and encouraging, sometimes not. But little by little, with the training sessions going hand in hand with literature work, people did seem to be growing in the faith and appreciating the Word of God more and living by its light.

One such encouraging Teaching Day was when we went to a faraway village in the Dewar District. It was a farm community all by itself, in the land of the monkey and the mongoose and big, big very old tortoises. We found the people all assembled, dressed in their uniforms, the big girls and boys assembled as a choir with bow ties, and the minister, Rev Vumindaba, had prepared for a Communion service as well. Some of the girls in the choir were already doing the Bible School Correspondence Courses and one was waiting for her certificate of completion of one full Course of ten lessons!

On another such day we went very early to Somerset East. Breakfast of tea and scones and jam was ready, and then Bill had a meeting with the elders and Elizabeth with the women and big girls. Then the church service and after that a youth service to help set up a Youth Fellowship and Youth Club.

3. Correspondence Courses

There was a third arm to the Bible School – the Correspondence Courses. This would be known today as 'distance learning'. After a lot of thought and comparing methods used in different Bible Schools, a system of ten lessons per Course seemed the best.

Each lesson was in the form of a separate booklet, and as the lesson went on responses had to be written in the book after each important statement or block of statements. This was followed by a restatement of the response so that the truth being emphasised was clearly stated. Along with each lesson booklet there was a question paper which had to be completed and sent to the School to be corrected and then the following lesson booklet was posted out. Along with each one was a sign-up paper for any friends who wanted to study the Courses themselves. After ten lessons had been successfully completed a certificate was posted to the student. The hope was that the sets of ten booklets would form a tiny library which could be referred to again and again. Then the student was encouraged to begin another full Course of ten lessons.

The courses were available in Xhosa and English.

Eventually these were the ten-lesson Courses which could be studied:

1. Know Your Bible
2. Know the Way of Salvation
3. Know the Doctrines of God's grace
4. Know the book of Paul to the Romans
5. Know the letter of Paul to the Thessalonians

These Correspondence Courses went in and out in hundreds. Some of them were studied by ordinary men and women by paraffin lamps on the table at night, some went to men in the mines, some to senior school children, but by far the most enthusiastic students were prisoners, all over Southern Africa. Sometimes complaints would be received that one prisoner had pinched the communal Bible and was sleeping with it under his pillow. Sometimes we were warned to be careful in sending Bibles requested by prisoners as Bible paper made very good cigarette paper!

Students often sent letters in with their returned lessons asking questions which were bothering them. It became quite a ministry just answering these.

Sipho

The most poignant letter, which came one day in with a completed lesson, was this:

"Don't send me any more lessons."

These words were received one day in a letter from a man we will call 'Sipho'.

He was a prisoner in one of the prisons in which we have many Correspondence Course students and he became one of them.

As Sipho began to study and to read Gospel literature we sent, the Lord truly worked in his heart. He used to write us long letters – often these would be full of Scripture and showing that a real work of grace had taken place in his heart. There was evidence of real repentance for the crime he had committed and a deep concern for his own family.

Sipho was transferred to a prison not very far from Dimbaza. And it was from that prison that he wrote the words, "Don't send me any more lessons, for," he said, "I have my date now." Very soon we learned what that meant.

Sipho was a murderer. One could only be appalled at the crime he had committed. But one could only marvel too at the grace which had come to touch this man's heart and to bring him to repentance and to seek forgiveness in Christ. When Sipho found that grace he did not keep the news to himself. The change in his life was evident to all. Another prisoner wrote asking if he too could receive what this man had found through the Gospel. Sipho was to be executed for his crime.

Then came that fateful letter. With it he enclosed R1 (50p), saying "to help the work of the Bible School. Thank you for all you have done for me. Please pray for my parents."

We wept for this young man – and yet for him this ending was to be much better than the life he had led.

One day the prison chaplain walked into the Bible School in Dimbaza. He said, "I thought you would like to know how Sipho died." He said he had been with the prisoners early on the morning of their execution (there were three of them). Their worry was that they had not confessed every sin. The two other men to be executed along with Sipho had also confessed their sins and trusted in Christ. Then they wanted to sing. So all three went to their deaths we believe as Christians, singing praise to God for His grace to them.

And a sequel

The village to which Sipho belonged, and where his parents lived, has had a Christian witness for a very long time. His parents were professing Christians. But Satan had been busy in that place too. Some weeks after Sipho's execution, a Christian Students' Mission went to work in the village. On the opening night of their campaign a young woman was brought into the meeting. Her friends said she was possessed of a devil, and this indeed proved to be the case. They asked the students to cast out the evil spirit. The students prayed for this young woman that, in the name of Jesus, she would be freed from this demon possession. They heard the demon speak. It said it would pull down their meeting tent. But in the power of Christ, the demon was cast out of the woman.

One or two nights later a gale force wind sprung up and the large meeting tent was indeed blown down. The very heavy metal poles, which were the centre supports of the tent, were snapped in two. Three students always slept in the tent to guard it. They usually slept on the left side. That night they had changed their bedding to the right side of the tent. Those great poles fell on the spot on the left where the students had slept on previous nights. Next day they took the poles to King William's Town where a Christian man welded them together without taking payment, and soon the tent was erected again. That night and during the remainder of the mission crowds from the village came to hear the Word of God, through what God had done for that demon-possessed woman.

Many people responded to Sipho's plea that we should pray for his parents. Was all this an answer to those prayers? So often Satan overplays his hand.

LITERATURE WORK

In those three ways the Bible School set out to give training to those both in and out of the churches, but especially to those who were already preachers or teachers of the Word of God.

But there was another aspect of the Bible School work and it became more and more prominent, especially when the political unrest made it uncomfortable for people from other villages to come into Dimbaza. This was the printing and distribution of various types of Christian literature. Although people could not come to be trained, training books and preaching helps could make their way to them anywhere. Actually, the literature work began even before the Bible School was formed. After investigation, we found that there was very little Christian literature already in Xhosa except the Bible and the Pilgrim's Progress. The Bible was in an older form and in small writing and was quite difficult to understand, and there was obviously a great need for help in opening up the precious message of the Bible to the people.

Daily Notes

For this reason we began by preparing books of quarterly Daily Readings, which covered the Bible in three years, with explanatory notes and a prayer or thought for the day. They were called **'Isondlo Somphefumlo'** which means 'Food for the Soul'. In English they were called **'Living Word'**, and in Afrikaans, **'Lewende Woord'.** We wrote it in English, had it translated and checked in Xhosa, and later in Afrikaans when there was a demand for this. At first we printed them at home, but quite soon we found a printer in East London who printed the pages for us at a very competitive price, and for years Mr Cooper was a real friend to the Bible School. After the Bible School was opened and the work became better known, other churches, and one Roman Catholic priest, gave orders for copies of the Notes. Afrikaans speaking churches and schools wanted them in their language and sometimes we were collating and stapling about 2000 copies each quarter of Xhosa, Afrikaans and English Notes. An architect friend made beautiful black and white drawings for the books, and later other friends with artistic talent (from as far afield as Scotland and Peru) supplied excellent drawings too.

Weekly Bible Studies

Along with the Daily Notes, we produced Weekly Bible Studies by taking one of the daily notes or a theme from each week and making it into a full Bible Study, which could be used by the Women's Christian Association groups. These groups met in every church in most denominations each Thursday. Members took it in turns to lead the meeting. We heard tales of how she might just open the psalm book (because the Bible was 'too difficult') where it happened to open and preach extempore from that place. But with no training or Christian books to help her, she couldn't always bring an accurate or helpful message.

At first using helps to lead the meetings or to read the Bible at home was an innovation too much, and we would find all the books under the shelf in the pulpit unused! But gradually this changed and the Thursday meetings were feeding the people's souls much more because the leaders had something to say. Preachers were also using the Studies at times as sermons on Sundays, and some were used in sermons on national Radio Xhosa. As time went on the studies were collected together into books e.g. "David and his Psalms", "The life and letters of Peter", "People who Prayed", "Daniel", "Marriage", and finally 100 Bible Studies divided into themes to be used when visiting the sick or bereaved people, for a time of danger, for encouragement, or themes from the Old Testament and the life of Jesus.

Other Books

Many other books followed over the years in Dimbaza.

Books for office-bearers included a book of basic doctrine called "Understanding the Christian Faith", (in Xhosa: *"Ukuqonondisa Inkolo yobuKrestu"*) for use by elders who taught candidates before they were admitted to membership; a book of Bible Themes: *"Iingongoma zeBhayibhile"* which was a skeleton Systematic Theology in the form of a topical Concordance designed to help preachers find the Biblical references for all the main doctrines of Scripture; a book on "Marriage and the Christian Home" (in Xhosa: ***"Umtshato neKhaya lamaKristu"***) which proved to be very popular – indeed it was serialised more than once on Radio Xhosa. Rev Nelson Mpayipeli helped us with this book, especially in the chapter on whether boys should go 'to the forest' (for circumcision, a rite of passage from youth to manhood). Rev Bryce Taho also helped with advice in our various books.

There were **classic books** on the Christian faith, which had been reduced to basic English for easy translation into other languages.

Then there were books of lessons for **Youth**, and later a whole series of **Sunday School Teaching Lessons** spanning four years, with pictures to colour in.

Evangelistic tracts were produced and distributed, and one found its way into each correspondence course as it was returned corrected to its owner.

One little red book ***"Molo",*** which means 'Hello' in Xhosa, was published in tens of thousands. Because of donations for its printing we were able to put boxes of these books into clinic and hospital waiting rooms to be taken away free. It told the story of two men in a hospital waiting room chatting while waiting to see the nurse, and the Gospel story of sin and salvation was woven into it. On hospital visitation we used to take these books to give away and it was gratifying to turn round at the door on the way out and see each black head above a white bedcover engrossed in studying this little red book! One travelling clinic nurse paid for 10,000 of these books to be printed and she took them to distribute wherever she went. Only the 'Day' will declare if any really put their trust in Christ after reading 'Molo'.

The Gereformeerde Kerk had a Xhosa magazine "***Umthombo Wamandla"*** (Spring of Water). After some time we were asked to take over the publication of this magazine, and in it we were able to have a round-up of church news, sermon outlines, a children's page with story and puzzles, book reviews, and sometimes recipes!

Imvo *newspaper*

A quite unusual series of contacts led to the writing of an article each week for the Black newspaper *Imvo*. The paper had a circulation of about half a million and had a Christian editor for some time. He had started asking his readers to write to the paper if they had requests for prayer or matters for which they wished to express their thanks to God. The response was almost overwhelming so the Editor asked us to take the letters each week, to pray over the many requests and then to write an article dealing with some of the problems raised by the letter-writers. The articles were written under the pseudonym *Mncedisi* (the helper) and they continued for as long as that particular Editor was in place. The memory of some of the matters raised in the hundreds of letters we prayed over will remain with us for ever. One in particular we could never forget was from a man in Paarl, near Cape Town; an ordinary Black man who must have thought much before he would put pen to paper and write to a newspaper. "Please pray that my boss will treat me like a human being," he wrote. We pray the Lord granted his request.

Three Year Course in Christian Studies

This course was designed to help those who were preaching on a regular basis. For a time the Free Church in South Africa considered appointing part-time ministers, such as teachers or other educated people, and the three-year course was considered helpful for training such men. The course was conducted by correspondence and was 'pitched' at a higher level than the other Correspondence Courses and also incorporated some of the 'Christian Classics' mentioned above. Over time up to about 50 people were studying this course but eventually it was overtaken by the full-time classes which began in the next phase of the Bible School's life.

HOW WAS ALL THIS FINANCED?

The Free Church in Scotland paid the salary of Bill as Principal and extra money was also sent by the Foreign Missions Board to help with the salary of the Xhosa typist. The Gereformeerde Kerk gave money too, as well as providing the land on which the Bible School was built. Once a year every congregation of the Gereformeerde Kerk received a letter from the Missions Committee of the Gereformeerde Kerk East London asking for financial support for the Bible School and several congregations responded with generous donations.

For this we were very grateful, and also to the Presbyterian Church of Eastern Australia (from which Lex Colville and Dr and Mrs Andrews had come), to the Evangelical Presbyterian Church of Ireland, to the Reformed Congregation at Edmonton, Canada, *l* and to many other good friends, rich and poor.

Back at the start of the Bible School in 1979 the ladies of the W.F.M.A. in Scotland made it their project. And on July 9 1986 we had a meeting in the School attended by about 90 people and the special guests were Rev Prof Douglas Macmillan and his wife Mary. During this meeting Mary handed over another gift from the W.F.M.A. in Scotland – R15, 000 (£4,000) and more to come. This was for the refurbishment of the Bible School kitchen. A red letter day indeed!

'The cattle on a thousand hills'

Yet nevertheless there were times when money was in very short supply.

In Psalm 50 verse 10 the Lord says, "The cattle on a thousand hills are mine." At these times we cried out to the Lord, "Please, Lord, won't You sell one of your beasts?" And we were **never** disappointed. Sometimes it was a beast in Canada he sold for us, sometimes in Scotland!

On one occasion we had a delegate from the Board staying with us. After a few days he went up to Transkei to visit the mission there. While he was there, we had a phone call from our good friend Mr Cooper, the printer in East London, to say he was retiring. This was a body blow, as we knew we could never afford to have our literature printed at the going commercial rate. Depression! But, we said, if the Lord wants the work to continue, he will send the means. Back from Transkei came the delegate, and we told him our story. "Oh," he said, "I forgot. The young people of the church in Scotland told me to look for a project for them for the next year. I think there will be about £5000." This was a fortune in South African terms and our difficulties were solved. We were able to buy printing equipment in East London, and, as Dimbaza was too dusty, from then on we set up the end of the corridor in our house in King William's Town as a printing room and did our own printing. For this we hired the help of a young man named Ebenezer (was this appropriate, since his name means 'Hitherto hath the Lord helped us'?) The table tennis table in the garage became an excellent place to collate all the pages, and many times our children and their friends went round and round this table collating the pages when we had an extra big printing job on hand!

On another occasion we returned late on a Sunday afternoon from being out in the district churches to find a bicycle propped up in our sitting-room. It bore a note which said that this bicycle was to be used in any way we liked for the Bible School and enclosed was an envelope with money in it. For a long time we wondered who our anonymous donor was, but we were very grateful to him. One day, in a roundabout way, we thought we knew – he was a young student away at university, and he was having to walk everywhere there because, said his mother, "his bicycle had mysteriously disappeared!"

So many times we proved that the Lord knows and supplies our need according to his riches in Christ Jesus.

Why move away from Dimbaza?

Eventually, in the mid-1980s, Dimbaza began to get a little hot for comfort – politically. On some days, a high-ranking policeman used to phone us to say to stay at home today – 'they are shooting' or 'they are burning'. One day someone passed by the Bible School and said 'We are making toast today' – referring possibly to the custom of the time of 'necklacing' some unfortunate – by placing a tyre around their neck and setting fire to them. Who was to be the toast that day? One day the cleaner asked Bill to go home as they were burning the school up the road and she feared for him and for her. Day conferences had almost stopped in the Bible School as our people from the villages feared to come into Dimbaza where they were not known. They much preferred to be in King William's Town.

We began to wonder if the Bible School would not be more useful if it were located in King itself? The town was a hub from, and to which, all roads led. If we could get somewhere down near the bus and taxi ranks, that would be good. There was a little Anglican church down in Leopold Street. Was it still in use? But it was not for sale ...

The Lord knew ... so watch this space!

ON REFLECTION

Looking back one can see so clearly the Lord's hand in bringing together the vision of the Free Church and the Gereformeerde Kerk in the formation of the Bible School. While the Free Church provided the staff and were involved in most of the day-to-day running of Dimbaza, the Gereformeerde Kerk provided the location and much financial and practical help

It also became obvious that it was the 'right' time to start Correspondence Courses of the type we produced and the other literature as so many people used them and found them helpful over the next few years.

Dimbaza was a good place for the Bible School to be in its early days as it would not have been possible for such a venture to be located in King William's Town due to political restrictions at that time.

Independence 1980–1989

CHURCH ACTIVITIES IN THE EIGHTIES

The Church becomes fully independent

Probably the biggest event in the history of the Free Church in South Africa was its full independence which came about on 9 July 1983. There were other events in church and missionary life which were momentous too in their own way, but everything was different after 9 July. Strong links with the Free Church of Scotland were to remain, the Board assured the South African Church of its continued commitment to the work there, and the missionary staff were also to remain - as seconded personnel – but the Africans were to take the lead, the missionaries to help.

A Form of Agreement between the Free Church of Scotland and the Free Church in Southern Africa was agreed by the Board at their meeting of April 1981.

In February 1983, the Board said that the Free Church of Scotland would give "what help she can to help the African Church reach the goals of spiritual growth and financial independence". They also said that they would be happy to help with the travelling expenses of African ministers to enable them to visit all parts of their Districts more regularly, and this the Board did.

So a committee of Presbytery met at Ibika, Transkei, on 19 March 1983. The Board's letter with the draft Agreement for Independence was to hand for this meeting and was agreed to with only slight adjustments. The Presbytery set out its own proposals for the structure of the Church after Independence. The main proposals were the creating of two Presbyteries, a General Assembly which would meet every year in May, starting on Ascension Day and closing not later than noon on the Saturday following, Commissions, and the various Committees required to facilitate the business of the Church throughout the year. All members of the two Presbyteries, which were to be called the Transkei Presbytery and the Southern Presbytery, were to be members of the General Assembly.

The Service of Independence

An Office-Bearers' Conference was arranged in Dimbaza Bible School to take place for two days before the Independence Service, on 7 and 8 July 1983. Two delegates from Scotland had arrived and were present. Two Free Church of Southern Africa (FCSA) delegates came from Cape Town, three from Somerset East, three from Dordrecht and the rest from Transkei and Ciskei - 37 men altogether. The Scottish delegates were Rev Prof A.C. Boyd, Secretary of the Board, and Rev John Macleod, Moderator of the 1983 Free Church of Scotland Assembly. The Board suggested that when Prof Boyd was in South Africa he should meet with the African ministers on their own to hear their views on missionary involvement in the church and on the political situation.

Then, still in Dimbaza, on 9 July, under beautiful clear skies, came the day of the Inauguration of the Free Church in Southern Africa as an independent church, and its first Assembly. Eighty people gathered in the big hall of the Bible School. First a general meeting of the Church approved the terms of the new agreement with the Free Church of Scotland and the calling of the first General Assembly of the Free Church in Southern Africa. (It was called 'Southern' at this stage because South Africa was a separate state from the homelands of Transkei and Ciskei. After the homelands were disbanded following the General Election of 1994 the name reverted to the Free Church in **South** Africa). Rev David Fraser was appointed to occupy the Chair and constitute the General Assembly.

The Assembly's first item of business was to elect its Moderator and "with warm enthusiasm", to quote Prof Boyd, appointed the

Rev Bryce M. Taho. It then appointed Rev Albert Sliep as Senior Clerk of the Assembly and Rev Nelson Mpayipeli as Junior Clerk.

The Forms of Agreement between the Churches were signed by Rev Prof A.C. Boyd and Rev John Macleod, and by Rev B.M. Taho and Rev Nelson Mpayipeli on behalf of both Churches. So at last the apron strings had been untied and the beloved child of many prayers was released to walk alone.

Prof Archie Boyd reports

Prof Boyd wrote feelingly and understandingly of the pressures and problems faced by the young independent Church. At that time there was a particularly bad drought – cattle and oxen had died and crops failed completely. When the drought eventually broke the changes it forced upon rural people especially were long lasting. Cement blocks began to replace mud and wattle for building, and stoves for cooking instead of dung fires. Many people stopped looking on cattle as their wealth and banked what money they had instead.

In 1980 a sum of R12000 (about £8000 at that time) had been received from a Canadian Christian for a relief fund. A Committee under Rev Joseph McCracken was set up to give grants within the amount available each year. The Fund was named *The Sarah Shields Bequest* Fund after the donor. This fund helped many in dire poverty over the years. A few months after Prof Boyd's return to Scotland the Foreign Missions Board sent £1000 from the Free Church Disaster Fund to help those affected by the drought. Prof Boyd said:

> For five weeks in June and July I had the privilege of visiting the Free Church in Southern Africa, worshipping with her and meeting and discussing with her pastors and people her progress and her problems. We had heard about the drought and we knew that the Transkei and Ciskei were suffering. To see it was a different thing, to see it and its effects was to bring it all home in a different way ...

Our sister Church in Southern Africa finds herself working and witnessing in the midst of an enormously tense and complex situation, socially, politically and economically. While the majority of the church people live in either Transkei or Ciskei a considerable number live in South Africa itself but, of course, in the segregated black locations. Under South African rule, apartheid; under homeland governments, no apartheid, and the Free Church straddles both.

Steady work

Throughout the decade, Presbyteries and General Assemblies, Committees and Commissions met regularly, and the work of the young church went on apace.

In 1981 the Burnshill District held a week of special meetings in which ministers and missionaries of several districts took part. The first day was sunny and after a morning of visits in the community a children's meeting in the afternoon brought the whole local school in attendance, teachers and all! The next and following days were wet and stormy, and meeting attendances were disappointing. 'Why?' Then we realised that everyone was at home sheltering from the storm instead of working out in the fields, and so a great time of visitation followed, with good meetings held in the church at nights at Mnyameni. Several professed conversion and the people were thrilled with the joy of evangelising. A joint Communion service which included baptisms and restorations of backslidden members followed on the Sunday. That was just one among many efforts in the various districts of the Transkei and Ciskei.

The second General Assembly of the Church in 1984 was held in Ibika Church, Butterworth and was addressed by the Transkei Minister of Education, Mr Bubu. A Transkei newspaper reported on his speech. It said: "Mr Bubu commended the Free Church for its approach to the dissemination of the Word of God in such a manner that they completely disregarded the colour of a man's skin ... The Free Church had rid itself of what constituted a great temptation for other churches in South Africa ... Great care was brought to bear upon the instruction of the young in this church. 'Your booklets dealing with Biblical matters have been beautifully simplified and could be used as additional reading material of an elementary nature in schools. If ever there was a time when the Word of God must be brought within easy reach of youth, it is now'." It was good to know we were doing something right!

In 1984 an invitation had come from the ICRC (the International Conference of Reformed Churches) inviting the Free Church in Southern Africa to apply for membership. This invitation was taken up and the Church became a member church of the ICRC. In September 1985 Rev Nelson Mpayipeli went to Edinburgh, Scotland as a delegate when the Conference was held there. He was joined by Revs Alejandro Tuesta from Peru and David John from India, and together they made a historic journey to various congregations of the Free Church in Scotland. They also took in the Summer School in Theology and were able to have fellowship with some of the ministers.

Bibles and Psalm books

A new version of the **Xhosa Bible** was being prepared under the direction of the Bible Society of South Africa. Rev Bryce Taho was among the team of well-qualified men and women who acted as consultants during the preparation of this version which was based on the Bible Society Text for the *'Good News Bible' (Today's English Version)*. The South Africa General Assembly of 1984 commended this new translation with some qualifications but stated that it was particularly helpful for the younger generation growing up in the church.

It had been hoped also to produce a revised edition of the **Xhosa Psalter** with a tunes supplement, but the cost proved to be prohibitive and the old Psalter was reprinted. Unfortunately in 1986, 700 copies of this Psalter were lost in a fire at the printers.

Dimbaza Bible School produced a **Handbook** for instruc-tion in Church membership and it proved to be very helpful to those who used it, but it takes a long time to change ingrained habits!

In 1987 the Free Church of Scotland Board sent out a great number of **books for pastors**. They contributed a sum of £100 per pastor and the Banner of Truth Trust doubled that amount in the value of books. This was a great help to men who had access to very few preaching aids at that time.

SIGNIFICANT LANDMARKS OF THE EIGHTIES

Pirie Mission Anniversary

At the beginning of this decade in 1980 the Church was looking back, not forward. It was the *150th Anniversary of the founding of Pirie Mission*. A Conference was held at Dimbaza on 25-26 October to commemorate the putting down of roots and the beginning of Gospel witness in our areas. Rev Joe McCracken was asked to prepare a commemorative booklet to mark the occasion and the Bible School produced it.

Rev Nelson Mpayipeli

At Mnyameni on 12 March 1983, *Mr Nelson Mpayipeli* was ordained and inducted to the Burnshill District and the family moved into the manse in Keiskammahoek. The 12 March was a hot, sunny day, but Mnyameni's usually beautiful hillsides were burned brown with the maize crop in a sad state. Nelson Mpayipeli had been a student at the Evangeli Xhosa Bible School, Kentani, Transkei. He was accepted as a student for the ministry of the Free Church and went to study at the Decoligny Theological College in Umtata. On completion of his studies there he was an assistant in the Burnshill District for a year. During that time the people had got to know and respect him and the Lord had given him encouragements in the different congregations in the District. Rev B.M. Taho conducted the service at the Ordination and Induction, and speakers from several parts of the church spoke words of encouragement and welcome. On the following day Mr Mpayipeli was 'introduced' to the District at a service in Ngqumeya. He was welcomed as a member of Presbytery at its meeting on 19 March, at Ibika, and was accepted for the panel of radio preachers in Radio Xhosa.

Rev Bryce Taho

On 4 June 1984 **Rev Bryce M. Taho** resigned as minister of the Knox District as he had joined the Religious Broadcasting staff of the SABC (South African Broadcasting Association). He was given the status of Minister without charge but with a seat in the Southern Presbytery and the General Assembly. In 1985 Rev Bryce was appointed a Chaplain to the Ciskei Defence Force, his status as a minister of the Free Church with a seat on the Presbytery remaining as before.

Evan Macdonald visits

On 27 June 1986 **Mr Evan Macdonald** arrived for five weeks to give advice on promoting Youth Work in the South African church. A 'live-in' Conference for youth leaders and older youth was held at Debe Nek when Evan gave much advice and encouragement in the development of youth work. 60 people attended the full conference and from 10 to 20 people came in during the day. One night at the Conference the young people held an *Imvuselelo* (Revival meeting) and it was thrilling to see the way they chaired the meeting, testified and preached. It was hoped that a movement to be called *Abavuseleli* (The Up and Coming Ones) might eventually take shape. However, in the climate of the times this did not develop but Evan's visit and good advice was really helpful. Evan travelled far and wide in Transkei and Ciskei to help prepare youth leaders to set up youth groups and his input, while not able to be developed at that time, may have played its part in establishing the successful youth movements of today. Three organisations were set up at the Conference in Debe Nek: Campaigners (*Abavuseleli*), a Youth Organisation, and a Free Church Association for everybody.

Evan described a visit he made to the congregation of Mnyameni one Sunday morning:

> The Mnyameni church bell rings out, scarcely, it seems, making any impression on this sleepy, peaceful

Ciskei village. But a sizeable congregation had already gathered and we can hear the harmonious strains of Xhosa singing filtering through the open door as we wait outside. At the service, the first Psalm was 122. The volume, harmony and rhythm of Xhosa singing has to be heard to be appreciated. How they enjoy their singing! One of the elders has been asked to lead in prayer. His prayer begins softly and deliberately but ends on a note of loud urgency. His 'Amen' is the signal for the whole congregation to join in singing the Lord's Prayer – its chant-like form providing a moving contrast to the African version of *St Magnus!* ... As two of the younger men pass the offering plate round, the choir and the congregation sing again, this time with body as well as with soul. To join the choir you simply have to be the right age! Young people in their teens and twenties constitute the bulk of its members. The girls look really smart with their blue bow ties, white blouses and black skirts. While these young men and women are singing so heartily, I find myself wondering how many of them have experienced the transforming power of Christ? Some, I know, have. I recognise several faces from the Conference on Youth Work ... Will any of the young promising Christian lads respond to the need for African ministers? The Church so desperately needs them. So many of these young people are keen to become involved in the affairs of the church. Will the recently formed Free Church Youth Association help harness and direct their spiritual energy and vision? Will they possess the grace to stand up for what is right in the face of insidious intimidation? So many questions! So many problems! How we praise God for the saving, sanctifying and preserving power of the Holy Spirit.

... The closing Psalm, ... the shaking of hands ... the singing, singing, singing until everyone is standing outside in a long snake-like line in the bright, hot sunshine. What a lovely way to end an unforgettable service!

As we drive back to King William's Town, my thoughts are still wandering ... wandering back to the pioneering days of the Gospel in a place like Mnyameni. If only those pioneers could see the church now! And I began wondering what the church at Mnyameni will be like in ten or twenty years' time. God is building His church, and the gates of Hell will not prevail against it.

Lovedale Reopening

After a complete refurbishment by the Ciskei Government, **Lovedale College** was reopened as a college for the upgrading of teachers' qualifications. The reopening ceremony was held on 1 September 1989. It was a nostalgic day for the many 'old Lovedalians' who were present. During the proceedings Mrs Pearl Magodla, herself a teacher and former student of Lovedale, presented a number of books to the College library on behalf of the Free Church of Scotland. The Church also made a gift of books available for an annual prize in the Biblical Studies department, the prize to be called *The Ross Memorial Prize*. The day finished with traditional dancing, much singing and a very fine meal.

Mrs Vumindaba

At the end of September 1989 Mrs Vumindaba, minister's wife of the Dewar District, was knocked down and killed in King William's Town when making her way to Grey Hospital to see about her eyes. Her large funeral was held in the open air outside the new Geju Church, on 7 October, the one perfect sunny day among many rainy ones. She had been a most competent minister's wife and President of Dewar District Women's Christian Association, and was preparing to host the following Convention in Gqumahashe, Dewar, so her death was a sore loss to the District as well as to her husband and family.

Delegates from the Board, November – December 1989

Missionaries and African church members enjoyed a very happy and helpful visit from **Rev D.K. and Mrs Nina Macleod, Kingussie**, and **Mr Alastair Fraser, Kyle of Lochalsh** at the end of 1989. They came at a time of great rain, and started their visit in Transkei, staying with missionaries and meeting with the African ministers and office-bearers. They spent time with each missionary family on the field and visited widely in the Districts. They also met the President of Transkei, and were most impressed with the fact that he conducted a spiritual conversation with the Free Church delegation and asked one of them to lead in prayer. He spoke with great gratitude of all the Free Church had done for his people on a material level as well as on the spiritual.

The delegates returned from Transkei for the two-day office-bearers' conference in Dumisani which preceded the Thanksgiving celebration of 10 years of the Bible School. There were gatherings for the delegates here and there, with the Free Church folk now living and working in Bisho, and with the ladies in Whiteville Church. One day they were shown all over Lovedale Institution by the Principal. On their very last evening, a Sunday, all the missionaries who could, gathered in the house which Kenny and Coleen Macdonald were to occupy in a few days and Rev D.K. Macleod held a fatherly family service. Next day a large group of well-wishers gathered at the airport as they returned home, mission accomplished. One result of their visit was that from then on the missionaries gathered in one of the homes for a family service and fellowship on Sunday nights.

NEW CHURCHES AND CONGREGATIONS

The Eighties were busy years for the building and opening and use of new churches and the establishing of new congregations.

Mr Neil Maciver from Callanish in Lewis was a wonderful help in this. He came out for months at a time and undertook the work of whichever church was being built at the time. He was a blessing from the Lord to the Church there.

Cape Town and Eastern Cape

Gugulethu **Church, Cape Town** was the first to be opened in this decade. The opening day, a day of pouring rain, was 28 June 1980. It was built by Rev Angus Alex Macdonald who was not just overseer but 'hands on', living in Cape Town for long spells at a time. During Rev M. MacRitchie's visit as Moderator he visited the site and was present when the foundation stone was laid on 10 November 1979. The people of Lewis and Harris, hearing Mr MacRitchie's inspiring messages about his time in South Africa, supplied the lacking finances to complete the church.

A special bonus was the fact that Rev Joseph McCracken was able to be there at the opening in spite of his failing health, as he had pioneered the whole project and it was due to his tireless efforts that the site was acquired. He began the service with a brief outline of the steps leading to the formation of the congregation. The first entry in the Minute Book of the congregation had been made on 4 May 1968. This was the result of a letter Rev McCracken received from Mr Wellington Sobili who, with a handful of Free Church people, had moved to Cape Town in search of work. When their numbers reached between 20 and 30 Mr Sobili requested that a congregation be set up in Cape Town. Having received permission from the Foreign Missions Board Mr McCracken then set about collecting funds. So after many trials, it was a great day and a milestone to have a Free Church building in a Cape Town location. The weather cleared for the Communion Service held in the new church the following day.

Zwide **congregation, Port Elizabeth.** In late 1980 the Presbytery was informed that a new congregation had been formed in Zwide, one of the Port Elizabeth locations.

Dordrecht **congregation** came under the wing of the Free Church in August 1982 when the Presbytery agreed to a request from a group of people that a congregation of our church be established there. It became a separate district of the church in 1985. At first the people worshipped in the school but much later in 1992 they built a small church of their own.

Transkei

***Ibika* Church, Butterworth, Transkei** was opened in style on 24 July 1982. This was one of the churches helped by Mr Neil Maciver, though it owed so much to Rev David Fraser, minister of the district and also Rev Angus A. Macdonald. A team of young people from the Gereformeerde Kerk in Potchefstrooom helped with the foundations of this building. They spent so long on the foundations, they said they were building the underground church! Prof Donald Macleod was visiting at the time of the opening and he put some finishing touches to the building and then preached at the opening.

Albert Sliep had explained to the Board when he was on home leave how important it was to have a place of witness in this growing town fast becoming an industrial centre of Transkei. He said that the Reformed Witness was again attracting many people who were seeking for security in a world of continual change and uncertainty along with disappointment with the shallow and often misleading teaching of some of the other denominations and of the many cults and sects. So it was a special blessing to come to the day of opening of a Free Church in Butterworth.

***Ntshiqo* Church, Transkei** was opened during the visit of Prof Archie Boyd in July 1983. It was the first church building in an almost entirely heathen community. Until that day services were held in the home of the first convert in the area, John Ntsibantu. The church was packed on that opening day, the majority of the congregation being heathen. The stalwart Evangelist Nenemba had pioneered this work, as he had done in many other communities.

***Godidi* Church, Transkei** was another of Mr Nenemba's works for the Lord. It was opened on 5 November 1983, to the joy of, among others, NoEngland, whom Prof Boyd described as "an unforgettable Christian lady". Rev David Fraser was tireless in his efforts in building these churches with as small an outlay of funds as possible.

***Nkanini* Church, Transkei** in the Embo District was opened in August 1986. Again Mr Nenemba, along with David Fraser, did much of the hard graft in this building work. Mr Nenemba was an ill man by the time it was finished but he came out of hospital the day before the opening and helped to put finishing touches to the "congregated roofing" as he put it, and the guttering. Mr Evan Macdonald, who was in South Africa at that time, officially opened the building.

Ciskei

Ngcamngeni (or Isikhali) in **Ciskei** Church opening followed shortly after Ibika. This happened on 14 August 1982. This congregation was one which owed its origin to the work of Mrs Lex Colville and progressed under the help of Elders Mr Theophilus T. Nocanda and Mr Wilson Mtishe, and was nourished by the ministries of Dr Campbell Andrews and Rev Bryce Taho. At the opening Rev Bryce Taho spoke of his debt to Dr Campbell Andrews, "whose son in the faith I am", and he wanted the church to be known as the *Rev Dr J.C. Andrews Church.*

Geju **Church, Ciskei** was built under the leadership of Mr Neil Maciver, and was called "The McCracken Church". Gaelic and Xhosa phrases were traded as the building proceeded. It was built on a hillside and, like the Sea of Galilee, sudden great winds funnelled down through the hills and into the valley causing the partly built walls to collapse twice during building operations. The women of Geju then said, "We must meet in the building to pray." This they did, and before the benediction the wind came down in force. However, the building held together, the roof was erected and Mr McCracken himself was well enough to open the door on 29 October 1983 and to preach at the service on the following Lord's Day.

Rev David Fraser also started work up in *Umzimkulu* on the Transkei/Natal border, several hours drive away from his other congregations, and also in another direction at *Maclear* on the Transkei/South African border. The work at Maclear did not function for too long but the work at Umzimkulu progressed, and a church was built there under Rev Ian and Mrs Maryanne Wylie in 1993.

The Gereformeerde Kerk and the Free Church

There was ongoing contact with the Gereformeerde Kerk whose Missions Committee felt that their work among the amaXhosa would be better carried out under the general guidance of the Free Church but with both churches keeping their own identity. In practice it followed the suggestion that the co-operation would be best served on a local basis according to the wishes of the congregations. Although the G K was politically conservative it was proactive in building bridges between the different races in South Africa and in reaching out to countries to the north of South Africa. A joint Conference of office-bearers of both churches was arranged in King William's Town from 6-8 February 1984 and again in 1986 when it was good to see an obvious change in the attitudes of several of the Gereformeerde Kerk men to the Black people.

In Dimbaza the two churches worked together sharing the building and literature and sometimes joint conferences. When the Bible School moved to Dumisani in King William's Town, the G K was fully involved again.

Life IN the Churches

While all those church buildings were being completed and the old ones were in constant use, what was happening in the spirit and soul of the ordinary members who made up the congregations in the churches?

Here are some examples from one district in the Ciskei:

This district is greatly affected by the migratory labour system, with a lack of young and middle-aged men in the congregations. Yet there were about three dozen men on the preaching plan and some are really faithful men of God who stand firm in the faith and preach well. Some of these men have been going out with bands of helpers to evangelise their own people.

One of the new members in one congregation was a gentle old man, illiterate but with a simple trust in Jesus for his salvation. This man had twin grandchildren, a girl and a boy. They were about twelve years of age. One afternoon the young boy was sent into the veldt to bring home the cattle, something he did very often. This day he hurt his foot on a large thorn. The wound became septic then gangrenous and eventually the wee boy died. On the day of his funeral the whole school gathered at the family home to share the sorrow of the family, especially of the old granddad. As was apparently the custom with twins the little girl was laid in the grave first and then taken out, possibly in a gesture of identification with her brother. The old man began to tell the cause of the boy's death and as he did so he broke down in tears and could not go on. For a brief moment there was silence and then, as one, the large crowd began to sing a hymn, softly and with a sympathy that was palpable, and the old man composed himself to continue his story.

After the death of the elder in that congregation 13 people were enrolled in the Catechism class, and were taught each Friday using the new book from Dimbaza for this purpose. So at the Communion, there were 13 new members in that small congregation and one lapsed member restored. Two of those who were received were the daughters of the late elder, and both of them had gone astray and caused much grief to their parents. However, the Lord brought them back in His covenant mercy and both spoke of the influence of their Christian upbringing and parental example in showing them the way to Christ. One said that what caused her to seek the Saviour was the way she saw how God undertook for them as a family after the death of her father.

In another village, some men introduced a stranger to the minister. "This man, umfundisi, was lost but has returned again." The minister was glad to see this modern prodigal and asked him if he had truly returned to the Lord to trust him for his salvation? His answer was strong! "Yes, mfundisi," he said, "with power." He meant he was fully trusting Christ for his salvation. The joy of the other men was evident. They were to hold a Thanksgiving Service in the home of this man's brother and then, after an all night service on the Saturday, they would accompany the returning 'son' to the church on the Lord's Day. "*Rejoice with me for I have found that which was lost.*"

So the Lord was still working in the lives of the ordinary members of the churches.

POLITICS IN THE EIGHTIES

Ciskei Independence Day – 4 December 1981

It was not only the Free Church which gained its independence during the 1980s.

As has been mentioned in connection with Dimbaza the policy of establishing 'independent' states within the country of South Africa was in full force at this time. These states were not recognised outside South Africa – they were part of the apartheid policies of the Nationalist Government – and many blacks did not want to be citizens of an unrecognised tiny state, they wanted to be South Africans. But yet many people did benefit from the independence and there was great enthusiasm for the sense of identity it brought to the people. Outside the homelands racial discrimination was still rigidly applied, and blacks were in effect a disenfranchised people. The South African Government continued to remove people from areas designated as 'white' and to deposit them in places within the homelands which were sometimes completely strange to them. Ciskei and the other homelands had their own defence and police forces, civil service, philatelic service and their own elaborate government structures. The homelands were a hugely expensive 'solution' to the problem of race as the Afrikaans authorities thought of it.

King William's Town where most of the Ciskei missionaries lived was to be just outside this new state and still in South Africa, but Bisho, a new capital for Ciskei was built just up the road. It was very new, modern, smart and expensive, with a Parliament building and mansions for Chief Sebe the President and for government ministers, a shopping mall and a good hotel which became a casino. Casinos were not allowed in South Africa so it became a magnet which drew so many good people into debt and addiction from both Ciskei and neighbouring South Africa.

The celebrations in Ciskei started with a National Day of Prayer and a well attended service in the new Bisho stadium on the cold Sunday prior to the Day of Independence. The following day, Monday 30 November, Maitland Road was like Piccadilly Circus with buses of singing children and lorries of adults going up and down to Bisho from dawn to dusk. There was a National Agricultural Show during the celebrations, and stalls and displays of all kinds studded the area. Dimbaza Bible School was exhibiting too – and it won a silver cup for its display!

At the official opening there was the reading of Scripture and prayer, and the first act after the raising of the flag at midnight on 3 December and the firing of 101 guns was, again, the reading of Scripture and the offering of prayer. And so the new country of Ciskei was born.

Independence Day (4 December 1983) was hilariously happy. People turned out in colourful traditional Xhosa garb with intricate beadwork. The events were unmarred by any violence and there was a sense of a new beginning. It was a hot day with the threat of a thunderstorm which did not materialise, and the 50,000 people at Bisho were happy and orderly. An aeroplane went over leaving a smoke trail of blue and white, the Ciskei national colours. The next day there was tribal dancing before the crowds thinned and went home to digest the fact that they were now Ciskei citizens and not South African any more.

The Christian Church in Ciskei, including Dimbaza Bible School, had not been slow to seize the opportunity for evangelism presented by this special occasion. Teams of young people, black and white, presented tens of thousands with the Gospel, through tract distribution, testimonies and meetings. Many came to the Bible School to enrol for Correspondence Courses.

Political tensions

Political tensions became hotter and more violent as the decade progressed. Schools, universities and colleges were special targets as they represented authority and government. Several of our elders and preachers were also head teachers of schools and for them this was a tense time. We well remember getting a phone call from a principal of a school in the township of Duncan Village outside East London city saying "They are coming for me. If I don't come home tell my wife what happened," and then the phone went down. We waited and prayed and eventually heard that when his school was torched he had escaped out of a back window and made his escape. But the scars remained for a long time. Another teacher, an elder, and his family found their clothes and furniture had been removed and burned.

One 77-year-old lady who had been a teacher for 37 years had been a councillor in a black township. One Monday a letter from her was published in a local newspaper. In it she appealed for all the "mistakes" of the year to be buried, for everyone to enter the new year with "a clean sheet asking the good Lord for guidance". She wrote that in 1985 the people had gone astray and had turned their backs on their Creator: "All we need to do is to go down on our knees, bow our heads and fervently ask for forgiveness and guidance. He is always willing to help us, but we have to be loyal and true and enter 1986 with love for one another as God's children irrespective of colour," she said. A day or two later she heard that one or two of her fellow Black residents were accusing her of being an 'informer'. She lifted her pen again to deny this "contemptible lie". By the time this letter was published her home had been petrol-bombed, a pile of tyres soaked in petrol was put on top of her and set alight, and she was already with her Creator. At the same time, a 19-year-old girl, daughter of another Black councillor was stoned and set alight. She died next day of 100% burns.

Each time we travelled to a nearby town we passed the charred remains of a beautiful big Xhosa church. One of its elderly members, a deeply religious man, had been sleeping in it to guard it from mobs at night. He had been warned of danger but he loved God's House too much to leave it unguarded. It too was petrol-bombed by local youths and as he escaped in flames he was attacked and killed with a spade he had earlier used that day to tidy up around the church.

So much of the violence seemed to be Black on Black. Why didn't they turn on the Whites who were subjecting them to such racial abuse and apartheid? Why didn't they turn on us who were going in and out of Black locations and yet experienced only kindness? It was a strange time of turmoil and political uncertainty.

MISSIONARY MOVEMENTS

For some of the missionaries this decade brought momentous changes.

Mrs Lex Colville

One of these was Mrs Lex Colville. She had been ill during the latter part of 1979 and was unable to drive after that, but in 1980 she began holding a meeting in her home, 22 Maitland Road, for the leaders of the Girls' meetings and Sunday Schools. She gave them the outline of a message which they used in the classes and reported on the following week. She looked forward to this gathering, usually making a big plate of pancakes in preparation.

In July the missionaries held a dinner to commemorate her arrival on the mission field in July 1955, 25 years before. Later in the year the South African Church held a proper celebration in her honour. The big church at Mdisa was all decorated, there were gifts of all kinds, and speeches which took a long time. Lex had had no intention of retiring, (although she had just had her 78th birthday) but more than one speaker, mindful of her health, said, *"Hlala phantsi ngoku, Nomaka"*, Sit down (retire) now, Nomaka. At the beginning of the following year Lex felt she should go back to Australia to look after her sister. She took a 3-month return ticket – but she never used that return. Instead, she became a wonderful ambassador in her home church in Australia, which became more of a prayer and financial support than ever to the Church and Bible School in South Africa.

She did revisit her old haunts with Dr and Mrs Andrews and a friend Miss June Harris for three months in 1982. Then they left for Australia in January 1984, and that was the last time any of them set foot in South Africa again. Lex took ill in 1987 and after a short illness she died on 9 November - just 4 days before Joe McCracken. So those two warriors almost entered glory together.

Rev Joseph McCracken

Joe took ill in the middle of the year 1987 and was in hospital for some time. At times the nurses had to wheel his bed out of the ward at night because he was singing and preaching as he 'took a service'! He died on Friday 13 November (he always said the best things happened to him on Friday 13th) and was buried in King William's Town next to his predecessor, Rev Alexander Dewar.

At Joe's funeral, the pallbearers were all office-bearers of long standing in the Church, who had worked with Joe over the years. There was a large congregation. One interesting point was the number of white men then in the ministry who testified that it was Joe's encouragement and influence that had brought them to that point.

So for Joe and Lex the missionary movement was upward!

The Albert Slieps

These months were a mixture of sorrow and joy. Just a few weeks before Lex and Joe gained glory we had a celebration of thankfulness for Albert and Pat Sliep's 25 years of faithful service on the South African mission field. A year later people gathered in Ibika, Butterworth, from many parts of the Free Church in Southern Africa to mark their retirement from the active work in a district. Albert had ministered in Ciskei and Transkei, he had served as General Treasurer of the Church and as Senior Clerk of Assembly and as Clerk of the Transkei Presbytery. He, along with Pat, had been faithfully trying every method of getting the Gospel to the people in the most effective way through week-by-week preaching, evangelistic outreaches and camps, children's work, nutrition programmes etc. He served as Secretary of the Transkei Evangelical Association, was Chief Scout of Transkei and was closely associated with the Bible Society of Transkei. It was surely time to take off his boots and relax a little.

Albert and Pat retired to East London, then moved to Cathcart where Tom went to school and they looked after the congregation in Dordrecht when they could, before returning to East London. They later moved to Durban to be nearer their daughter Mary, and later the Slieps with Mary and her husband and family relocated to Cornwall in the U K.

The **Angus Macdonalds,** the **Frasers** and the **Grahams** continued their work as before.

Angus and Helen Macdonald were kept busy with the care of all the churches in the Pirie District, which included 11 congregations, and Somerset East and Cape Town.

Their manse was open to all and often had enquirers having tea as they came to ask about some problem. Helen was most active in taking Thursday women's or girls' meetings, quarterlies, pre-funeral ladies' meetings and so on.

The Slieps and the Frasers had exchanged districts in 1984. This meant that the Slieps were now in Butterworth in the manse which had become too small for the growing Fraser family with the birth of Daisy Joan, Marion Faith, and later Suzanne and Martin. The Frasers were in the manse in Umtata. There they were busy with the congregations of the Embo District, and also David started work some hours away to the East in Umzimkulu and to the North in Maclear. Marion also carried on a faithful work among the women and girls, often taking meetings with the latest baby being happily passed around among the women in the congregation! She wrote a small book about the life and testimony of Mrs Jemima Ngceba, a bright Christian lady near Butterworth. Mrs Ngceba's life was hard, but shot through with a love of the Lord and his servants. She died in May 1985.

The **Grahams**. We were fully occupied with Dimbaza, later with Dumisani work, and also for a time the Knox District.

Rev Ken and Joan Cameron do 'locum'

From May to October 1988 Rev Ken Cameron, followed later by Joan, came to do locum for the Frasers while they were on home leave. They greatly enjoyed their time in Umtata, identifying with the people in the various locations, and especially with the children. They say, *"If you have drunk of the water of Africa, you will always come back."* And so they did – in 1991.

The Glover family arrive

On 1 December 1988 welcome reinforcements arrived in the form of the Glovers.

It was with great thankfulness that the Foreign Missions Board at its meeting in January 1988 received and accepted an application from Rev Ian Glover, then minister in Bishopbriggs, to serve in South Africa. The Board recommended that Mr Glover be "used partly in Dumisani, being available also for pastoral work ..." Their farewell was held in Glasgow on 3 September and they arrived on 1 December 1988. Quite a contingent of missionaries gathered at East London airport to meet the family – Ian and Sandra with their children, John-Mark, Rachel and two-year-old Catriona. They found it all so new and different at first, but soon settled in and the children enjoyed being able to play barefoot in the warm climate.

A few weeks after, on 14 January 1989, Sandra was formally 'dressed' as a member of the Women's Christian Association at a Knox District quarterly meeting. Mrs Taho took as her text *"Welcome (her) in the Lord":* Philippians 2: 29.

The following day Ian was present with others at Bebula, and then on to a Revival Meeting at Mamata. It was a great meeting with several professing faith for the first time and several recommitting their lives to the Lord.

More reinforcements – the Millers and the Macdonalds

The Thursday of the Assembly of the Free Church of Scotland in the year 1989 was somewhat taken over by South Africa. The Moderator was Rev Ken Cameron, who was thanked for his period of service in South Africa, as were Rev Albert and Pat Sliep who were now retiring after so many years of service. There were two sets of new missionaries to commission – Rev David and Mrs Meg Miller, not long married and not long ordained – and Mr Kenny and Mrs Coleen Macdonald, with their sons Mark and Greg. Kenny came out as a builder and property overseer and was a tremendous help in the building of churches – as nearly every missionary had at least one church he wished to build! We, Bill and Elizabeth Graham, were also present on our way from some weeks of deputation in the Presbyterian Church of Eastern Australia. Rev Huite Sliep dedicated all the missionaries in prayer to the God they were to serve. Rev Ken Cameron said, quoting Bunyan, "*I wished myself among them!*" But before long, he and Joan were setting out also for a more lengthy period of service on the same field.

The Millers, Macdonalds and Grahams travelled out on the same plane to South Africa and were met by a 'phalanx' of missionaries, and we to a welcome in the Bible School – about 60 people waiting there with gifts for '25 years in the ministry'.

After settling in, it was down to business. David and Meg Miller were to take the place of the Slieps in Butterworth in the Ngcingwane and Kentani Districts. The Macdonald family were also in Butterworth for a few months but had to move to King William's Town because of lack of accommodation.

But while the Millers and Macdonalds were still together in Butterworth, Kenny wrote home an account of one of their first visits to a church service, still held in a house but with the hopes of a church to be built soon, in Ndlambe.

> ... Eventually we reach the village of Ndlambe passing on the outskirts the proposed site of the new church, local headman and officials permitting. The women seem to be busy doing their daily chores, including carrying to their homes water-filled containers of all shapes and sizes taken from the nearest stream or pool. We are so aware that here the Lord's Day is as any other to many of the people.
>
> We see women sitting in a group smoking their long-stemmed pipes and we resolve to speak to them on our return journey. What they are wearing as head covering indicates to us that they are heathen women.
>
> So we arrive at our meeting where we are met by four young Xhosa students from the Kentani Evangeli Xhosa Bible School who have been taking Sunday School with the local children.

We enter the one-roomed house and are surprised at the spaciousness of it, and we see that it has been prepared for our visit ... The service begins with a Psalm in Xhosa followed by Patrick leading in prayer, and then we settle down to listen to the sermon. Within a few minutes of Rev Miller starting we are distracted by some new arrivals, women and some young men. Despite this distraction we praise God for such who desire to come to hear the Word. Once again we seek to concentrate on the message, but a few minutes later one of the children decides to get up from where he was sitting quietly eating from a bowl of rice. Eventually after he had spilt some of it on the floor he was finally persuaded to sit down again. Unfortunately a couple of hens with their chicks passing by the open door spied the spilt rice and quickly darted in to enjoy the unexpected fare.

Our prayers are now with Rev Miller as he seeks to continue preaching and tries to ignore the goings on around him. Truly Satan comes in different guises!

And so it went on: visits from two dogs, a cat which jumped out through the window after being attacked by a hen, and of course the inevitable stream of children coming to see for themselves what was going on. Thankfully this did not seem to disturb our hosts as much as it did us and some of them seemed to be taking heed of the great truths set before us.

The service over, we once again stepped outside into the hot sun, and bidding farewell to these kind people we set off on our return trip to Butterworth with the haunting sound of the Xhosa Psalm-singing still following us.

The roadside smokers? Well, they had moved on, and so another opportunity to witness for our Lord and Saviour had passed. Maybe next time, D.V.

REFLECTIONS

- The Church's Independence; perhaps it was unfortunate thatwhenthetimeforthechurch'sindependencecamethere was still a large missionary presence relative to the number of African ministers. This may have given an impression to the ordinary members that nothing much had happened – independence seemed to bring little change other than a few new committees!

- The high hopes we had for a Youth Movement did not immediately materialise but it did develop later and is very active today. It is still hard to get the Church to take the spiritual needs of its children seriously.

- In considering the progress of the work, we had always to assess whether we were communicating *effectively*. We also had to take more seriously efforts to help the office bearers who were preaching in most of the pulpits on any given day.

- The growing awareness of Dumisani and the supply of its staff resources was a significant pointer to the development of future strategy.

- The Lord's goodness to the Church and the missionaries during increasing political tension, and the Church's stance, is a matter for thankfulness.

13

Dumisani Bible School

HOW IT ALL BEGAN

Remember that little Anglican Church down in Leopold Street, quite near to the bus and taxi ranks, but not for sale? It was called St Chad's and had had a chequered career. It had been built in the 19th Century for the 'other ranks' of British troops stationed at the garrison in King William's Town and for those of them who had retired and were housed in that part of the town, which became known as 'Pensioners' Village'. In time a Black congregation of Anglicans worshipped in the building and when they relocated to Zwelitsha a Coloured Congregational group used the building and it was also converted into a series of offices.

A For Sale *Board*

On the night of 31 July 1986, we, the Grahams, were at a meeting in King William's Town. A friend asked us for a lift home. As we dropped her off in Leopold Street, we noticed – a *For Sale* board on the little church! A telephone call to the estate agents in the morning revealed that, "Nobody wants a church in King William's Town. You could probably get it for the price of the land. It is on two plots." With some missionary colleagues we went snooping round it, climbing on backs so that we could see inside the high arched windows. The rain had come in and the ceiling and floor were in need of repair but otherwise it seemed sound. There was quite a lot of land to the back and a big, shady jacaranda tree, some bushes and a pomegranate tree. The estate agent came to show us round. We conferred and consulted with our own church people, the Bible School Board, the Foreign Missions Board, the Gereformeerde Kerk, the house agent and the architect. We debated whether we would be given town planning permission for a change of status to an educational institution. We waited while other offers were rejected. We held our breaths while a karate club put in an offer at the very last minute. But at last, on 21 August, the Bible School Board's offer was accepted and the St Chad's Anglican church became converted to a Bible School. The church was bought for little more than the wonderful gift of R15, 000, which the ladies of the WFMA had given us to upgrade the kitchen in Dimbaza!

Fitting Out

The Gereformeerde Kerk (Afrikaans congregation) became joint owners of the building, undertaking to fund the repairs to the church, which cost more than the building, on condition that they could use it as a church on Sunday mornings. Until this time they had met in the living room of one of their elders or in a school hall.

The Church people from the villages were delighted with the new location as they had long been uncomfortable going into Dimbaza "with these politicals" and they were concerned about us working in there too. In most cases it involved only one minibus taxi journey for them to get to King William's Town and they could get shopping done too when they came to meetings. Just at this time, several houses in Dimbaza were burned down and the big security spotlights had been fused. Did this confirm the rightness of the move?

Work began on the building. The rotten timbers in the roof were torn down and the floor underneath was replaced. As it had been an Anglican church, it was in the shape of a cross. We put up partitions allowing a double sized office at the top and two offices each in the two arms of the cross. There was already an office behind a partition at the other end of the building which had been the headquarters for Steve Biko, leader of the Black Consciousness Movement, whose death at the hands of the security officers would play such a big part in the bringing down of apartheid. That office became the printing room, and we moved the work from the end of the corridor in our house into it. Painters redecorated the whole building. Carpet layers fitted carpeting throughout the building, and went home with a job well done. But next morning, we found a neat piece had been cut out of the carpet which obviously just fitted the needs of someone! So it all had to be done again. We fitted a tiny kitchen in the back porch with a small sink, a small worktop, cupboard space and a stove. It proved to be adequate for many meals for training days and conferences in the days to come. The main body of the church formed a big area for holding day conferences for the Bible School and for the Gereformeerde Kerk to have church on Sundays.

Dimbaza Bible School gets a new name

So, all you people, 'Praise the Lord!' – 'Dumisani uYehova!' But having moved from Dimbaza, the Bible School could no longer be called '*Dimbaza Reformed Bible School*'. It needed a new name – so that is exactly what the new Bible School came to be called – **DUMISANI** - which in Xhosa means "Praise". When the Bible School Board approved the new name at a meeting in February 1987, *Dumisani Bible School* was born.

A printing press as well

The Board's offer for the St Chad's church was accepted on 21 August 1986. At the end of this same day came the news from the Superintendent of the Church of the Nazarene Mission that we were to have as a gift a very large printing press, along with a paper cutter, stencil-maker and electric guillotine. It had been intended for use by their church organisation but sadly the missionary who was to have used it had died. After Dumisani was up and running it was duly installed in the office which was now our printing room. But – however did this big machine work? It used plates, chemicals and had several idiosyncrasies! After many despairing efforts and much prayer, we found that an American friend, Dr Clinton Tatsch, a retired man who had come out with his wife to help as a Baptist missionary, had been President of a Technical College and knew most things about our new machine. He helped to get it going and again we could only say, 'Praise the Lord'!

Saying 'goodbye' to Dimbaza

While all the renovations were being made to the new building in King William's Town, work was still carrying on in the long, low building with the red zinc roof in Dimbaza. Correspondence Courses were written, translated and went in and out by the post; letters were written in answer to problems or questions about the Christian faith; Biblewomen's Days were held, but not so many conferences as the political situation was so volatile and people really did not like coming into this place where they were not known. The closing day at Dimbaza was 12 December 1986. There was a real pathos about this last staff meal together with eleven of us sitting round a long table. Most would be coming in to the new building in King William's Town after the holidays, but Mrs Nduli, the caretaker who lived across the road, would miss the Bible School sorely. Round the table with us were a Gereformeerde student on placement, the printer from our house in King, the translators and correctors, Mr and Mrs Bunguza, and the typist, the gardener, the caretaker ... The eight years spent in building up the Bible School in Dimbaza had been a learning curve filled with prayers and answers, trials and errors, and in spite of the good leading of the Lord it was hard to leave. It was the sort of feeling one would have on leaving the first small home of one's own for a bigger and better house. But the words came spoken so long ago: *"Fear not little flock, it is your Father's good pleasure to give you the Kingdom."* So we could go into the move with the feeling that the Lord Himself had ordered it all and was coming with us. And the doors of this place in Dimbaza would still be open each Lord's Day, for the Xhosa congregation of the Gereformeerde Kerk would be using it as their church as before, and during the week a children's nursery would make use of the building.

Wednesday 4 February was the moving day and on 11 February 1987 the doors of Dumisani were opened for business.

THE FIRST PHASE

Mr Neil Macleod

We were due for leave in March, just a month after opening, and so Mr Neil Macleod, from Dingwall, arrived to hold the fort for part of the time that we were away. He must have wondered what was before him, as in the early morning after he arrived there was an attempt made to assassinate the President of the Ciskei, Mr Lennox Sebe, whose palace was just a mile up the road from our house. However, Mr Macleod was made of stern stuff and he went on to forge ties of real affection with both the Bible School staff and the Free Church in South Africa. He answered many letters dealing with questions on morality and Christian conduct, and he went on to frame a new correspondence course on 1 Thessalonians, to "keep the correspondents working" until the new course *Know the Doctrines of God's Grace,* was fully prepared. He thought that the three-year Diploma Course was very good and so he recommended it to the South African Free Church General Assembly as a qualification for evangelists.

Mr Macleod travelled to visit several areas of the church in South Africa and particularly enjoyed preaching in the Knox District. He was also a frequent visitor to the table of Angus and Helen Macdonald who lived nearby, and Helen saw that he was not hungry for long! As a keen member of the *Gideons International* he was very pleased to take part in Bible Distribution work in several schools in the King William's Town area.

The Grahams return

During our leave, we were able to visit congregations all over Scotland and some in Northern Ireland to present the needs of the Bible School for the prayer and care of the Church. People were very kind and interested and also generous in their gifts for the School, and we found much to encourage us for the work in South Africa. But it was hard to leave family and friends in Scotland and as the plane took off the words of Jesus were in our minds about leaving "*home and brothers and sisters ... for my sake and the Gospel's*". We returned to a warm welcome and a meal from missionary colleagues, and in the Bible School we found the staff and many of the Biblewomen gathered there to greet us with flowers. So we knew the truth of the rest of that verse *"Everyone who has left houses or brothers or sisters ... for my sake will receive a hundred times as much and will inherit eternal life."* And there was more. A heart-warming gift of R23 000 (about £6000) had come from the Reformed Missions League in the Netherlands, to be used for the development of the buildings for the Bible School. So sometimes we felt that when we asked the Lord to sell one of his beasts on a thousand hills, he sold a whole herd!

Ian and Sandra Glover

It had been obvious for some time that one man could not cope for much longer with all the work of Dumisani if it were to expand, and if the dream of training full time students for the ministry of the Free Church were ever to be realised. It was a real answer to prayer, therefore, when the Glover family arrived at the end of 1988.

Ian was particularly interested in being involved with the Bible School and took up the work enthusiastically in Dumisani when it reopened in January 1989 after the holiday break. Mrs Sandra Glover had her hands full with looking after three young children, but it was great to have her help in both Biblewomen's Days in Dumisani and in taking W C A meetings in the Knox District, and later she was able to take classes in teaching in the Bible School.

The Early days

February 1989 marked the 10th anniversary of the Bible School work. Ian Glover wrote an article for the *From the Frontiers* magazine, introducing readers to the Xhosa colleagues who were working in the school at that time. Early letters and reports home from new missionaries are always fresh and interesting, and Ian's article gives a flavour of what the early days of Dumisani were like. He said:

> The School opens at 7.30 a.m. and the first to arrive is **Mrs Eldah Maseti**. She is responsible for all the mail, and given that at the moment most of our work

is by correspondence, you can imagine there is a lot of it. The various course answer sheets are separated into Xhosa and English groups. I receive the English papers, whilst external examiners mark the Xhosa ones. The occasional Afrikaans paper is marked by Bill Graham. When the papers have been corrected the marks of each student are recorded, and the corrected lesson is returned to him along with the next Lesson and answer sheet. A Certificate is sent to each student who successfully completes his course of ten lessons. He also receives the first lesson of another Course. About 8000 students have enrolled for the various courses over the years, though quite a number have dropped out as their particular course progressed. Nevertheless we are thankful for the large number of students who have persevered and completed their courses, and for the benefit that they have testified to having received. Mrs Maseti will take a large bundle of letters to the Post Office each day, and invariably returns with as many again. Our weekly budget for the mail is R150 (£40), which represents quite a lot of mail considering that most letters cost either 18c or 30c to post. (5p or 8p)

Not long after Mrs Maseti, **Mr Gladman Sonkosi** arrives. He is responsible for the stock of literature in the School. All of the material used in the School is prepared and printed here. Bill attends to the printing and is assisted by Sonkosi, who then puts together and staples the various booklets ... The greatest pressure on the publishing department occurs just before the beginning of a new quarter, when the *Bible Study Notes* have to be prepared ready for distribution. There is of course the on-going work of maintaining our stocks of literature in both Xhosa and English.

The next person to arrive is usually *Miss Lungisa Koko*, our typist. She has the unenviable task of deciphering our scripts, and of typing what we have written. Her work is never done! Naturally she is bi-lingual (Xhosa and English) – which is a great blessing!

Mrs Pearl Magodla comes in next. She works here three mornings a week, and translates any private correspondence we receive. Sometimes these letters are applications for our courses, and sometimes they are requests for help in understanding the Faith. It's a rewarding part of my job to do the necessary research and attempt to answer these questions, as well as being a useful discipline in the art of simple and concise answering.

The final member of our staff I would like to introduce to you is **Mrs Esther Kleinbooi** who comes in every Friday to clean the School.

Comments from correspondence

Some comments from correspondence received at Dumisani may illustrate how those participating in the various courses receive the work:

"As one of the women of Gugulethu (Cape Town) I want to do something for my Lord. I see some of the women spreading the Gospel to others, so I would like to follow them ... I want to learn from Dumisani Bible School. Will you please send me the first lessons that will enlighten me about the Lord."

"Will you please help me so that I can be sure I am child of God?" (From Grahamstown).

"My heart is full of joy because of the many things God has done for me ... thanks very much for the Certificate I got for the first course of lessons" (from Transkei).

A letter from Zululand asked permission to translate the book, *Marriage and the Christian Home* into the Zulu language to be used among young adults.

Visit to Australia – March to May 1989

From the early 1940s and before, the Presbyterian Church of Eastern Australia had been deeply interested in the mission work in South Africa. From them had come Dr Campbell Andrews with his wife Ruby and family, and also Mrs Lex Colville. After the setting up of the Bible School and especially after Lex's return and excellent ambassadorial work on our behalf, the PCEA directed many prayers and much interest and very generous finances to the work of the Bible School. In 1989 they invited us (Grahams) to come to Australia to visit the churches and tell of the work first hand.

A day or two before embarking on this adventure, five Knox Biblewomen came into the Bible School. They met with Ian Glover and ourselves in one of the offices. They made a speech: "We have no silver or gold, but we give you our prayers. May God be with you, lift you up in the air, keep you safe under his wings." We sang Psalm 23, verses 3 and 4, and Mrs Mlanjeni prayed. Then they felt we were ready to go! How grateful we often were for the prayers of the people of the church in South Africa!

Soon after our arrival in Australia we were able to attend a camp at Toowoomba up in the hills above Brisbane with the church there, and then to attend and address the PCEA Synod in Taree. After that we were able to visit almost all of the churches up and down the eastern seaboard of Australia and Tasmania. It was good to be able to thank them personally for their kindness and to bring news of the latest developments in Dumisani. We were particularly pleased to stay for two nights with Dr Campbell Andrews and Ruby and just talk and talk ...!

It was sad that Lex Colville had passed away by that time, but we stood by her grave in Maclean and remembered her with very great thankfulness.

Ten Years' Celebration

Although the Bible School was ten years old in February 1989 and the Glovers had arrived a few weeks before that, things move slowly in Africa and it was only on 17 November 1989 that these events were properly celebrated. An Office-Bearers' conference was held in Dumisani that day, and it was attended by two delegates from the Foreign Missions Board, Rev D.K. Macleod (and Mrs Nina Macleod) and Mr Alasdair Fraser. The following day a celebration was held giving thanks for the Glover family being with us and being so involved in the work of both Dumisani and the wider Church, and for the ten years of the Bible School's work. Prof Bennie van der Walt, Potchefstroom, was the guest speaker (as he was at the inauguration of the Bible School in 1979) and well over 100 people attended.

The title of Prof van der Walt's address was *Relevant Christian Education for Africa.*

Rev D.K. Macleod in his report noted some of what he said:

> "While at the beginning of the 20th century there were only about 3 million Christians in Africa, this has grown to about 200 million (from a population of 400 million). At present the growth is going on at a rate of about 4000 per day. If this increase should continue, one could think that by the end of the century there could well be 350 million Christians on the continent – more Christians than in Europe; even more than in USA and Canada together ... A Black African recently said that the problem of Christianity in Africa is that it looks like a river which is 2 kms wide but its water is merely 2 cms deep."

Rev Macleod commented that, "This is the very thing that Dumisani is concerned about." In response to that need the Foreign Missions Board pledged £200 per year to pay expenses of office-bearers attending training courses at Dumisani or other centres at which the Dumisani staff presented the courses.

THE EARLY PROGRAMME

The Three Year Diploma Course

By the following year, 1990, there were 35 students enrolled for the three-year Diploma Course, some of them from different African

Independent Churches. This was a great opportunity, as many of these churches had no institutions of their own to help them. The Independent Churches vary greatly both in membership numbers and in orthodoxy. Some of them have the ear of the people and have huge memberships so it is the greatest of privileges to teach their preachers and present to them the Saviour Jesus Christ as the *only* Mediator between God and men – the all-sufficient Saviour. This is a hard fact to grasp if, as some of these folk do, one believes in a multitude of "intercessors" in the form of the ancestors and other mediums.

The Biblewomen

One of the early requests from the Free Church in Southern Africa's General Assembly was to ask the Bible School to train Biblewomen. This was a particular pleasure and the Biblewomen's Days became a regular feature of the calendar each month. For a long time one lady in the Knox District had been the only Bible-woman and had done a great job. She was paid a small sum each month for her labours. Now two Biblewomen were to be chosen from each area. Early in January 1987 at a Quarterly meeting of the W.C.A. two more new Biblewomen were to be chosen from the Knox District. The question arose as to how we were to afford a small sum for several Biblewomen. Then one lady stood up and reminded us of the sacrifice Christ had made for us, and she said, "Surely we ought to make sacrifices as Jesus did? We don't need pay." Wonderful! She was later chosen as one of the two new Bible-women and remained a shining light for the rest of her days. We made the decision that each W.C.A. where the Biblewomen took the meeting should provide tea and refund their bus fare, and this became the norm. When they came to the Biblewomen's Days in Dimbaza / Dumisani, their fare was repaid by the Bible School and breakfast and lunch was provided.

Mrs Pearl Magodla's report

One of the early Biblewomen was *Mrs Pearl Magodla*. She was asked to write an account of her work.

I am very happy to tell you about the work of a Bible Woman in the Free Church in Southern Africa. I have been fortunate to be amongst the first trained Bible Women in this country under the Dumisani Bible School ...

We visit different stations. We do home visitation, hospital visitation and we also visit heathen homes for evangelism. This work needs perseverance, patience and humility, because we meet many different characters. Some people are highly educated, yet are ignorant of the Word of God. Others are illiterate and they too are ignorant of the Word of God.

However, the main difficulty is the distance between the congregations. At times we have to leave home as early as 5.00 a.m. to get the first transport and we do not return home until 7.00 p.m. Nevertheless the work is progressing. We look to God to lead us and to provide the skills we need.

Who should be a Biblewoman?

The obvious question arose as to who should be a Biblewoman. What qualifications did she need? A book produced for the Biblewomen states:

1. A Biblewoman should be:

    A woman who is a mature Christian and loves the Lord;

    A member of the Women's Christian Association in good standing;

    A woman who wants to serve God above all;

    A woman who is not quarrelsome;

    A woman who can read the Bible fluently and can conduct meetings well.

2. A Biblewoman should be chosen by her President and Committee, with the approval of the office-bearers, and should be set apart at the Annual

Women's Christian Association Convention, or similar gathering.

3. A Biblewoman should not be held in reverence and given a special place; rather she should be a servant of Jesus and follow him closely in humility and in service for others, using the gifts which she was given by him. (Philippians 2:2–8; Romans 12:3–5, 7–8).

Biblewomen's Days

Once a month on the last Wednesday of the month the Biblewomen gathered in Dimbaza or Dumisani. This was a time that generally all looked forward to.

One day during report time one lady said she was very sorry that she didn't have enough money for her fare that day to get in to the Bible School. She would have got her return fare back at the end of the meeting but she had nothing for the journey there. She put on her apron to do her housework instead and there in the pocket she found a coin which was enough to get her there and here she was! She saw that as a direct answer to prayer.

After breakfast, singing and prayer we had the Report Back. One of the team of two Biblewomen from each area reported on their work in the last month. At first these were discouraging. One woman after another said she had been very busy that month and had not managed to go out at all. So we opened a book of 'Encouragement' for all reports of encouraging encounters or meetings and gradually it filled up with items of real progress. One good day, several told of attempts they had made to reach outsiders with the Gospel. One had given Bible School books to an alcoholic teacher whose husband had left her and whose children were begging for bread. Now the teacher had found a job and wanted more books. A few weeks later that Biblewoman died suddenly and 1000 people attended her funeral. What a loss she was to the whole church!

Quite often the Biblewomen visit members who are 'weak', i.e. who have not been attending meetings for some time. One of the Biblewomen told the story of one visit to a woman who had been very slack in her attendance at the meetings and was therefore due for visitation. When she saw a procession of women in blue and white uniforms making for her house she quickly jumped into bed. When the women gathered round her bed, she spoke in a weak voice and was obviously not well. She was duly encouraged and admonished and prayed for. The question which worried the ladies was, 'Do we wear our uniform to your funeral or not?' Then she was asked to pray. Now, no Xhosa will pray in a horizontal position, so she had to get up to kneel in the bed – and was discovered to be in full dress, apron and all!

During the troubled times we often admired the Biblewomen who went about faithfully doing their job. They told of going to comfort the family of a man in the village who had died when his home was burnt down. Some told of terror in the big townships. Sometimes it was a danger to be in their WCA uniform in the minibus taxis and sometimes it was a protection. Often they had attended pre-funeral Thursday meetings in the home of the bereaved and brought comfort, or attended homes where someone was sick.

These Report Back sessions were followed by a time of open prayer.

Biblewomen's Training Sessions

After the prayers there was a training session. This included such themes as:

> How can you know that you are a Christian?
> How do you explain the way of salvation to others?
> How best can we lead a meeting?
> Visiting the sick, Christian and non-Christian – what Psalms and Scripture to choose.
> Why does God allow his people to suffer?
> Visiting a home where there has been a bereavement.
> What does the Bible teach about heaven and hell?
> Speaking to God in prayer.
> Listening to God through the Bible.
> Bringing up children for God.

The Christian woman and her home.
What about old tribal customs?

On one occasion one of our wise African Free Church ministers, Rev Bryce Taho, was invited to speak about our attitude to *Old Tribal Customs*. It was a day of sleet, even snow, and mud and we expected a minimal turnout, but it was one of the best attendances ever. Women braved the cold and the muddy roads to get their minibus taxis, and were more glad than ever of the mug of hot, sweet tea and breakfast. There is still a lot of confusion even among Christians as to whether it is really sinful to turn to a witch-doctor if the other doctors give no hope for the medical condition of a loved one. And what should the Biblewomen say to a woman who still wears a necklace of hair from the 'cow of the home' as a protective charm? They needed to be sensitive and understanding, but to encourage strong faith in a loving God who is in control of all events in his people's lives. So there was a lot of interest in that subject for study.

Cookery session

Some of the themes for training sessions were compiled in a book for Biblewomen. At the end are some recipes used in the cooking sessions, which followed lunch and were usually taken by Mrs Helen Macdonald. These were much appreciated. They featured inexpensive but nourishing dishes which gave a change of diet and could be made on a Calor gas stove if necessary, such as Spanish omelette; French fried toast; Rice with pilchards; Corned beef patties; Sausage hot-pot; Pumpkin fritters; Mealie jelly pudding; Fruit crumble and even Scottish pancakes!

Then came the scramble to give out travel fares and hurry for the taxis back to the villages, some quite remote, and maybe to get some shopping done on the way.

Sunday School Teachers' Days

The Bible School held a similar training day for Sunday School Teachers about three times a year, usually on a Saturday. This was especially good as the attitude in times past used to be that children didn't really matter until they reached maturity. Teachers found their way to Dumisani from as far away as Port Elizabeth – about three hours or more in a minibus taxi.

Each session included a Report Back so that good ideas could be shared with others. Teachers from other denominations came to these Training Days with enthusiasm, and some of them had huge classes of children to teach. After the reports, the training session might take the form of a sample lesson, with the audience of teachers being the children in the class! They learned and sang new Scripture songs or psalms.

We gradually built up books of lessons for teaching Sunday School classes, 12 lesson books for three years, along with two pre-school books as well by special request. Day school and pre-school teachers also used the books. Lois Mackay, daughter of Ian and Maryanne Wylie, our missionaries in Transkei, produced beautiful outline drawings for each lesson.

So there was usually a good turnout of Sunday School teachers for the January Training Day when the new lesson books for the year were given out along with the drawings and the opportunity to buy crayons etc and each teacher usually went away also with a bundle of cards sent from the UK with a Xhosa text stuck on, to use as an incentive in their classes.

At the end of the year children from all over the area took part in Sunday School exams. In 1999, 810 children sat the exams.

Dumisani Study House

Always there was the hope that soon it would be possible to open the Bible School for the training of full-time students for the ministry. Because there was so much room at the back of the Dumisani building, it seemed sensible to build two classrooms and a printing room out there. An architect friend drew up excellent plans for this – but the cost was great.

Just at this point, an estate agent was seen leaving the house directly across the road from the Bible School, No 18 Leopold Street. On enquiries, it turned out that the house was to be for sale. After consultation, the Bible School Board put in an offer for the

1st f/time student

house and, following various formalities about the change of use to educational purposes we were able to take possession of the house. This provided us with classroom and library space, better kitchen facilities and a room at the back of the house, which Mr Kenneth Macdonald quickly converted into a very suitable printing room. This freed up space in the main church building. The Board was able to buy the property, now called the 'Study House', with the money donated by the Reformed Missions League in Holland and gifts from the legacies of Mrs Colville, Rev Joe McCracken and a friend in Scotland. *Dumisani*, (Praise), once more, to the Lord!

With the problem of accommodation settled, preparations began in earnest for the start of full-time classes early in 1991. The General Assembly of the Free Church in Southern Africa had asked the Bible School to undertake the provision of theological and extra-mural education for its students for the ministry. Ian Glover and Bill Graham prepared course outlines and submitted them to the Senate of the Free Church College in Edinburgh for advice. Later the Southern Africa Free Church Assembly agreed to the programme of courses.

FULL-TIME STUDY, STAFF AND DEVELOPMENT

So on 28 January 1991 Dumisani Bible School's new session began. It opened with a Fellowship Conference for all the ministers in the Church along with the three students who had been approved by the Training of the Ministry Committee of the Free Church in Southern Africa and had come to study full-time for the ministry of the Church. They were Patrick Diniso, Joseph Mbembene and Zukile Nyokana.

Joseph was the youngest and most inexperienced but so willing to learn and to be helpful. Richmond Gotywa joined them as a private student.

This was the beginning of the vision when Dimbaza Bible School became a reality twelve years before – the training of men for the ministry of the Word of God among the Xhosa-speaking people. The task of teaching the main subjects in the Ministers' course was shared between Ian Glover and Bill Graham, and

Elizabeth Graham taught a practical English and a Social Studies Course. The plan was to bring in other lecturers as required. Mrs Coleen Macdonald gave valuable help with the administration work and the African colleagues continued with the other aspects of the School's work such as the printing and correspondence courses. Mr Kenneth Macdonald was very helpful in overseeing other business connected with the practical running of the School. We planned two semesters, the first from early February to mid June and the second, early August to end November.

Bill Graham became Moderator of the Free Church of Scotland General Assembly in May 1991 and Ian Glover shouldered the full burden from May to July when we were in Scotland. While in Edinburgh we had a letter from Joseph Mbembene beginning, "Dear Mum and Dad ..." He said he was missing us, and the sound of our voices. We returned on 29 July in time for the second semester . The Glover family left for home leave on the last day of September and David Miller came from Transkei to help out for most of October. Before the Bible School closed for the holidays in December there was a closing service and a meal, and there was a sense of real thanksgiving to God for setting us on the road to becoming the Dumisani Theological Institute and Bible School.

Highs and a very low

At the Closing Service at the beginning of December, a happy occasion, all four students got their certificates of passing their first year, and all gave their testimonies. We said to Mrs Mbembeni, Joseph's mother, 'You must be very happy today'. She said 'Yes, but I always pray that he won't go into the world. There are so many pressures today.'

On December 14 our daughter Ruth Graham and Robert Howard were married in Dumisani. It was all dressed up for the occasion and our missionary colleagues and many other friends from far and near made it a supremely happy wedding day for the young couple. That was a real 'high'.

The very next day, December 15, the very worst possible thing happened. Joseph Mbembene, youngest of the students died by his own hand. He was found hanged, in a little wood between Mdisa and Knox. We were stunned, finding it impossible to believe. WHY??? As far as we know, nobody has yet found out why. He came from a good home with a Christian mother. Who knows what temptations he faced when he studied away from his home. Could we have been more aware that he was suffering? Could we have done something? What would the youth of the Church feel for he had preached often? How would it affect the Bible School and its perception in the community? Did we push him too hard? Or did he feel he was not suited to the ministry but didn't see how he could turn back?

He was buried quietly. Then on December 28 1991 there was a huge memorial service in his home congregation of Mdisa. It was a beautiful hot day with a little cool breeze, and the big church was packed with hundreds of people. The family sat on the floor filling the big space in front of the pulpit. On the left was a phalanx of men, and on the right a great crowd of the youth, including his rugby team in their black and yellow strip. It was a heavy, per-plexed, comfortless funeral. A woman took an epileptic fit in the middle of the service. No one knew why Joseph had done this. All spoke of how good he had been at home, building up the youth, getting them to open and close their meetings with prayer, helpful in the lodgings he had been living in. It was a hard task to preach at this funeral. What could we say? Certainly we do know and could testify that a Christian never needs to feel he cannot cope – always there is strength from God and his promises are true ... There was pleading with the young people, to come and take his place.

After the service everyone walked a long way to the grave, where we sang, Rev David Miller led in prayer, and Rev Bryce Taho read from Revelation 21 and 22, and pronounced the benediction so that 'this thing might now be "cimile" – extinguished'. But the picture of that poor, little, Joseph-shaped mound of rough sandy soil with thorn-branches stuck in it to keep the animals away – that picture will never ever be extinguished.

Later sessions and the need of more help

The new session of 1992 opened with six full-time students, four of whom were from the Free Church of Southern Africa. Talks were still going on with Professors of the Gereformeerde Kerk about the possibility of Dumisani becoming a satellite college of Potchefstroom University. In September of that year the Foreign Missions Board in Scotland sent out a letter to all the ministers of the Church appealing for at least one additional staff member for Dumisani now that there were different teaching levels to cope with. Bill and Ian shared all the theological classes, and Elizabeth Graham and Sandra Glover did two classes each of English Bible and English language. Extra help was even more necessary as, towards the end of 1992 Bill suffered a slight stroke and had to curtail some duties for a time. And a few months later, the need for help became desperate as Ian Glover was off work from March to June 1993. His ill health was mainly caused by trauma resulting from a violent situation in one of the congregations in the Knox District due to inter-political strife in the area. In June he and the family had to return to Scotland for good. Both full-time and correspondence students expressed their regard for Ian as a teacher and for the benefit they had received from him. Ian himself appreciated the 'great understanding' shown by his missionary colleagues and said how much he had learned of the Lord's care during his illness. There were several farewell occasions and we all missed them very much. Later, when the political situation had calmed down, the people expressed sincere regret at the effect this had had on Mr Glover.

THE MACIVERS ARRIVE

During this time the Bible School had to be closed for a day or two occasionally due to political disturbances. Sometimes it was taxi wars – literally, shots were fired, people killed, and everything came to a halt! Students and staff could not get to Dumisani, and the doors had to be closed. More often it was strikes or marches. So on one of those days, while we were working at home, we were surprised to find that the postman was delivering letters – but he did, and he delivered one to us. It was a letter from Rev Donald

Maciver, minister in Cumbernauld, telling us that he had offered his services to the Foreign Missions Board for work in Dumisani! That was thrilling news and we sat down and praised the Lord first and phoned the colleagues to tell them next!

Meanwhile while we were still alone with the teaching schedule in the Bible School, our other colleagues, who all had districts of their own, did their best to help out in this difficult situation. From Transkei the Millers came in August, the Wylies in September and the Camerons in October.

Then on 21 October 1993, Donald and Isobel Maciver with young Marcus arrived at the East London airport and were met by quite a deputation of missionary colleagues, who all shared a meal together that evening. The Macivers had left their two older children, now university age, behind in Scotland and in the care of the Lord. And on the Saturday Albert and Pat Sliep came to join the welcome team. Best of all, after settling in to their new home in Alexandra Road, King William's Town, Donald was ready to take on a full teaching load in Dumisani Bible School. In due time he also established important contacts with the University of Potchefstroom.

So the Dumisani Graduation day on 27 November 1993 for the final year students was a day of great thankfulness to the Lord. In spite of everything, we had reached that day and it was wonderful to see that students were going out into the world having completed their course in the Bible School. About 150 people attended the Graduation Service, which was followed by a meal together, using the Study House for extra eating space.

Correspondence Courses continue

In the midst of all the problems of 1993, the literature work and the correspondence courses carried on as usual. That January a newly released prisoner visited the Bible School. He had been the one delegated to distribute the mail in prison. He told of how eagerly men awaited their course lessons and what positive good they were doing. God was changing lives in there. All praise and the glory to the Lord.

As well as helping with all Dumisani Biblewomen or Sunday School Days, Mrs Isobel Maciver corrected the English language correspondence courses and at one time she noted down some of the encouraging answers given in response to the invitation: "Write down any part of the Bible that you have found helpful and tell why." Among the answers given was this; "Psalm 23 – This is the part of God's word that helped me find the right way in my life. Before I was a fool who followed fools, but now I follow Jesus and I am praying that God will help me to come out of my sins. I want God to help me and my family." Another wrote; "'*Though my father and mother both forsake me, the Lord will not forsake me.'* I know what it is to lose both my father and my mother and to be left a cripple. But I praise God every day, every night and every time because the Lord found me and I am his and he is mine and he cares for me."

Prof Clement Graham comes to help

From February to March 1994, Prof Clement Graham came at his own expense to help by giving a series of lectures on Christian Ethics, Homiletics and Ecclesiology in Dumisani. He was a benediction to us all. At first he found that the lectures he had prepared were expressed in language too technical for those for whom English was their second language. He immediately set to work to remedy this and the result was great appreciation on the part of the students and great satisfaction and delight on the part of the lecturer! He took a fatherly interest in the students and their situations. Each Friday the students came over from the Study House for coffee and eats together before a time of worship. On the last Friday of Prof Graham's visit, their deep voices could be heard singing as they came across the road into the other Dumisani building bearing a parcel which they presented to him with singing, dancing and handshaking! It was a painting of a Xhosa village beautifully done. He was thrilled with it and it was a constant reminder to him to the end of his days of the very happy time he spent at Dumisani.

When he reported to the Board in Scotland on his return he said that he had delivered 37 lectures at Dumisani, attended two Presbyteries, two Conferences, one for lay-preachers, one for ministers, and the Commission of General Assembly. He said he felt Dumisani was not merely a Bible School, nor even the centre for Correspondence Courses, but the Headquarters of the Church as well as the place where everyone came for help. He felt there was a need for another worker at Dumisani and the emphasis should be on the training of national pastors. Among the students who started that year were Buntu A. Mtishe and Khulile Davids.

There was sunshine and shadow for the missionaries during the time of his visit. Andrew Miller was born to David and Meg in Transkei on 27 February 1994 and was a great joy to the whole missionary family, and towards the end of Prof Graham's time with us, Elizabeth Graham had to have another operation in hospital in East London. He was so considerate and helpful not only at home but in insisting on giving company in the car to go down to East London to visit on a road which at that time was not so safe for whites to travel alone at night.

The Millers move to help in Dumisani

In response to this need for more staff, the General Assembly of the Free Church in South Africa and the Foreign Missions Board agreed to a request from Dumisani to release Rev David Miller from his work in Transkei to join the Dumisani staff. This he did on 1 October 1994 and the family settled in to a suitable house in 12 King's Road, King William's Town and became part of the Dumisani team. As well as lecturing, David took over most of the administration work. A condition of David's move to Dumisani was that he would remain on the Transkei Presbytery and be responsible for arranging lay-training and on-going ministerial education programmes.

Student worries

We were always thankful for the way our students conducted themselves at Dumisani, but we did have one incident which caused real worry and concern to us. We had to suspend a Free Church student on the grounds of immorality. The other students were really upset by this action, but the staff were united in resolve that a stand for righteousness had to be made. When the facts were laid before the students the unrest subsided and we were able to continue as before with much thankfulness to God. Throughout the country troubles were erupting among students. At the nearby Teachers' Training College at Zwelitsha there was some very serious rioting in which several staff members were badly injured. One of them was a lady who was a good friend of ours and a lovely Christian and who was always keen to help the students. That College had to be closed, so we were extra thankful that we were able to continue. In all the work of Dumisani we were greatly helped by the local King William's Town and the East London members of the Gereformeerde Kerk. Ds Johan Myburg, the minister, was keenly involved in the work of the Bible School and gave valuable assistance as a lecturer.

Donald Maciver looks back

When Donald had completed a year (1994) as lecturer and member of staff in Dumisani, he wrote of his experience. "The first year has been demanding, as expected, in that new lectures had to be prepared for Old Testament, New Testament and Homiletics (preaching). There is a lot of interaction with the students in class largely through "problem questions" and there is no end of them! But it also helps to find out where they are in terms of knowledge and understanding ... The challenge to a teacher is there all the time." Donald went on to show that this challenge came both through teaching in English when the first language of the students was Xhosa (all secondary and tertiary education throughout the country was conducted in English or Afrikaans) and in trying to get students to think analytically when all their education had been dominated by rote learning.

The Graduation service at the end of the year was a happy affair attended by about 100 people. As well as Free Church students there were private students from other churches and their friends

who always added colour and warmth to the graduation ceremonies!

Dumisani Theological Institute

In April 1995 the Dumisani School Board decided that, for
theological training purposes, the name should be changed to
Dumisani Theological Institute. As far as correspondence
courses and literature purposes were concerned it would continue
to be **Dumisani Bible School**. One of the denominations who
had three students attending Dumisani and were considering
sending more wanted the name change because they said the work
done was of a much higher standard than would be offered by a
Bible School!

Along with the teaching side of the work, the literature work
kept going. By the end of the year there were 12 books, one for
each quarter, of the three-year Bible Reading Notes completed and
undated so that they could be re-printed each year if necessary.
Seven books of Sunday School teacher's lessons, three for the
primary children and four for the older groups, one book for each
year, were ready along with their sets of pictures and they too
could be reprinted. About 500 children wrote the Sunday School
exams at the end of 1995.

At the Graduation Service at the end of 1995, one of the
outgoing students, speaking on behalf of those who were leaving,
gave a warm address in which he stressed how well the students
had knit together 'in a spirit of oneness and fellowship'. He spoke
of Dumisani as a place 'where the dignity of each student is equally
respected regardless of denominational backgrounds and where
every student feels secure'. He said they regarded their lecturers
as their friends and this close relationship made them grasp
their lessons very easily. "We have learned how to interpret the
Scriptures and to apply the Word of God to the nation as God-
committed men."

This was important as in Africa in some denominations
people could remain without a deep understanding of the moral
and ethical implications of the Gospel because the preaching had

not really addressed these problems and there may not be much doctrine in the sermons either. So the Dumisani teaching was designed to prepare their ministers-to-be to apply the Gospel to the people in the pew. The students asked that the standard be upgraded to degree level as soon as possible although this was already an ongoing issue with the University of Potchefstroom.

The growing list of Free Church in South Africa students associated with Dumisani at that time included P. Diniso, A.G. Ngaki, C. Xabadiya, B.A. Mtishe, K. Davids, F.F. Mva, L. Piyo, W. Ledwaba, R. Gotywa (who came into the Free Church later). Some had already finished their courses.

MORE STAFF CHANGES

Goodbye to the Grahams

In late October 1995 Elizabeth Graham was seriously ill and required further surgery for cancer. The surgeon said she had to have a full course of chemotherapy to have any hope of long-term survival. But that was problematical there at that time. Eventually the decision was made that it was time to go back to Scotland to complete the medical treatment. The Board insisted that she should not come back first while Bill followed later, so there were only three weeks available to wind up all our work in Dumisani, and pack all our belongings to be sent home by sea by the end of January 1996.

While in hospital for two nights having the second dose of chemotherapy there was an interesting incident. "After supper I heard lovely Xhosa voices singing psalms or hymns in harmony. I pushed my drip trolley out and went to track it down. The women patients (about 16) in the main ward were having a service and they said I must come and join them – and preach to them! I went back for my Bible and some copies of the little red book 'Molo' I had brought in with me and joined them. We sang. Then they **all** prayed at the same time. As the volume died down and the last Amen sounded they looked at me expectantly! So I spoke to them – first comfort to the con-verted from Deuteronomy 31: 8 '*The Lord goes before you **and*** *will be with you'* and then to the unconverted, urging them to accept the Lord. I gave them all a 'Molo' booklet which explains the way of salvation through a story of two men who meet at the outpatient clinic. Then we sang again, and I departed during the singing of Amens, with waves all round. Next evening there was no singing – I think some had been operated on and some may have gone home. But a Coloured lady came into my ward and we got talking. She said she was not a Christian because she kept putting off and saying 'another time'. I said I would probably never see her again as we were going away, so maybe God had sent me to her to urge her once more to accept Him, as his Spirit does not always strive with us. She said she would go and do it that very night."

A wonderful surprise farewell was arranged for us at such short notice. We were overwhelmed by the love and the gifts given to us. "At one stage all connected with Dumisani invaded the podium to present the Grahams with gifts and to literally wrap them together with a colourful linen in a very fitting, symbolic and moving gesture."

Because of flooding the Burnshill District transport was unable to get out to come to the farewell. But they braved dreadful road conditions next day to find us in King William's Town, hold a service with us and give us their lovely gifts. We never heard that they had arrived home safely! It was hard to leave.

Over to Rev Donald Maciver

Yes, it was hard to leave, but it was a great blessing to have someone of the wisdom and experience of Donald Maciver to take over the responsibilities of Principal so suddenly, and he was duly appointed to the post. It was hard for him to have to take up this work at such short notice, but he shouldered the burden and did not allow Dumisani to suffer.

The Macivers were due for home leave in June but in a wonderful provision Rev Peter Gadsby from the Presbyterian Church of Eastern Australia, along with his wife Lindy and their two younger children Marcus and Jennifer, offered to give six months service in Dumisani. It was good for David Miller, also an Australian, to have another from 'down under' to keep him company! The PCEA kindly bore all expenses for this help. Peter Gadsby gave lectures on Doctrine, Old Testament and New Testament subjects as well as Homiletics. Lindy gave considerable help in reconstructing the library.

The Christies arrive

The negotiations with the University of Potchefstroom came to a successful conclusion in August 1996, so it was important that Dumisani should have suitably qualified lecturing staff. The University had made a major contribution to Christian education in South Africa and, very especially, in encouraging colleges like Dumisani to raise the level of theological education offered to African students in various parts of the country. As the level of school education increased so there would be a greater demand for tertiary education and the church would have to take account of this also. As congregational members had more education, they would not be so tolerant of a pastor who did not.

For this reason the Foreign Missions Board in Scotland invited Rev Ronald Christie to consider offering for work in South Africa. Thankfully he accepted the invitation for work in Dumisani and in the Free Church in South Africa. He and his wife Morag were farewelled from Govanhill and Ronald was inducted to the South African mission in Govanhill on 11 September 1996. They travelled there in November.

Before they arrived, two delegates from the Board came to visit South Africa from 29 October for three weeks. They were Rev William Macleod, Portree, and Peter Morrison, Secretary of the Board, with his wife Marion. One of their recommendations on their return was that the Constitution of Dumisani be reconsidered since, although its main role would always be to provide training for ministers and leaders of the Free Church, it was now providing theological training for the students of many other denominations. This was in line with one of Donald Maciver's own recommendations when the Board interviewed him during his home leave.

One very worthwhile new development was that Donald Maciver now conducted 'workshops' with preachers in nearby congregations after the morning church services and another was that the elders in these congregations were encouraging all the over 18s to study the Correspondence Courses. It was hoped that Dumisani would be able to continue and develop such contacts with the congregations.

Increase in interest in Dumisani

The 1997 session in Dumisani began encouragingly with 17 students, eight doing the new B.A. course. Donald Maciver wrote: "Although we have hardly started this first year of re-vamped courses it is clear that we will have to do some hard thinking by mid-year to come up with a scheme to change our timetables so that students can study at Dumisani in the early evenings ... We have had many requests too from people wanting to do Correspondence Courses as a result of advertising ... We hope the interest in Dumisani is spiritual and we seek to stress this to the students. But this interest is also part of a wider movement in South Africa referred to as the *culture of learning*, which is trying to make up for the inequalities of the past. We have to take advantage of the present climate in which learning is gaining importance and make ourselves known to a wider constituency but our prayer is that the right students will find their way to Dumisani and for the right reasons."

Meanwhile Rev Ronald Christie seemed to take to the Dumisani situation like a duck to water! He was soon lecturing and preaching in the districts and adventuring into understanding Xhosa, while Morag soon found herself involved in helping out in all sorts of situations, especially with the Bible Women.

While the Millers were on home leave in 1997 Rev Norman and Mrs Angela Reid of the EPC of Ireland came to take their place – indeed they were able to be at Dumisani for most of the 1997 session. When they were thanked on their return for all they had contributed to the work in South Africa it was said that "perhaps they should not settle too long in Ireland"!

The Macivers return to Scotland

In mid-January 1998 the Macivers found it necessary to return home to Scotland for personal reasons. The Foreign Missions Board expressed its gratitude to Donald for the work he had done in Dumisani, particularly in overseeing the development of the accreditation process with the University of Potchefstroom for Christian Higher Education so that Dumisani students could have the opportunity to study towards a Theological Degree. They recognised that the Macivers went out at a particularly difficult time and at a considerable sacrifice as far as their family was concerned, and prayed for the Lord's blessing on him as he took up ministry again in the home church. Mr Maciver was inducted to the congregation of Fearn, Ross-shire on 28 May 1998.

Another new Principal

As Donald and Isobel Maciver and Marcus returned to Scotland, a new Principal for Dumisani was needed. But there, by the goodness of God, was Rev Ronald Christie. He was appointed Principal and although he also had to take over the reins at short notice and in difficult circumstances he was equal to the task and took Dumisani on to the next stage of its development. There were 13 students at various stages of study in 1998. The Miller family returned from leave in time for the opening of the new session. Ds Andries Coetzer of the Gereformeerde Kerk helped with the teaching programme during the first semester of the year.

In the meantime **Rev Alex Murdo Macleod** was asked if he would go to Dumisani for a short period and this he did, accompanied by his wife Chrissie, for the second semester of 1998. He enjoyed the experience. Writing after he returned to Scotland, "Although a short-term worker's feeling, I would say, that if I were in a congregation at home I would wish to 'adopt' some mission work, and none would be more attractive to me now than Dumisani College. Whatever is true of this land, it seems to me to be in dire need of the College and the Gospel."

Rev John MacPherson, **Rev Kenneth Stone** and **Mr Ernest Brown** and **their wives** also gave valuable help during this period.

The Reids come back

Rev Norman Reid was contacted and he agreed to return to South Africa to work as a lecturer in Dumisani as from January 1999. Remember – *'if you drink of the water of Africa, you will always come back!'* Norman Reid would remain a minister of the Evangelical Presbyterian Church of Ireland and that Church agreed to support him financially while he was seconded as a Free Church of Scotland missionary. So once again we were deeply indebted to the Irish church for excellent missionary help.

The Reids were set apart in a service in Finaghy EPC Church, Belfast, on 12 December 1998, and in that service reference was made to Norman's 'long pastoral experience in a church planting situation which will be invaluable'. And indeed it was, as have been Angela's 'gifts of friendship and spiritual counsel.'

Norman and Angela Reid returned to South Africa along with their son Stephen who continued his school and later university studies in South Africa. Norman was to be centred in Dumisani but was to give valuable help in the Free Church in South Africa as well. Norman began work in Dumisani when the new session started on February 2, 1999.

Norman wrote shortly after his return to South Africa:

> Dumisani seems twice as busy as the last time we were here. I am enjoying teaching very much, though it is certainly hard work, like preparing ten sermons or Bible Studies every week. It is a great joy to see the increase in the number of students. They are keen to learn and there is a good spiritual atmosphere.
>
> A few days ago I was teaching Ministerial Studies and had 10 men in the class. We had completed six lectures ... so I decided to give them a test for an hour. When I was going over to the classroom I could hear singing ... what sounded like a Psalm in Xhosa. When

I went into the classroom I waited until they were finished, then I said, "You all sound very happy. It must be because you are looking forward to the exam." One of them answered: "Oh no, we are not happy; we were just singing a prayer for help in the exam!" They have a good sense of humour and are keen to learn, so it is a pleasure to teach them. However, it is awesome to think that I have some responsibility for their entry into the ministry.

Additional welcome help

The Free Church of Scotland's Missions Board had pledged finance for three lecturers but a fourth was needed. So it was a great pleasure that **Rev Bryce Taho**, on retirement from the Army Chaplaincy, was now able to give some assistance in Dumisani.

Prof Andries Kruger, a retired professor from Pretoria, and **Ds Johan Myburg** of the Gereformeerde Kerk, East London gave very valued help also at this time. Prof Kruger, who had wide experience of theological education in Africa, had to undergo major heart surgery but he returned to Dumisani when he was well enough to do so.

Mrs Julia Campbell, a trained teacher, who had come with her husband Douglas to work initially in the district work, was also teaching two classes in English language. And the other Dumisani missionary wives, Mrs Morag Christie and Mrs Meg Miller, played a very active role in the training of the Biblewomen, Sunday School Teachers and work in connection with the Correspondence Courses and the Library.

A NEW MILLENNIUM

The Twenty Year Landmark

In February 1999, Dimbaza/Dumisani Bible School was twenty years old. Twenty years of the Lord's faithfulness and goodness! Twenty years of God's Word going forth by training or distance learning or full-time study! Twenty years of sacrificial giving and much prayer from far and near!

As if to mark the anniversary there was a considerable increase in the number of students attending. In all there were 18 full-time and 10 part-time students.

Eight of these were at different levels in degree programmes; five were in the Diploma Course; thirteen were doing the Certificate Course and two were admitted on a special basis. Seven of the students were Free Church, one new student being Mr Mxolisi Mafuya, and the others were from a wide spectrum of the Christian Churches of South Africa, one was a Bishop from one of the Ethiopian Churches (African Independent Churches)!

The range of subjects taught in Dumisani provided students with a comprehensive theological education. Those students who entered the degree programme were taught Biblical Hebrew and Greek as well as Dogmatics, Apologetics, Church History and Practical Theology subjects. The Diploma and Certificate courses varied according to the needs of students and had to be altered over the years. These courses came to serve as access routes to the Degree programme for students who did not initially have the required academic entrance qualifications.

As well as the day-to-day teaching of the students, there were elders' training programmes in Ciskei and Transkei. After Donald Maciver left for Scotland, Ronald Christie began a series of such meetings at the request of the King William's Town District. The Transkei 'Preachers' Days' had to be organised by the Presbytery, using public holidays, as Saturdays were far too busy for extra meetings. The Sunday School work had also increased. At the end of 1999, 810 children sat the year-end Sunday School exam. They came from 27 different Sunday Schools. As David Miller said: "Whatever the pressures and difficulties might be (with only a few staff to do it all) there is a tremendous encouragement just in being part of such a ministry to so many parts of the Southern African Christian Church."

At the same time, under the care of David Miller, the Correspondence Courses were still coming and going in their hundreds, and improvements were being made in the literature field too. Some of the literature had already been computerised with the help of friends around the world, and the filing system for the correspondence students had also been computerised, and was much more useful as a result. Dumisani was getting ready for the 21st Century!

Entry into the new Millennium

In 2000 a 'study day' for all former and present students of Dumisani was introduced, to encourage them to keep up their habit of study. The theme for the first meeting was 'The Eldership'.

Norman Reid also had a new experience when one of the students, a builder to trade, asked him to go with him to visit the prison and to tell the prisoners about the Correspondence Courses. It was a maximum security prison with over 900 prisoners, a very sad place because most were serving life sentences. He said: "It was a great thing to be able to preach to them. There were about 70 at the service, many of them carrying Bibles. They all sang heartily and listened very attentively. I preached on Matthew 11: 28 'Come unto me all you who labour and are heavy laden and I will give you rest.' It was strange to look these men in the face and know that most of them were murderers and yet to have a message to bring to them that was true and that could give them hope.

After the service we gave out some Bibles and the first lesson of one of our Correspondence Courses. Then we went to the prison hospital. There we met about a dozen patients and also gave them a Bible to share between them and some Correspondence Courses."

There were 33 students enrolled in Dumisani in 2000, so Ronald Christie had his hands full to manage to match classes to lecturers. Some were full-time, some part-time. About a third of the students came from Presbyterian denominations, a third were Methodists and the rest from a variety of ecclesiastical backgrounds. There was an age range from early twenties to mid-fifties. There were three Free Church students studying in Dumisani at that time and one minister completing a degree course. With such a diverse body of students it was a matter of thankfulness that a spirit of harmony existed.

The end of the century but not the end of the road

With the year 2000 we have come to the end of our journey with Dumisani, but this is not the end of Dumisani!

Towards the end of the century Rev Ronald Christie wrote a perceptive article telling what the view from Dumisani was like now that it was twenty years old. There were men on the Diploma Course, many more on the Certificate one year Course, a few on the Degree Course and wondering about help to go on to Post Graduate studies, and many, many from prisons and elsewhere writing the Correspondence Courses. There were several Kirk Sessions which would welcome a lecturer from Dumisani who had time to come and take special sessions with the office-bearers to help them with their preaching and taking funerals ... Everywhere one looked there was much land yet to be possessed. But so much which had been accomplished only with the help of the Lord.

A local newspaper article published in January 2000 said, "The two main features of the Institute's ethos are humble devotion and practical scholarship." And this surely will characterise its work into the future. **Dumisani uYehova!**

ON REFLECTION

One understands the feeling of being neglected on the part of those districts which are geographically far away from Dumisani. We have not always served them well. One hope which remained unfulfilled in the period we have been looking at, was the establishing of regular training on a Theological Training by Extension (TEE) pattern. However, on occasions when courses were held, there was not always a good response.

• It has been good to see the way God has used each successive principal and staff member for the steady progress of Dumisani. God has tuned his servants to the needs of the hour. While the facilities are limited we are thankful that the quality and Biblical faithfulness of the teaching has been consistently high. This has continued so that increasingly Dumisani has become a vital centre of Biblical and theological education in the Eastern Cape Province, and its influence is felt well beyond that.

- The original focus of the Bible School in producing correspondence courses and other literature, now updated, is still a positive influence for good.

- Whatever had been achieved by Dimbaza/Dumisani up to the year 2000 it was due, under God, to the faithful help and encouragement of a multitude of friends and to the support of the Free Church of Scotland International Missions Board, the University of Potchefstroom (now North West), the PCEA, EPC of Ireland and the Gereformeerde Kerk.

14

The Free Church in the New South Africa 1990–2000

The 1990s were momentous years for South Africa. It moved from being a Republic where the relatively few privileged Whites still tried to tell the rest what to do, to being a democracy where everybody had the vote and the Government was largely Black. Indeed, there was almost apartheid in reverse, as under an 'affirmative action' employment policy, black applicants would usually get preference.

How did this happen? What happened in the political field to so change this country?

POLITICAL CHANGES

At the turn of the decade change was in the air. First Russia began thawing (Glasnost), religious prisoners were freed; the Berlin wall tottered, broke and collapsed; Poland, Czechoslovakia, Romania ... broke the shackles of Communism, with 100,000 voices in the Square in Bucharest shouting 'God is alive'. In China too there were pro-democracy demonstrations when thousands of students rallied in Tiananmen Square in Beijing but they were ruthlessly bulldozed down. In Africa, South West Africa gained its independence and became Namibia. Now it was South Africa's turn!

On 2 February 1990, in a 'watershed speech', Mr F.W. de Klerk, the President, announced the beginning of the 'New South Africa'. Political prisoners were to be freed, the ANC (African National Congress) and other organisations were unbanned, negotiations were to be entered into, and Nelson Mandela would be freed. And he was – on Sunday 11 February! There was jubilation everywhere, apart from some bad rioting in Cape Town. Mr Mandela made a speech in which he said the ANC must now intensify its struggle, and world opinion towards South Africa did a complete u-turn.

The Ciskei Coup

There had already been a peaceful military coup in Transkei in 1988 under General Bantu Holomisa. Now in Ciskei, as we slept in the early hours of Sunday 4 March 1990, while President Sebe of Ciskei was away in Hong Kong, there was a take-over of power by the Ciskei Army in Bisho, just up the road from King William's Town. Brigadier Gqozo was now in charge and a Council of State was formed. All was quiet at first. But in the evening and next day there was a trail of destruction in Mdantsane, Dimbaza and Zwelitsha – houses and factories burning and 18,000 jobs lost – and it seemed as if all of Ciskei, hanging on to lorries and buses hooting their horns, made their way to the Bisho Stadium. Nelson Mandela came to King William's Town and Bisho and at a huge rally urged the need for discipline among his people. All quietened down, but friction developed between the ANC and the PAC (Pan African Congress) which impacted on our areas. The PAC wanted power, not power-sharing. In some of our villages there was war between these two organisations and sometimes a low missionary profile had to be maintained. Village headmen were targeted by the ANC who wanted to set up village committees in place of the traditional 'inkundlas' or councils which followed a more tribal way of doing things and which were presided over by Headmen officially recognised and appointed by the Government.

South Africa comes in from the cold

As the year 1990 progressed, events tumbled over themselves to get into the history books. President de Klerk and Nelson Mandela met and talked as friends many times, each seeming to have a high regard for the other. They both made triumphal world tours. Astounding news was that the National Party was to become non-racial, and the schools, the beaches and the cafes followed when the Separate Amenities Act was abolished on 15 October 1990. Finally the Group Areas Act was abolished in February 1991 and we had almost arrived!

Daily we saw a thawing in world attitudes to South Africa. America and Europe were considering lifting sanctions and sports restrictions, and the Rugby Board, the Olympics Committee, and British TV all welcomed the 'new South Africa'. A Springbok (South African) cricket team had a 3-day cricket series in India with a rapturous welcome and world record crowds.

Still the violence continued with inter-party fighting and a terrible death toll. Every news bulletin was a dread to listen to as blacks butchered blacks or a white farmer a day was murdered. In Natal, violence was mainly between the ANC (mainly Xhosa), and Inkatha (mainly Zulu). There were some atrocious mass murders in villages there too. The leaders of the main black organisations blamed the police and "The Third Force" – a mysterious shadow whether of substance or not we did not know, but they said it was behind the violence, stirring it up. In some of the villages in our church areas there seemed to be almost anarchy – youths leading in everything. 'Young people must camp in the school', 'young people must NOT go to church', and then rival gangs murdered each other. Our church young people were afraid to join the other youth and afraid not to do so. Some gruesome 'necklace murders' took place too for the most trivial of reasons.

In Transkei there was an unsuccessful attempt at a coup on 22 November 1990. A great deal of violence and toyi-toyi marches took place in Butterworth and Umtata and at times the missionaries and other white folk felt quite intimidated.

The Bisho Massacre

During 1992 there was much jockeying for power on the part of the Nationalist Government and the ANC and other organisations. Mass action was called for and days of national strikes. The ANC really wanted to unseat the Gqozo government in Ciskei and to gain control there, so there was much unrest. A march was arranged to Bisho on August 4 1992, to hand over demands to Brigadier Gqozo. He refused to let them in. After frantic telephone negotiations the huge crowd streamed away peacefully although they had not got their way.

But on 7 September 1992 another ANC march on Bisho was organised. Every agency in the country tried to stop them but they said the march would go on. They agreed just to go into the Stadium unarmed. However, some of the marchers got through a gap in the razor wire and a crowd followed, heading for the Government complex in the centre of Bisho, and the Ciskei troops stationed on top of the Government buildings just fired upon them. Twentynine people were killed, and others injured. The crowd fled back down the road into King William's Town. The South African police and army formed a barricade on the road outside the missionary home at Maitland Road, but soon hooting vehicles from among the fleeing people had to get through to the hospital. A Red Cross ambulance was first – so full of badly injured people that the nurse was hanging out of the window. Then followed cars full of injured – even one lady in the open boot of a car!

Meanwhile the crowd headed for the Victoria Park in King. Later they regrouped and held an all-night vigil on the Ciskei border, but after dark many groups came back down to King. There was an eerie peace till midday next day. ANC officials were addressing those up at Bisho and Bishop Desmond Tutu held a service on the road. A chanting crowd with banners came down Maitland Road to the King Stadium where Nelson Mandela addressed them. There was calm after that and the crowd dispersed, but there was a great deal of violence to houses and people when they returned to their villages.

Next day there was a mass funeral service held in the Victoria Park in King, with 29 coffins lined up and a crowd of about 40 000 people. The rhetoric was chilling: "Kill the bosses." "Keep the fires burning after we go." Chris Hani, the leader of the armed wing of the ANC, was one of the most fiery. There was a large notice calling Mr de Klerk and others "The Butchers of Bisho".

One good thing which resulted from the Bisho Massacre was that even the more moderate leaders of the ANC were shocked at the vehemence of the violence of their own people. Talks were resumed between the ANC and the Government, which, in turn, stirred up the other political factions to even more mass action!

On Easter Saturday, 10 April 1993 Chris Hani was assassinated. Once again South Africa seemed to be teetering on the brink of disaster. There was a massive funeral and several inflammatory speeches. Everyone held their breath wondering what would happen when the crowd left the stadium where the funeral service was being held. There was a lot of anti-white talk and action but eventually it all settled down.

However all of this activity did mean that Dumisani came into its own as several church events had to happen there. The Assembly was changed from Port Elizabeth to Dumisani; the celebration of Angus Alex Macdonald's 25th anniversary in the ministry was changed from Pirie; the Knox Communion service was held there, and all Assemblies and Commissions were to be in Dumisani until further notice.

The election at last

As 1993 drew to a close big things were happening politically. After very many ups and downs the new Constitution was at last voted in. Campaigning started in earnest for the first 'free and fair' election in which all members of South African society could take part. The date was fixed for 27 April 1994.

In the run-up to the election, there were waves of violence – both criminal and political and at times it seemed impossible that an election could ever take place.

A big 'Jesus Peace Rally' was organised, and behind the scenes an intermediary was arranging meetings between warring factions. Christians of all denominations prayed, sometimes round the clock, and the Lord heard those prayers - for the atmosphere on Election Day, when it eventually arrived, was almost a party one. Long queues of voters of all colours and races waited in the sunshine, chatting together, for their turn to vote at last. There was goodwill, patience, camaraderie and an almost peaceful election which saw the ANC win a huge majority and Nelson Mandela as President.

He was installed in a spectacular Ceremony attended by royals and dignitaries of the world, and the euphoria lasted for some months after. Everyone settled down to live again, and for the rest of the decade there was a working out and settling in. Nine regions were formed, each with its own capital and Parliament. Bisho became the legislative capital for the Eastern Cape Region. So "Peace – blessed, blissful, unbelievable peace" settled on the 'beloved country' and its people who had been crying for so long.

There had to be some 'trying of wings' or 'flexing of muscles' after this transition to democracy, and it came in the form of a wave of strikes. Everyone in every section of society seemed to want to know what it felt like to rebel and be free to do so. Students rampaged and trashed campuses; people were taken hostage, nurses spread infected blood over ward floors and walls ... Then suddenly everyone seemed to get tired of it and most wanted to settle down to being good citizens. Unfortunately criminals have made cities dangerous places to live in. Big dogs, high railings and razor wire have become the norm in the suburbs at least. But by the end of the decade and century, South Africa had stabilised and taken its place among the free nations of the world.

A Multi-Faith Society

The religious situation in South Africa changed quite dramatically following the transfer of power from the predominantly Afri-kaans Nationalist Government to the new ANC led Government. The former regime favoured Christianity and gave it a real place in education, the broadcasting media and in public life generally. The new regime had come to power through the help of move-ments and governments, many of which were not Christian and as a result South Africa became a 'multi-faith' nation almost over-night. The public place given to Christianity was, if not altogether withdrawn, certainly reduced. Several of the leading figures in the new Government were Muslims. South Africa was undergoing changes that were far more radical than the political emancipation which was catching the headlines. There was, and still is a battle for the soul of the country in progress.

MISSIONARY MATTERS AND MOVEMENTS

A Field Council is set up

There was a lot of missionary comings and goings during this decade. The Camerons, Wylies, Macivers, Christies, Reids and Campbells came, and the Glovers, Kenny Macdonalds, Grahams, Angus Macdonalds, Macivers, Wylies and the Frasers went. The Millers moved from Transkei to Dumisani. Mr Jimmy Gunn from Rosskeen Congregation came to help for three months.'

One result of the visit of the delegates from the Foreign Missions Board in 1989, (Rev D.K. Macleod, with his wife Nina, and Mr Alasdair Fraser) was the holding of a Sunday evening service for the missionary families. The first of these was held on January 14 1990. There were 19 present, including the children. This tradition continued for many years.

Another result was the setting up of a Field Council for the missionary families in South Africa. The first Field Council meeting was held in May 1990. This proved to be a good forum for discussion of matters which referred to the missionaries, but not to the South African Free Church.

Dena Macleod

In the early 1990s Miss Dena Macleod, from Lewis, was working in Umtata as an accountant. While she used her gifts and training in her work there, she was also a good friend to the missionaries and the Africans. She was actively involved in the local congregation of the Free Church and had a good-going Sunday School.

Dena wrote about her experience in the following letter, which was published in the Monthly Record:

"What should a young Free Church member do who feels called to work on the mission field somewhere abroad, but is not a minister or teacher? One answer would be to apply for a post you are qualified for and become a 'support worker' within the church rather than a full-time missionary ... Why do it this way?

1. The company would normally provide accommodation.

2. The financial burden would not fall on the church.

3. A new sector of the population could be reached.

4. The labourers are few."

Dena went on to point out some of the drawbacks, including the fact that it can be lonely and sometimes the hours one has to work may curtail the amount that can be done in the church. Dena herself was the best advert for what could be done and there were many other avenues of opportunity at that time, especially in Transkei.

Two new missionary couples

Rev Ken and Mrs Joan Cameron

Welcome reinforcements came on 22 January 1991 in the form of Ken and Joan Cameron, this time as full-time missionaries. They arrived in East London on a night of heavy rain and mist and were met by most of the missionary families. There was so much of news to catch up on from Scotland, and in anticipation so much to tell about the work in South Africa. Two days later fourteen of the missionaries gathered for a meal followed by the usual Thursday prayer meeting. There was much for which to thank the Lord that night.

Meanwhile, Rev Thyson Nkwelo had retired from the Tabase District, Transkei, on 1 December 1990. The Transkei Presbytery therefore decided that the Camerons should minister in the Tabase District, and after a short time in Umtata Ken and Joan moved to live at Efata, a few miles outside the town. The Church officially welcomed them at a joint WCA Convention held in Mdisa, Ciskei, and Ken preached at the Sunday morning communion service.

Very soon the Camerons were deep in the work. They had seven congregations to look after in their district, as well as the work in Umtata. The Sunday School work often suffered from neglect in our Free Churches in South Africa, and Ken and Joan gave a lot of attention to this aspect of ministry in their own district. Six new Sunday Schools were up and running, but as Ken said, "It is one thing to get them started and quite another to keep them going – and coming, both teachers and pupils!" Work with teenagers in an organisation like the Campaigner Movement did well for a time but then gave way to meetings of the Free Church in South Africa Youth Organisation. This was designed for the age group 18–40 but teenagers were also welcome at the popular monthly rallies held in different churches. The Camerons felt this was perhaps one of the most valuable things they had been able to do for their youth. Singing was interspersed with talks and questions and the Tabase District Choir learned many a new psalm tune with a Scottish flavour!

Inasmuch Fund

Ken and Joan had a very compassionate heart for the need they saw all too clearly in the villages and homes they visited. After some time Joan set up the *Inasmuch Fund*, which helped to provide housing, education, food, clothing and much more for the needy people in their area. People in the home churches were extremely generous in their response, and it was amazing how many people this fund helped. The children looked forward to classes held for them each week in different places and were ready to meet the car as it arrived – sometimes a very long way from Umtata. Some of these children went through school, and later even university, because of the *Inasmuch Fund*.

One such young man was Kiviet Zide, who returned the Camerons' help to him by translating and doing whatever else he could for them. Although he had polio at the age of 4 years he was the first in Transkei to gain the Scouting Springbok Badge. He was converted, perhaps after reading Bunyan's *Pilgrims Progress*. So it was a devastating blow when, after graduating BA from Transkei University and just after getting his first job and car, he was killed in a car crash. As the Camerons said, "He proved a faithful pilgrim who, we believe, has reached the Celestial City and entered into the joy of his Lord." Death was common in South Africa and Transkei at that time and some of the deaths in the Tabase District were particularly deeply felt by Ken and Joan. Indeed Joan was unable to continue in the work for a time because of the effects of the many traumas they had experienced. As in all the other districts, HIV/AIDS was taking a terrible toll, especially of the young. Lifestyles were such that the young people were dying but no cause was given. Hospitals in Transkei at that time, many of them originally mission hospitals, were poorly maintained, with a great lack of adequate staffing.

Brighter days

But there were also many bright Christians in the congregations whom they came to write about and to appreciate so much. As Ken said: "The Lord has his people even in dark days and difficult places." At one Easter Convention which Tabase District was hosting, the theme was *"The Christian and his Saviour"*. Joan Cameron wrote that the people were welcomed with the Saviour's words: "Come and see" (John 1:31), and they were sent on their way with the angel's instruction, "Go and tell" (Matt 28:7). Many young people attended, choirs sang and the emphasis throughout was on Christ – Redeemer, Royal Master, Returning King. "The food was excellent," they said, "but the preaching was better."

When the Camerons returned from leave in June 1998 they found all the congregations of their district gathered in Tabase under a big banner saying, "Welcome Mfundisi and Mfundisikazi, this is your home!" And that is what they felt too. An elder said on another occasion, "It was no waste of time, Umfundisi, coming here. I have been enriched and Christ has found me!" Ken Cameron and his colleague Ian Wylie held Preachers' Days when practical advice was given on preparation for worship as well as on the preparation of sermons. On the initiative of their office-bearers they would study part of a Dumisani correspondence course together, leaving the men to finish the lesson at home and bring it to the next Kirk Session.

The Umtata Church

One of the big projects in Ken's ministry was the building of the Umtata Church. It was difficult to build up a congregation there as several of the people liked to go to their family homes in the country over the weekends. Ken felt an African pastor in Umtata would be beneficial, and he stressed that the building would enable the Transkei people to have "Dumisani by extension." Because the church was in a big town it had to comply with stricter building regulations and consequently cost more to build. There were frustrating delays, but in December 2000 a very attractive building was ready for services. It was officially opened on 24 February the following year and has been much in use since.

At the Opening Day Ken said that the hope was that "it will become a centre of Gospel influence in the important centre where it is placed". Such an influence was sorely needed. Ken referred to a TIME Magazine report that 50% of South African 15-year-olds were expected to die in the next decade (from 2000) and since 51% of the Transkei population was under 15 years that surely spelled disaster for the area.

However, he said, "We are ploughing in hope and, although, here and there, there are a few green shoots the harvest seems a long way off. But our God is mighty, His Word will certainly not return to Him void and we covet daily, at the Heavenly Throne, the Youth of Transkei for the Kingdom of our Saviour Christ."

Thirteen years passed quickly in the various ministries of the Tabase District before the Camerons retired to Scotland in 2004. Again, it was very hard to leave, but good to leave it all in the Lord's more than capable hands.

Rev Ian and Mrs Maryanne Wylie

The second new missionary couple who brought help and encouragement to Transkei were Rev Ian D. Wylie and his wife Maryanne, both South Africans. They became interested in the Free Church's missionary work in their country through correspondence with Rev Joe McCracken in the mid-60s and Ian later trained at the Free Church College, Edinburgh, in the early 1970s. But when he finished his course there he received a call from his former congregation in Johannesburg and he felt he should accept it. However his interest in the missionary work did not grow less and in 1990 he applied to become a minister of the Free Church of Scotland

and a missionary seconded to the Free Church in South Africa. His application was gladly accepted and at the 1991 General Assembly in Scotland he was accepted as a Free Church minister. He and Maryanne brought a valuable new dimension to the mission, as they were working in the country of their birth and they didn't need to adjust to a new climate or apply for passports and visas. At one time Ian had worked in the mines and knew the trials and temptations that would assail those of the Transkei men who worked up there and came home only for Christmas. Ian and Maryanne could also speak Afrikaans, and had given several years of ministry in the Gereformeerde Kerk, so they were a good link between the two churches in South Africa. They had five grown-up children living in South Africa.

Embo District becomes vacant and is filled

The Transkei Presbytery was asked where it wanted Ian to be placed, and decided on the Embo District. This district was vacant because Rev David Fraser had asked the Foreign Missions Board to allow him to transfer to Cape Town. They agreed on condition that the Free Church in South Africa also agreed to the move. The Transkei Presbytery was very reluctant to do this, particularly as the impression was given that the decision had already been taken without prior reference to them. The Board apologised to the Presbytery with the assurance that no slight had been intended to the independence of the Presbytery or the General Assembly of the Free Church in South Africa, and the Fraser family move to Cape Town went ahead.

And so Ian and Maryanne came to live in the manse in Stanley Nelson Drive, Umtata, and became used to the good people and the long distances of travel to the nine congregations of the Embo District. They too were especially concerned about the teenagers of their district. They wrote to ask for special prayer for them, as they didn't own their own Bibles or have much Bible knowledge, and often fell into immoral ways and, because of their culture, they were not encouraged to discuss their concerns with adults. So the Wylies built up a good ministry among the young people, and through the kindness of friends in Scotland they were able to supply Bibles to several of them.

Old Traditions

The Wylies found a warm welcome wherever they went in their ministry. They were encouraged by a fine choir festival with 8 choirs and 75 young people. But at the same time there were so many problems. Professing Christians still had such difficulty in making a complete break with the non-Christian beliefs of their culture. Maryanne says: "Ian baptised a child recently and only afterwards did we notice a charm around his neck. We asked the mother to remove the charm as the little one was now to be brought up for Jesus. But she hesitated and said, 'This is something we do. I will try but it is very difficult'. The mother had answered the questions well at the examination with the elder, and yet, here she was, finding it difficult to part with the old way of life." It was easy to be discouraged, but the whole environment was so unchristian.

As they told of this incident the Wylies also asked prayer for South Africa in general. "Because the dishonesty, corruption, violence, immorality, laziness and godlessness which are on every hand affect us all. Our people are fearful, traditional religion is on the increase – we see this in every District of the Free Church in Southern Africa. Please pray for a movement of the Spirit in the congregations."

The Building of Umzimkulu

The Wylies were also able to give practical help to several people in their district and to develop different projects because of gifts given by God's people for the work. They rebuilt the house of one of their key helpers; they held a camp for the young people, attended by 43 children; they helped widows and their children and provided 22 winter tops for toddlers. They were able to use Christian films and video recordings which helped in the work. But one of the special projects for which they received help was the new church building at Umzimkulu. The previous one had been built on the flood plain and was washed away, so the new one was built higher up.

Umzimkulu is about 162 miles from Umtata near the border with Natal, so if Ian had forgotten his screwdriver he couldn't go home to get it! There were many troubles in the building of this church, and many long treks to see to the construction, but at last in 1993 it was complete and opened for public worship. The congregation there was encouraging. They praised God for the growth of the congregation, asking prayer particularly for the young people. "Life can be difficult and dangerous, especially for girls, but we praise God for those who are testifying to God's saving work in their lives."

Encouragement and disappointment

In 1998 Ian asked for prayer for Xolani Damane, a young man who was 'Embo District's first prospective student for the ministry'. (Xolani did train in Dumisani and on completion he succeeded Ian as minister of the Embo District. Sadly, however, he died after only a short time of ministry.)

One great and sad disappointment at this time was the tragic death of one of their most able elders Doctor Sigodi (Doctor was his Christian name). On 22 September 1998 he was involved in a serious motor accident caused by the sheer recklessness of a drunken taxi driver. About a fortnight later he died because of severe burns and other wounds. A Colonel in the Correctional Services, he was the Assistant Director of Prisons in Transkei. Doctor Sigodi had been a special person and a great help to the Wylies in many ways. He was only 46 when he died, and the church lost one of its wisest and best elders. Why? We know the Lord knows.

Maryanne and the READ Educational Trust

Maryanne was involved with what is called the READ Educational Trust. The aim of the projects run by the Trust is to help underprivileged children learn English language skills, as English is the language of the classroom in many areas of South Africa. Maryanne was involved with projects in rural schools. A portable box library containing dictionaries, fiction and non-fiction books, and other attractive materials was placed in each school. Maryanne's job was to see that these books were used responsibly and to train the teachers and principals to use the resources effectively. Many times there were disappointments – the school walls or roof had fallen down, the books had been stolen, the teachers were away attending a Teachers' Union meeting – but when the books were being used well, the results showed a dramatic improvement in the class-work. She tells of two of her many visits:

> At one school the vice-head is a sangoma (witchdoctor) so she usually grumbles under her breath when I arrive because she knows I am a Christian. The children there wriggle and their eyes sparkle as they see me take those beautiful Christmas cards sent from Scotland out of my bag. A card can bring so much joy. Last year this school didn't make much progress because their roof was blown off but they do remember some English they learned and they sing it as I arrive, "*Rejoice in the Lord always and again I say, Rejoice.*"
>
> At another school things are going well. One lad asks me, "What is your favourite football team?" Another lad asks, "Ma'am, are you saved?"
>
> There are disappointments and frustrations but there is also a sense of being involved in something worthwhile, encouraging something that is bringing hope to our children. Many of the teachers are Christians but the chaos in education de-motivates them. There are many opportunities to share the Gospel. Please pray that the Lord will water the seed sown.

Ian and Maryanne Wylie visited Scotland for two months from September 1999, and were warmly thanked for their service in Transkei, on their last leave before retirement in March 2000.

David and Marion Fraser

The Frasers started the decade in Umtata, where David graduated BA from the University of Transkei. They moved to Cape Town in 1991, bought a house in the Monte Vista area and began work with the congregation in the Gugulethu church building which had been erected by Angus Macdonald. David had plans for the training of the office-bearers. Meantime with a view to expanding the work, the congregation bought a site in the adjacent township of Khayelitsha. Quite extensive alterations had to be made to the church in Gugulethu to meet with 'Health and Safety' regulations. Extra emergency doors for exit were needed on either side, but as David rather ruefully remarked, "They were only to provide easy entrance for intruders, first to take the crockery, then the communion vessels, now the electric cooker. What next?" Life was not easy in the great townships of Langa, Gugulethu and Khayelitsha and our members there tried to live out their Christian lives surrounded by much violence, drug-taking and vice. The Free Church in Cape Town has always had the benefit of some fine elders who came from both Transkei and Ciskei; for example, David's right-hand man was Mr Johnson Tetani, a most gracious and self-effacing gentleman.

Help and cooperation with the Free Reformed Church

The Frasers soon made contact with the Reformed Churches in the Cape Town area and this led to interesting interaction between members of the Free Church and people from, among others, the Free Reformed Church of South Africa. They helped with provisions for a Youth Camp which the Frasers held in December 1992 with 30 children and helpers attending. One never knew with camps – sometimes they planned for a certain number and half turned up, sometimes double! As the political situation and violence and intimidation in the townships became worse, it was unsafe for David and Marion to go in to the area at times. Schools closed down, causing great gaps in the education of the pupils. So David set up the *'Khayelitsha Coaching Clinic'* to help those pupils, and the Free Reformed Church in Belhar provided their building as a base, while pupils from Edgemead High School and the Free Reformed Church came to help with the teaching. About 70 black pupils took advantage of the Clinic and altogether it was an excellent way of improving understanding between the races. The 'Festival Outreach Café' held in St Columba's Free Church,

Edinburgh helped towards the expenses of this project. Although both Marion and David travelled many times to take meetings in the townships when it really was not safe for whites, there were times when Marion especially, couldn't go into the townships to take her women's meetings. So the women came out – and they held their meetings in an area to which they could travel. During the time when the Frasers couldn't go into the Cape Town area, they made contact with farm workers in the surrounding areas where many Xhosa people are employed.

Khayelitsha Church opened

By the end of 1994 the Khayelitsha Church building near Cape Town was opened. There was more than usual thankfulness for this as the project went ahead in the most difficult circumstances due to the recurring violence all around. But the political situation, after the election, had changed and David said he saw Cape Town as the most strategic part of South Africa. While previously people were encouraged to return to their rural roots once they had retired, now people would be making their homes permanently in city locations. The church desperately needed ministers willing to work in these environments, but most of our Free Church ministers have been born and bred in the country and feel unfamiliar with life in the townships. Yet without the vision for evangelising the multitudes there, our own church will also perish.

Work in Cape Town District

True to his vision, David Fraser started a training class for office-bearers and others who wanted to deepen their knowledge of Scripture and doctrine. Along with Rev Jan van Straaten, an elder from the Monte Vista Reformed and Presbyterian Church, he arranged preaching classes for the elders and deacons.

In September 1995, Marion, meantime, in addition to the work among the women, was holding children's meetings in Khayelitsha. Some of the women from the church helped her in this, and the children were invited to come to the church services.

Sometimes these meetings were held in the garden of a home and all the children in that street would attend! They memorised Xhosa choruses and heard stories from Scripture. Then there were meetings in other locations. The need was so great and our labourers so few.

Marion was interviewed in Gaelic for a programme which was broadcast on Scottish TV in September 1997. Scenes from the townships where she and David worked were shown. She was commended for the way she promoted the work of the church in Cape Town and in South Africa generally.

Early in 1998 David and Marion Fraser and family moved their home to Somerset West. This gave them easier access to some of the townships and was also more convenient when they travelled up to King William's Town for Presbytery and other meetings. About this time David reported: "The congregation continues to grow in Khayelitsha and Gugulethu, with members numbering 180. Prayer meetings have continued to benefit the people. Many indifferent homes have been revived by them and youth also attend ... We have a large number of youth in Cape Town. It is an encouragement to see about 60 in Khayelitsha and 30 in Gugulethu. A good number of these profess faith after learning the abridged catechism I prepared."

And in Knysna and George

David was also in process of planting preaching stations in Knysna and George – towns on the Garden Route about 250 miles from Cape Town, between Cape Town and the work in the Eastern Cape. Rev Jan van Straaten was a great help and had now been seconded as a minister in the Free Church in South Africa. He said that there were several possible areas of extension to the work in the Cape region in South Africa but there was a need for African pastors with a heart for mission. In time, David put up a small church building in George and attended the first Communion Service held there, but before the congregation could be consolidated, he had left the mission and the Free Church.

The Frasers move on

In early 2000 David Fraser wrote to the Foreign Missions Board telling them of his wish to go to Zambia to set up a Bible School there under the *Frontline Fellowship,* an organisation based in Cape Town. There would be no financial charge on the Board. The Board urged David to stay at the work he was doing. Their hope was that an African minister could work alongside David to further develop and expand the work in places like George and Knysna. To move from all these developments at that time would obviously impact very negatively on the whole work in the Cape area. However, sadly, David tendered his resignation to the Board on 25 April 2000 and this took effect on 15 July 2000. Shortly after, he left the Free Church to join the Free Church (Continuing).

The Kenny Macdonalds

Kenny Macdonald was kept very busy building churches in different districts and being responsible for the care and maintenance of all the mission houses and properties. Coleen was a great help with administration in Dumisani and with day conferences held there. Kenny also began preaching in several congregations. Not least was their hospitality. All the missionaries met together socially on many occasions, and Kenny and Coleen were the main organisers of an occasional weekend away which provided relaxation and a getting together which was valuable in itself.

While on home leave in 1991, Kenny Macdonald had applied to the Training of the Ministry Committee and had been accepted as a candidate for the ministry. He did not envisage returning to the mission field. At the opening of the Zwelitsha church, which Kenny had built, he was presented with an inscribed parchment detailing the various building projects in which he had been involved during his four years on the mission. So in July 1993, the Macdonalds returned to Scotland for good. While ministering in Skye, Kenny joined the Free Church (Continuing) in the year 2000.

The 'Free Church of Scotland (Continuing)' was formed by a group of people who left the Free Church of Scotland in January 2000. Although this group contacted the Free Church in South

Africa, the South African Church expressed their strong desire to "continue in the fellowship with the Free Church of Scotland that has been enjoyed for so many years".

The Glovers

From 1990 till 1992 they were fully involved in their work – Ian in Dumisani Bible School training the first students for the full-time ministry, as well as in the Knox District, Sandra as President of the Knox District W.C.A.

Then in one of the villages in his district there was serious political faction fighting which directly involved some of the people in the church. The congregation was split in two. One faction took its stand in the church building and refused entry to the other side. Threats of murder were made and taken seriously – one man was severely attacked. Ian Glover tried to preach for four weeks in succession in that church to try to bring calm taking elders with him from other congregations. But no peace came, only more threats of violence. The Biblewomen went there to help but were threatened with violence. So it was that the Session of the District took the radical and decisive step of suspending from membership every member of this congregation. No minister or elder would come to take any funerals. They also directed the WCA committee that the ladies of this congregation must also be suspended from its membership, and at one sad meeting they all had to gather up their bags and go home. All the members were assured that the door was open for their return when they repented of what was happening and sought peace with one another and with the Church.

All of this so affected Ian Glover that he suffered from reactive depression, and as the doctor suggested that either the situation must change, or he must come away from it, he and the family returned to Scotland in June 1993 for good, just before Kenny and Coleen Macdonald and family. It was sad to say goodbye to these two families who had been so much a part of the church life in South Africa.

About a year later, a message came to the Session from the church of the village where the trouble had been. The people were asking for a meeting, and they came expressing their repentance before God and seeking reconciliation with the Church. At the following Communion in a neighbouring congregation in the District all the people from that congregation were there – not dressed in their uniforms like the rest of the people. A space was cleared before the pulpit and they were asked to stand there, some very young, some old and frail. Rev Bryce Taho spoke to them and then put to them the vows for church membership. The heads nodded and then bowed in prayer. Then the elders filed round, shaking hands with each one – and they were back, received into the fold again, joining with the others at the Lord's table – a people restored. About two months later at a WCA Quarterly Meeting on 6 August 1994 the ladies were restored to membership of the WCA and re-dressed – they put on their uniforms again. At the 'malihambe' taking up of the money, nearly every woman who had been restored made a little speech of contrition and the one who had been fiercest made reference to her shame at having caused such sorrow to Umf Glover. Their great relief after that was expressed in the volume and fervour of the singing.

Angus and Helen Macdonald

In September 1993, Angus and Helen had spent 25 years in the ministry, all in South Africa - first in Somerset East and then in the Pirie District, Ciskei. One of the meetings transferred to Dumisani during the political troubles was a celebration for this jubilee of Angus and Helen. Missionaries came and went, but Helen and Angus went faithfully on among their people, preaching, taking Women's and Girls' meetings, examining candidates, balancing the books, giving tea to endless callers and being kind to the many poor and disadvantaged among their people.

In connection with the place of the women in the Church, Mrs Helen Macdonald said:

"Women are a very important part of the Free Church in South Africa. They tend to be in the majority and in many places the church would cease to exist if it were not for the women. The main aims of the WCA are to build women up in their Christian faith, to witness to the Lord Jesus Christ and to win souls for Him. The women can easily become discouraged because of the many difficulties and hardships, which they have to face. We encourage them to take their strength from the Word of God and to love, care for and pray for each other as sisters in Christ."

Eventually in July 1997 Angus and Helen felt it was time to retire and to return to Scotland. The General Assembly of the South African church wrote to its counterpart in Scotland: "Our debt to the Free Church of Scotland is great and we deeply appreciate the continuing prayerful and practical support we enjoy at the hand of those who, over the years, have come to serve among us. At this Assembly we take our leave of Rev Angus Macdonald, who with Mrs Macdonald, has rendered sterling and unstinting service to the church here for well nigh thirty years. Only eternity will reveal what blessing has come to South Africa through what they have done so gladly in the service of their master."

When Angus and Helen returned to Scotland they set up home in Angus's native island of Lewis and were formally welcomed home in Stornoway on 24 September 1997. Since his return Angus has been busy taking services, especially in Gaelic, and in hospital visitation – not so much time to rest, but maybe he likes it that way!

The Grahams

On our return from the 1991 General Assembly in Scotland, when Bill was Moderator, almost the whole missionary family, 27 in all, went to Rainbow Valley near East London for a weekend away. On the first evening there we held a second 'Moderator's Reception' for all the colleagues, and who could say which was better?!

On the way to Cape Town to take a weekend training session in 1992 Bill suffered a stroke, which has left him without hearing in one ear and quite unwell for some time. After some time he recovered from this quite well, but due to Elizabeth's illness, we suddenly joined the exodus of missionaries from the South African mission field, and arrived back in Scotland at the end of

January 1996, with very mixed feelings; glad to be getting medical treatment, but dazed by the suddenness of it all and deeply sad to be leaving our good friends and colleagues in Dumisani and in the churches of South Africa.

The Millers

For four years the Millers gave the Ngcingwane and Kentani Districts all their strength. Their house was always open to their people, and their car available to take them to hospital or to help in any need. They cared for the people in the newly formed congregations, which David Fraser had started, and for the very long established church at Ngcingwane. Meg did a great work among the women and girls, driving the bakkie on tracks which could hardly be called roads.

Then on 1 October 1994 David, Meg and Andrew moved to King William's Town so that David could help in Dumisani with the growing amount of administration that needed to be done, as well as doing some lecturing in the Bible School. Meg also helped with Biblewomen's and Sunday School Teachers' day conferences. This took a burden off the staff who were coping with lecturing, literature work, printing, finance, administration, editing a magazine, and the usual extra work generated by students. David continued to look after the Kentani District although Rev Patrick Diniso, the first Dumisani graduate to be ordained, was now the minister of the Ngcingwane District.

So for the rest of this decade the Millers were a stable and helpful presence in Dumisani, and their home too was always open and hospitable. Quite often the Sunday evening service for missionaries was held in their home so a baby-sitter was not required. Later Ben and then John, brothers for Andrew, came to join the family.

The story of the comings of **The Macivers, the Christies, and later the Reids** has been told in the chapter on Dumisani. Surely the Lord had his hand on the work when he called and enabled each of these folk to come at just the right time.

THE CAMPBELLS ARRIVE

In November 1998 Douglas and Julia Campbell arrived to work initially in one of the Districts of the Free Church in South Africa. It was a great encouragement for the church to have a new and young missionary couple committed to the work. They settled in King William's Town and attended Xhosa language classes at the East London campus of Rhodes University. Douglas worked in Mdantsane and later in the Knox District, as well as being interim-moderator of other districts at various times. This gave him a good opportunity to absorb the culture, get to know the people and the workings of the Church, and practise his Xhosa language skills.

Douglas gave his first impressions of living in South Africa: "The Eastern Cape Region is regarded as the poorest region in South Africa and this seems to be borne out by the number of people looking for work ... In East London and King one can see men standing on street corners with little placards advertising themselves and their various skills in the hope that someone may hire them for the day. Poverty is rife ..." Douglas went on to speak of the impact of HIV/AIDS, of violence and how all of that was affecting the church as well as the rest of society. He concluded, "Pray for wisdom to step out in faith with a vision for God's glory."

Douglas had a special heart for the boys he saw standing around in the villages of his District but not in church. He joined a rugby club, playing along with them. This was a new and welcome side of the 'umfundisi' for the young and bore its own fruit. Later, Douglas too gave valuable help in lectures in Dumisani.

Changes in church and people

While political activities got hot and cooled, while missionaries came and went, the African ministers and office-bearers continued their work and witness – often at considerable danger to themselves. But among the black ministers too there was a great deal of movement, as students from Dumisani finished their training and were ordained and inducted to congregations within the Free

Church. Church buildings seemed to be built and opened under Kenny Macdonald's skills with great speed!

Umf Nelson Mpayipeli moves to Somerset East

At the end of 1989, Umf Nelson accepted a call from Somerset East. At a farewell on 9 December in Keiskammahoek he and his wife and daughter were left in no doubt of the affection of the people of Burnshill where they had ministered since 1983. They moved to Somerset East early in 1990 and into a new manse there on 10 November.

In 1993–94 the Mpayipelis travelled to Scotland where Nelson studied in the Free Church College for one year. They lived in Edinburgh while he studied, but were able to travel quite extensively and to meet many of the folk who felt as if they already knew him from contacts and many prayers over the years for the Free Church in South Africa. He also addressed meetings in different places during his time in Scotland. Speaking at the Scottish General Assembly in May 1994 Nelson said that he had enjoyed this experience and would have liked to study longer, but he hoped others might come for longer periods in the future. He thanked the Free Church for sending missionaries, saying that the church in South Africa still needed their assistance, finishing with the Xhosa saying: *Ningadinwa nangomso* (Don't be tired; do it again tomorrow!)

Umf. Wilfred Vumindaba moves to Burnshill

After Rev Mpayipeli's move from Burnshill to Somerset East, the people of Burnshill extended a call to Umf Wilfred Vumindaba, currently serving in the Dewar District. He was inducted to Burnshill on 24 March 1990 with his official welcome in October. Mr Vumindaba ministered there until his retirement in 1999. He had served the church well and faithfully over a large number of years.

Umf. Bryce Taho was invited to be the interim-moderator of the Dewar District as from January 1992. The following year the Missions Board asked him to visit Scotland in connection with the Disruption Anniversary celebrations, along with Rev David John from India and Mr Luis Torrejon from Peru. These three men spoke at special meetings in various venues throughout Scotland in September and their presence was a real encouragement to all who heard them. Before this they all had attended the meetings of the International Conference of Reformed Churches in Holland.

Umf. Ntla comes to Dordrecht – and goes

The General Assembly of 1990 was held in Keiskammahoek from 24–26 May. Umf Ntla, who had been a minister in Transkei, applied to join the Free Church and was accepted at this Assembly. He had been working, in a probationary role, in the congregations of Dordrecht and Mdantsane. As the Dordrecht District gave him a call, it was agreed to induct Umf Ntla on 28 July 1990. Unfortunately this ministry was not a success and when he left Dordrecht, Rev Albert Sliep took over the reins as interim-moderator although he was officially retired. The fact that the congregation was 'out on its own' geographically, 130 miles north of King William's Town, may have contributed to its problems.

Umf. Thyson Nkwelo retires

On 1 December 1990 Umf Thyson Nkwelo, one of the first Xhosa ministers of the Church, retired. He and Mrs Nkwelo were the guests of honour at a celebration to mark his retirement at Tabase Church, Transkei, where he had been minister for 18 years. He had started his service in the Church as an Evangelist, and during this time he had been a great help and encourager to Rev Huite Sliep. After studying at the De Coligny College in Umtata he was ordained and inducted to the Tabase District on 28 December 1972. Mr Nkwelo had a strong personality and had a deep concern for the salvation of his people and their growth in the Christian faith. His wife shared his vision and did a good work among the women and girls of the District.

Evangelist Nenemba dies

In July 1992 the church lost one of its brightest and best servants when Evangelist Penrose Nenemba died. He had grown up in Sidwadweni in Transkei, and been baptised by Mr Dewar. He was particularly used of God in his ministry to the 'Red' people and he understood very well how to explain the Gospel to them. He was himself what he wished others would be "a slave for God". He and David Fraser had worked well together on building up the churches both manually and spiritually.

What he looked forward to in heaven was "Jesus, to see Jesus". And in July 1992 the Lord granted him his desire.

Umf. William Ledwaba comes to the Knox District

The General Assembly of the Church in 1994 admitted as a minister Rev William Ledwaba. Umf. Ledwaba had been a Baptist minister at Whiteville and was well versed in Reformed theology. Originally from the far north of South Africa, he married a Xhosa lady from Peddie in Ciskei. He became minister of the Knox District until 2000 when he became a Chaplain in the South African Defence Force, while retaining full recognition as a Free Church minister with a seat on the Presbytery and General Assembly.

Umf. Patrick Diniso goes to the Ngcingwane District

Rev E. Mkaba, who had come from the Reformed (G.K.) Church had been in this District but had left after a short time. This was disappointing. Why did those ministers who were received into the ministry from other churches so soon wish to leave again? Was the screening process not careful enough? Were we sufficiently welcoming as a Church to these men? Or did they see something amiss in the Church they came to join? Maybe a mixture of all three.

But on 23 July 1994 Patrick Diniso, the first Dumisani graduate was ordained and inducted to the Ngcingwane District. It was a day of dry high wind and veld fires and unbroken sunshine. It was quite an emotional moment when Patrick knelt on a cushion and all the black and the few white hands of the members of Presbytery rested on his head and shoulders – here was the first-fruits of the Bible School!

He and Constance, his wife, with Loyiso and little Ziyanda settled in to the manse in Scanlon Street, Butterworth. The traditional hospitality of that place continued as Patrick and Constance worked with their people in the old church at Ncgincwane and the new at Ibika. But tragedy struck one day in 1998 in the street in Butterworth when a drunken driver mounted the pavement in his vehicle and knocked down little Ziyanda. She died in her father's arms. The whole church felt the devastation, but Patrick and Constance went to visit the driver and told him they forgave him. Great grace! Umf. Diniso ministered in the Ngcingwane District until 2000 when he also became a Chaplain, but to the South African navy at Simonstown, near Cape Town.

Umf. Khulile Davids, a probationer-minister, had come to help Umf. Diniso in the work in the District under the direction of the Transkei Presbytery in 1998.

Umf. Avery Ngaki goes to Port Elizabeth District

On 13 May 1995 another student of Dumisani, Avery Ngaki, was called, ordained and inducted to the congregation of Port Elizabeth. The service was held in the Khanyisa Blind School in KwaDwesa township and it proved to be an excellent venue. Bill Graham preached and presided over the ordination and induction; Umf. Vumindaba addressed the new minister and Umf. Mpayipeli the congregation. At the reception, the Principal of the School, Mr Elliot Takayi, an elder in the congregation had arranged for the blind children's choir to sing. They sang so beautifully, their faces transformed with happiness as they sang, "When I **see** the sunshine ..."

As the congregation did not have a suitable manse, an appeal was published for this in the Scottish Church magazine *The Monthly Record*. As a result the Youth Project for 1996 was to raise funds for houses for African pastors.

The work was being developed in Kwazakhele township, and it was there that a new manse was built next to the church, with grateful thanks to the Youth of the Free Church in Scotland, and Umf and Mrs Ngaki were able to move into this. The church there is surrounded by many informal settlements as well as more established housing, so there is ample scope for evangelism on their doorstep. Umf and Mrs Ngaki have given long service in that place.

Umf. Xabadiya goes from Mdantsane to Pirie

In 1996, when Mr Xabadiya finished his training in Dumisani he ministered for some time in his home township of Mdantsane, East London, but after Rev Angus A. Macdonald had retired from the Pirie District, they called Mr Xabadiya to succeed him as their minister. He was also appointed as interim-moderator of the Cape Town congregations, an area which he knew quite well.

Umf. Bryce Taho comes to work in Dewar District

It was good news for the Church when, in 1999, Rev Bryce Taho came back to his home in King William's Town after finishing his Chaplaincy Service, as he was able again to take a full part in church activities. While still a chaplain, he graduated with B.Th Honours, so he had kept his mind well occupied. He became the minister of the Dewar District once more (having been the interim moderator in 1992), which was just as well since, although he had been far away from them for some years, they still considered him to be their minister! His experience was of great value to the church and also to Dumisani, as he was now free to take some classes there.

Umf. Buntu Mtishe goes to King District

Meanwhile, also in 1999, Umf Buntu Mtishe, also a graduate of Dumisani, was ordained and inducted to the King William's Town District, which had been formed out of the Knox District. It was comprised of the congregations of King, Mngqesha, Gwaba and Mxaxo and a new congregation of Qhugqwala has later been added. Usually the Minister's wife became the local WCA President, but as Mr Mtishe was still single, Mrs Morag Christie willingly accepted the office. As the King congregation met in the Study House of Dumisani, the question of building a church of their own arose.

In town areas like King William's Town buildings and sites were so much more expensive, but a good site was found in King, on the road to Bisho. The Crumlin Evangelical Presbyterian Church of Ireland sent an initial sum of £1435.00, followed by a further generous amount towards the cost of building this church, which was a great help. However through lack of local finance and various hitches it was to be a long time before the congregation could actually worship in the building.

Umf. F.F. Mva goes to the Burnshill District

Mr Mva had been studying part time in Dumisani, but by 1999 he had finished his studies and was ready for a charge. As Burnshill District was vacant because of Mr Vumindaba's retiral, that District called Mr Mva and he was ordained and inducted there in 1999. Sadly he died after a short but productive ministry.

Umf. Raymond Gotywa goes to Dordrecht

Also in 1999 Umf Raymond Gotywa, having finished his training in Dumisani, was called to Dordrecht congregation, vacant since Mr Sliep had retired as its interim-moderator. It was good for these people who lived so far from their nearest Free Church neighbours to have a settled pastor.

Ministers' salaries

The salaries given to the ministers were very low, due to the lack of response from the people. In 2000 the South African Assembly apologised to the ministers of the church for this, stating it was due to 'the reluctance of the members of the church to contribute to their upkeep'. The Free Church of Scotland increased its subsidy in proportion to the South African church increases in giving so that the Church could raise the salaries.

Elder Mfaxa reminisces

One of the school principals who was also an elder in the Free Church was Mr P.P. Mfaxa. He once told us his story, and maybe it will illustrate how difficult it was for some African boys to overcome many obstacles in life.

Mr Mfaxa, as a toddler, moved around with his mother and father, who was a shepherd, and a red-blanket man. He worked in the Karoo area beyond the town of Somerset East, but he belonged to Kentani in the Transkei. When his mother died, his father left him with another man and returned to Kentani with three younger children. When the farmer who employed them gave up farming, Mr Mfaxa's guardian ended up at his home town of Lady Frere (in the north of Transkei).

There, eventually, his father found him and took him back to Kentani. He was now ten years old and although his people were 'heathen' he was sent to school and church. The teacher was busy preparing the Primaries 3–5 for the Inspector and had no time to teach the first class. So Mr Mfaxa prevailed upon the next class, Primary 2, to help him and he taught himself to read. He went on as top of the class to Blythswood Institution (founded by Richard Ross in the 19th Century) and became a teacher.

Most of the schools were run by churches, and the teacher was expected to be a member of whatever denomination owned the school, and to preach also. So he became Catholic, Lutheran, Presbyterian and Free Church, but he said he liked the Free Church best!

We asked him about Ntsikana the Seer who had lived and prophesied before Christianity was brought to the land in the nineteenth century. He said that he had foretold that white men were going to bring the Xhosa three things: "Buttons without holes" (money); "Smooth stones with something harmful in them" (bottles of drink); and "an umqulo" (a pile of things – i.e. a book, the Bible). He advised the people to keep the umqulo and throw away the other two!

New churches opened

Mr Kenny Macdonald was in the mission from 1989 to 1993 and in that time he used his building skills and energy to good advantage. The following new buildings were opened during the decade, many built with Kenny's help.

Vivi, on 24 November 1990, in the Pirie District, down by the sea, where a small tin church built by Mr McCracken was replaced by a small, attractive wood-lined church. The door was unlocked by Mrs Helen McCracken, then aged 80, who reminisced about the original tin building. She said she would unlock the door and we would all go in, but it was more important to know Jesus who said: "I am the door, whoever enters through me shall be saved." So she unlocked the door, an old elder knelt on one knee on the turf and prayed, and we all went in.

Dordrecht, 9 May 1992, a small building but adequate for the needs of the people. This must have been an encouragement to them as Mr Ntla had left a short time before.

Mngqesha, 25 July 1992. This fine big new building replaced a small one which was becoming unsafe and needed to be replaced.

No 1 Trust, 28 November 1992. This was a small church for a loyal congregation near Debe Nek, in the Dewar District.

Umzimkulu, 1993, as already mentioned, 162 miles north of Umtata.

Zwelitsha, 19 June 1993, built by Kenny Macdonald as mentioned above.

Khayelitsha, end of 1994, as mentioned above.

Umtata 2000, building overseen by Ken Cameron as mentioned above.

CHURCH MATTERS

Faithful witness in difficult times

In the middle of all the busy comings and goings of missionaries and pastors, in the middle of all the political upheavals and changes, in the middle of danger from different factions or taxi wars, the people of the Church kept faithfully on. They went to church, travelled in their uniforms to take meetings, witnessed to others and gave to sustain the Church in all its needs. Many times in travelling on minibus taxis they took their life in their hands. One sad day of a WCA Convention in Ciskei two minibuses were travelling from Cape Town when, about 100 miles into their long journey, one veered off the road and overturned three times. Two of the ladies were killed outright and several others were injured, some very seriously. One of those killed was Sophie Mdledle, described by Marion Fraser as "a Mother in Israel to our church people both in Khayelitsha and Gugulethu". Some months before, this lady had been injured in another road accident and when Marion asked her if she was not nervous about taking another long journey by road she replied that she would go with the Lord's people whatever the cost; "If I die, I die". For her "a springboard to the Father's House". The other lady killed was a young married woman, only 20 years of age.

Conference in Cape Town

From December 13 to 17 1995 an Africa Regional Conference of the International Conference of Reformed Churches was held near Cape Town. There were representatives there from Zaire, Benin, Kenya, Uganda as well as South Africa. At the Conference both the *needs* and the *opportunities* in Africa were highlighted. Rev David Fraser had a significant input in the organisation of the Conference and other Free Church members participated.

Delegates' visits

Revs Archie Boyd and Finlay Mackenzie visited the field as delegates from the Board in May–June 1993 to assess the developing situation in the Church. Finlay Mackenzie said that "at the General Assembly (of the FCSA) we were impressed with the small but growing number of young, able elders, pastors and student-pastors ...

In various congregations we were heartened to meet a few promising young men, some of whom would like to train for the ministry.

The delegates noted the encouragements in the work in Cape Town and highlighted the need for similar work in other cities, particularly in Johannesburg, where there are so many men and families from Ciskei and Transkei.

Another two Delegates from the Board who visited the South African church in 1996, **Rev William Macleod and Mr Peter Morrison** (along with Mrs Marion Morrison) commented on the rather inward looking attitude of the South African church and encouraged the Africans themselves to have a missionary outlook. "An African Church which regarded itself as having a missionary outreach would indeed be on a most hopeful footing." This is true, but it may be coming in the future. In the early part of this decade the Church began to appreciate the importance of its young people – who are both the present and the future of the Church. Who knows if some of them will carry the torch of the Gospel farther afield than ever their parents even looked?

Developments in Youth Work

A new and good development was the holding of **Youth Conferences**. One such was held in Dyafta in 1990 and was packed out, with several choirs taking part. This became a regular annual feature of the Free Church calendar.

The General Assembly of the South African Free Church in May 1991 was a happy affair with every Commissioner being involved in the deliberations of the various Committees and the debates in the Assembly itself. One of the major decisions taken was to appoint Mr Eric Mekute as *Youth Worker for the Church.* This was an excellent development, but sadly, Mr Mekute died very suddenly when attending a funeral in January 1994. However, it all showed that the church was beginning to realise the place and importance of the young people.

NOT THE END OF THE STORY

The story has covered one hundred years of work among the 'Ochre People'.

Although our journey ends in the year 2000, the story of the Free Church in South Africa has not ended, nor has that of Dumisani Theological Institute – both are still travelling.

This has been very much an account of missionaries rather than our African brothers and sisters but this book is dedicated to them – a people who have been patient with us and kind to us and whom we love.

One of the last WCA Conventions of the 20th Century had the theme "We want to see Jesus". At that Convention a young boy asked an old missionary, "Do you love Jesus?" "Yes." "And so do I! And I love the people of Jesus too." The place where that particular Convention was held, Gqumahashe on the Tyumie River, was near the place where the earliest missionaries started their work over 160 years before, and the bodies of the three little Ross children were laid nearby.

Was it all worth it? I think that if the Rosses and all who followed them could have been present with the hundreds of Xhosa Christians at that Convention, they would have said, "Yes, a thousand times Yes."

Looking ahead

While there are now no Free Church of Scotland ministers working in the Districts in the Free Church in South Africa, the Appendices show how an increasing number of African men are taking over these responsibilities. This was the aim from the beginning and it is a great encouragement to see it coming to fruition. These men will take the Church forward as they look to God for guidance and wisdom.

The Dumisani Theological Institute has become an invaluable help to the Free Church and other Churches in the Eastern Cape in their need to produce leaders who are both spiritually and theologically equipped to be the kind of people God approves – *"a worker who is not ashamed and who uses the true teaching in the right way"*. (2 Timothy 2.15)

Since 2000 when our story finished, Dumisani has increasingly become a centre for academic as well as spiritual advancement under the successive leadership of Rev Ronald Christie and Dr Alistair Wilson. With the addition of more staff it has developed a growing involvement with the local community.

We know the Free Church in South Africa will, in God's grace, continue to have its own story to tell. It is our prayer that she will become more vibrant in her spiritual life, with a missionary vision of her own, and, under God, will go on from strength to strength into the future.

Appendix 1

Important Dates 1900–2000

1900   Union of Majority of Free Church of Scotland and the United Presbyterian Church.

Request from Africans for the resumption of Free Church work among the amaXhosa.

1905   First post-1900 Delegation to South Africa from Scotland – July/August.

1907   Second Delegation from Free Church of Scotland – July.

1907   First post-1900 Free Church Presbytery of Kaffraria – Wednesday, August 29.

1908   First post-1900 Free Church Missionary from Scotland – Rev Alexander Dewar and family sailed for South Africa October 31.

1954   'Second' Presbytery of Kaffraria – June 4 (Presbytery resuscitated).

1961   The Republic of South Africa declared.

1968   Division of the Pirie District into two to form the new Knox District.

1972   Division of the Transkei District into three Districts, Tabase, Embo and Ngcingwane.

1974   Division of the Burnshill District into two to form the new Dewar District.

1976   Free Church in South Africa inaugurated as an Associate Presbytery of the Free Church of Scotland – July 24.

Independence of Transkei – October 26.

1979   Opening of Dimbaza Reformed Bible School – February 24.

1981   Independence of Ciskei – December 4.

1983   Independence of Free Church in South Africa – July 9.

1987   Opening of Dumisani Bible School – February 4.

1991   Full-time courses commenced in Dumisani.

1994   First General Election of the new dispensation in South Africa – April 27-29.

New name - the Dumisani Theological Institute and Bible School – April.

1997   Degree courses commenced at Dumisani in association with Potchefstroom University for Christian Higher Education.

Appendix 2

Missionaries sent out/ seconded by the International Missions Board of the Free Church of Scotland (from 1900 to 2000)

Rev Alexander Dewar	(1908–1943) (Died in service.)
Rev William Murray	(1912–1923) (Died on furlough.)
Rev Adam Macpherson	(1925–1929)
Rev John A. Macdonald	(1927–1928)
Rev Dr H. Mackay	(1930 [briefly])
Rev Joseph McCracken	(1944–retired in 1974) died in S.A. 13/11/87
Rev Huite Sliep	(1948–1970)
Rev Dr J.C. Andrews	(1948–1964 and from 1970–1975)
#Mrs S.A. Colville	(1955–1981)
Rev Angus A. Macdonald	(1967–1997)
Rev Albert Sliep	(1962–1990)
Rev W.D. Graham	(1976–1996)
Rev D.S. Fraser	(1977–2000)
Rev D.D. Miller	(1989–2002)
*Mr K. Macdonald	(1989–1993)
Rev K.W.R. Cameron	(1988 and 1991–2004)
Rev I.D. Glover	(1988–1993)
Rev I. Wylie	(1991–2000)
Rev D. Maciver	(1992–1998)
Rev R. Christie	(1996–2008)
Rev D. Campbell	(1998–2006)
Rev Norman Reid	(1999–)

'Freelance' but authorised Missionary.

* Artisan Missionary.

(Since 2000 the following missionaries were inducted to the work in South Africa, centred in Dumisani Theological Institute:
Rev Dr A. Wilson (2005) and Rev Dr J.S. Ross (2008)

Appendix 3

African Ministers of the
Free Church in South Africa – 1900–2000
Ordained or admitted to the Free Church

Rev Burnett Gaba	1907–1911 (left Free Church)
Rev N. Gaba	1907–1917 (left Free Church)
Rev Mazwi	1926–1970
Rev R. Damane	1912–1916 (left Free Church)
Rev Zokobe Taho	1955–1962
Rev Skozana	1925–1938 (left Free Church)
Rev Moses Baleka	1955 (intermittently until 1963 then left)
Rev L.L. Miza	1958–1959 (left Free Church)
Rev Thyson Nkwelo	1972–retired 1/12/90
Rev W.T. Vumindaba	1976–retired 20/3/99
Rev N.P. Mpayipeli	1983–
Rev E. Mkaba	1983–1984 (left Free Church)
Rev Ntla	1990–1992 (left Free Church)
Rev B.M. Taho	1968–
Rev W. Ledwaba	1994–
Rev P. Diniso	1994–
Rev A.G. Ngaki	1995–
Rev C. Xabadiya	1996–
Rev K. Davids	1998–
Rev L.O. Piyo	1999–
Rev B.A. Mtishe	1999–
Rev F.F. Mva	1999–2005 (died 20/08/2005)
Rev R. Gotywa	1999–

(From 2000 to 2009 the following ministers have been ordained and inducted; X. Damane (died 2007), M. Mafuya, W. Tshoni, T. Ngada.)

Appendix 4

Map of the Eastern Cape

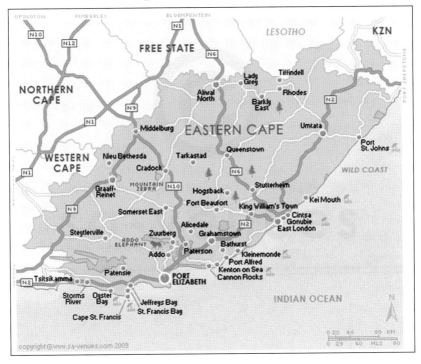

Appendix 5

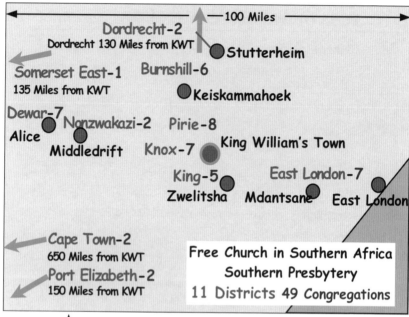

Dordrecht-2
Dordrecht 130 Miles from KWT
100 Miles
Stutterheim

Somerset East-1
135 Miles from KWT
Burnshill-6
Keiskammahoek

Dewar-7
Alice
Nonzwakazi-2
Middledrift
Pirie-8
Knox-7
King William's Town

King-5
Zwelitsha
East London-7
Mdantsane
East London

Cape Town-2
650 Miles from KWT
Port Elizabeth-2
150 Miles from KWT

Free Church in Southern Africa
Southern Presbytery
11 Districts 49 Congregations

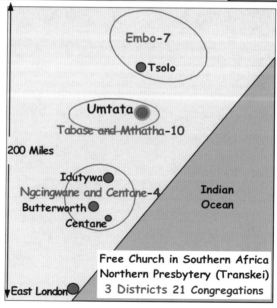

Embo-7
Tsolo

Umtata
Tabase and Mthatha-10

200 Miles

Idutywa
Ngcingwane and Centane-4
Butterworth
Centane

Indian
Ocean

East London

Free Church in Southern Africa
Northern Presbytery (Transkei)
3 Districts 21 Congregations

380

Appendix 6

FCSA Districts and Congregations – 2009

Transkei Presbytery – 21 Congregations

Embo – 7 : Rev B A Mtishe (Interim Moderator)

Nozibele	Ntshiqo
Mbongweni	Novukile
Sidwadweni	Sondelani (Umzimkhulu)
Nonzame	

Tabase and Mthatha – 10 : Rev B A Mtishe

Tabase	Mbolompo
Cicira	Mthatha
Nontando	Springvale
Nobhuhle	Lugxogxo
Gqabata	Nomzame

Ngcingwane and Centane – 4 : Rev Nelson P Mpayipeli

Ngcingwane (Ngcingwane)	Macibe (Centane)
Nqamakwe	Godidi

Southern Presbytery – 49 Congregations

King William's Town – 5 : Rev W Tshoni

King William's Town	Qhugqwala
Mxaxo	Mngqesha
Gwaba	

Pirie – 8 : Rev Clifton M Xabadiya

Pirie	Ginsberg
Jafta	Zwelitsha
Tyusha	Fort Murray
Rankin	Mdingi

Knox – 7 : Rev M Mafuya

Xukwane	Zikhalini
Zihlahla	Mdisa
Mamata	Bebula
Bulembu	

East London – 7 : Rev T Ngada

NU3	Tyhusha
Nonzame	Nqinisa
Tsholomqa	Zikhova
Masikhanye	

Burnshill – 6 : Rev M Mafuya (Interim Moderator)

Mnyameni	Ngqumeya
Geju	Kwamatole
Keiskammahoek	Mkhubiso

Nonzwakazi – 2 : Rev K Davids

Whiteville   Trust No 1

Dordrecht – 2 : Rev R S Gotywa

Dordrecht   Stutterheim

Dewar – 7 : Rev W Tshoni (Interim Moderator)

Upper Gqumahashe	Ngxwedera
Lower Gqumahashe	Umqhwashu
Lloyd	Sweethome
Sheshegu	

Somerset East – 1 : Rev N E Reid (interim Moderator)

Somerset East

Port Elizabeth – 2 : Rev G Avery Ngaki

Motherwell   KwaZakhele

Cape Town – 2 : Rev Clifton M Xabadiya (Interim Moderator)

Khayelitsha   Guguletu

Appendix 7

Schools that were formerly under the management of the Free Church in South Africa post-1900:

Pirie District:

Knox   Mxaxo

Mdisa   Ndevana

Dyafta *(Jointly managed with the [formerly named] Bantu Presbyterian Church)*

Burnshill District:

Mzantsi

Amatole Basin

Mnyameni

Umnqwashu (Farm School)

Transkei:

Ngcingwane

(With the exception of Umnqwashu all the schools became wholly managed by the Government in the 1950's and 1960's.) Umnqwashu, as a farm school was in a different category and the church remained as its 'manager' for many years until it fell under the management of the Ciskei Education Department. The teachers were always paid by the Government.

INDEX

E

F

G

Macleod, Rev D.K. 287, 312, 345

Macleod, Rev G. and Mrs E. 97-99, 102-104, 106, 139, 140

Macleod, Rev Prof J. 17, 21-23, 26, 72, 124, 279, 280

Macleod, Mr N. 307

Macleod, Rev W. 330, 372

MacRitchie, Rev M. 240, 245, 288

Macpherson, Rev A. and Mrs 75-78, 80, 82-89, 93, 123, 132

Madlokazi, A. Evang. 194, 233

Magodla, Mr H. 142

Magodla, Mrs P. 286, 310, 313

Mair, Mr A.M. 265

Makapela, A. Evang. 24, 194, 233

Mandela, President N. 11, 340, 342, 344

Matakane, S. Evang. 178, 194, 233

Matayo, William Mr 47, 48, 60-63, 66

Mazwi, Rev 78, 84, 86, 87, 93, 100, 101, 123

McCulloch, Rev Principal J. 17, 19-23, 124

McCracken, Rev J. and Mrs H. 102-108, 112, 121-124, 127, 131, 132, 134-136, 138, 139, 141-146, 159, 162-169, 177-183, 191, 195, 197, 207, 213-215, 220, 221, 223, 224, 226, 228, 237, 238, 256, 280, 283, 288, 290, 296, 297, 319, 349,

370

Mfaxa, Mr P.P. 226, 368, 369

Mfikile, Mr G. 142

Mgidi, O. Evang. 194, 233

Miller, Rev D.D. and Mrs M. 299, 300, 301, 320, 321, 325, 330, 332, 334, 335

Miza, Rev L.L. 164, 165

Morrison, Mr P. 330, 372

Mount Coke Hospital 216

Mpunzi, Mr P. 22, 33, 37, 56, 65

Mpayipeli, Rev N.P. 273, 280, 282, 283, 363, 366

Mtishe, Rev B.A. 325, 328, 367

Murray, Rev William and Mrs 53, 54, 57-59, 63-73, 75, 80

Mva, Rev F.F. 328, 368

Myburg, Ds J. 326, 334

Mzimba, Rev P. 19, 31, 56

N

National Suicide 12, 13

Nenemba, P. Evang. 152, 166, 219, 232, 289, 365

Ngaki, Rev A.G. 328, 366

Nocanda, Mr T.T. 132, 199, 200, 255, 256, 290

Nkwelo, Rev T.W. 188-190, 213, 219, 229, 232, 346, 364